DAY'S AT THE MORN

BOOKS BY SAMUEL CHOTZINOFF

DAY'S AT THE MORN
§
A LITTLE NIGHTMUSIC
§
TOSCANINI: AN INTIMATE PORTRAIT
§
A LOST PARADISE
§
EROICA

DAY'S AT
THE MORN

Samuel Chotzinoff

Preface by Sir Osbert Sitwell

HARPER & ROW, PUBLISHERS

New York·Evanston·London

48,784

Jan., 1965

FIRST EDITION

LIBRARY OF CONGRESS CATALOG CARD NUMBER: 64-21653

H–O

TO LISA, ROBIN, AND JENNY

CONTENTS

PREFACE

The first volume of Samuel Chotzinoff's autobiography was an unforgettable book, and the second, *Day's at the Morn,* is recognizably by the same hand and of the same quality, and it is impossible to give higher praise. It is a book carefully and beautifully written, and full of a humor and pathos that were all his own.

The first volume, *A Lost Paradise,* took us from the time when the author was an immigrant—at the age of seven—to the first day of his debut as a piano soloist with the Educational Alliance Orchestra. The second volume takes us from that point, when he was sixteen, with a great hatred of the rich and fellow feeling for the poor. There are many memorable scenes in this book, as, for example, when he goes to tea with a musical pundit and his wife, and sees sugar tongs for the first time; in a different way this was as important to him as the narrator's eating of a *madeleine* in Marcel Proust's *Du Côte de Chez Swann* (personally I am as fond of his subsequent meeting with these implements when, on being asked "How many lumps?," he replied offhandedly "Oh, the usual"). But indeed the whole book is full of humor as, too, it is full of pathos, both of them of a very personal order. Indeed, if I were to be asked what kind of pathos it was, I should have to go outside the range of literature to the films, to the feeling which is comparable to that constantly revealed in the earlier works of that great artist Charlie Chaplin and is particularly visible in such films as *The Gold Rush,* no less than in the more plainly pathetic *The Kid.*

Perhaps one reason why the book is so pleasant to read is that it is full of nice characters. The poor are more genuine, and in proportion more generous than the rich—for it can be as generous for a poor man to lend a dollar as for a rich one to lend a thousand dollars. Moreover, the poor are often more prompt in their response, and, further, are forbidden by their circumstances from showing any ostentation. Yet Mr. Chotzinoff never allows the niceness of the characters to become obtrusive. Thus the benevolent presence of his mother in the apartment is always to be felt there in the background, cooking or cleaning or sewing, though she is not often seen until the moment when her tender devotion to her son makes her flout every commandment in the Talmud and drive in a taxicab on the Sabbath to be present at her son's first public appearance in a concert hall. But the characters never cloy and, for instance, in the apartment there is also to be felt the brooding presence of the father, austere, ascetic and narrow-minded.

But it is the author's special understanding of artists which makes the second volume, as it made his life, most memorable. When he writes of them one can see his eager bird-bright eyes, and his occasional quizzical glance.

This is no mere success story, although he was a great success. In this volume we have his early meetings with artists and there is a memorable picture of his first meeting with Zimbalist. Zimbalist came from much the same background as Chotzinoff; but swift stardom had bestowed on Zimbalist at an early age self-assurance and a mastery of the social graces. There still clung to him, nevertheless, a primitive passion for statistics— " 'Do you realize, Mr. Chotzinoff, that the Ukraine grows more vheat than the rest of the world—even America! Do you know how many bushels of vheat the Ukraine sends out? Vell, how much do you tink? . . . Say what you tink.' I said two hundred thousand. '*Tree* millions!' he burst out triumphantly, and waited for the look of wonder on my face which he expected, and got." Chotzinoff soon learned to cut down the number of items to half what he would really have guessed them to be, because this plainly doubled Zimbalist's pleasure at astounding him with the real number.

I hope that we may, in due course, have a third volume. There is much in his later life one would like to know: among other things, for example, the secret of his great success as a friend, though such things are always hard to formulate. He was a great friend of mine, but I find it difficult to define, for instance, his charm; that he had a peculiar gift for friendship is undoubted. In it, he was as successful as he was as a musician and pianist, and now as a writer. Perhaps it was due to his modesty, a rare and tender quality, which enabled him who started life as an immigrant to end as a citizen of the world.

OSBERT SITWELL

THE ABYSS

In the closing chapter of my early reminiscences, *A Lost Paradise,* I related the circumstances of my debut as pianist in Mozart's Concerto in D Minor, with the Educational Alliance Orchestra conducted by Mr. Sam Franko, in the auditorium of the Educational Alliance, then, as now, situated on the corner of East Broadway and Jefferson Street, on New York's Lower East Side. The year was 1905, and I was sixteen years old.

My piano teacher, Madame Franko, Mr. Sam Franko's sister, had given me a scholarship, and had generally taken me under her wing. Her interest was not confined to my musical progress. Believing that musical progress alone would not ensure the career she had in mind for me, that my future depended also on such nonmusical factors as dress, deportment, social graces, and the interest and aid of what she called "the right people," her solicitude embraced also such factors as my life at home, my relations with my mother and father, the character of my friends and acquaintances, and my opinions on life, society and art.

1

I was grateful for her interest in me, though there were times when I was embarrassed by her close scrutiny of my clothes, and her pointed remarks about the importance of cleanliness. At those times I resented my poverty, which alone gave her the right to treat me as a dependent. For if I could pay for my lessons I would be under no obligations to her whatsoever. I could then say to her coldly, "Madame Franko, I am paying you to teach me to play, not to tell me to wash my hands or comb my hair or clean my fingernails." I was often tempted to tell her one of my cousin Nochum Flayshig's favorite stories, about the teacher in the kindergarten who wrote to the mother of one of her pupils, "Your boy needs a bath," and received the appropriate reply: "Don't smell my boy, *learn* him." I knew that my hair was generally disheveled, but I washed my hands and face each morning, and in the summer, oftener. In the matter of fingernails, I thought Madame Franko's suggestion to clean them each day a ridiculous excess of "society" elegance. Fingernails called, sometimes, for cutting, but I never knew of anyone who cleaned them daily. As for myself, I had long ago even dispensed with cutting them. It was simpler and pleasanter to bite them.

I minded very much Madame Franko's attempts to make me adopt her worldly, pragmatic social philosophy, which she held indispensable to the building of a successful musical career. My own social outlook had been shaped by the poverty I was born into and still lived in. From early childhood I had looked upon the rich as the "enemy." Madame Franko professed to have rich and powerfully placed friends whom she dangled before me as possible architects of my future. The mention of their names and Madame Franko's open speculation about the chances of their taking to me always irked me and made me combative.

Madame Franko painstakingly set about "preparing" me for presentation to these arbiters of the destinies of talented, but impoverished, youth. She planned to induce one of them to give a musicale and supper to launch me musically and socially. But before I could appear before "society," as Madame Franko called my future benefactors, I had, it seemed, much to learn about "civilized deportment." Many things appeared "wrong" with me, not least of which was my lack of social graces. But even more serious were my "views," my opinions on music, politics and economics, which Madame Franko held to be unorthodox, and as tending to offend the very persons in whose hands my career reposed. To change me, inside and out, became my teacher's purpose.

When I questioned the necessity of such a drastic alteration, Madame Franko invoked historical precedents proving that artists had always depended on the sponsorship of the noble and rich. She admitted that times had changed somewhat, that the artists of the present day could also rely on a mass audience not formerly available. But the mass audience too, she explained, was itself influenced by, and took its cue from, persons of leisure and taste. To become really popular an artist must first be "taken up" by the elite. The rest should follow. Madame Franko thought that I must count myself fortunate that my piano teacher was a familiar of this decisive set, and she was prepared to use her influence with it on my behalf.

After my lessons Madame Franko usually talked to me about the details of her campaign, adding new names to her ever-lengthening list of affluent or social persons she meant to enlist. By their names most of these appeared to be Jews. I wondered at the scarcity of wealthy Christian music patrons in so large a city as New York. A Miss Rhoda Lilienwald, who headed Madame Franko's list, was to be my chief patron. Miss

Lilienwald was a wealthy spinster, and a member of one of
the finest *German*-Jewish families in America. Madame
Franko's way of stressing the German side of German-Jewish
families irritated me. It was an oblique, indelicate derogation
of Russian Jews, to which category I belonged. Madame Franko
scarcely ever mentioned Russian Jews; and when she did talk
about a Russian-Jewish artist she managed to emphasize his
singularity. I had been brought up to regard German Jews
(with the exception of remarkable philanthropists like Jacob
Schiff) as out-and-out snobs who despised their Russian co-
religionists. Not that Russian Jews were altogether free from
snobbery, for we in turn looked down on Galician Jews. But
then we had every right to look down on *Galicianer,* for they
were all, without question, barbarians, and they spoke Yiddish
in the most outlandish fashion, with an accent and a singsong
intonation that were ludicrous. The German Jews, on the
other hand, rejected Yiddish altogether and were, therefore,
indistinguishable from the Christian Germans, as their syna-
gogues were hardly distinguishable from Christian churches
in their cleanliness and architecture. Unbeliever that I was, I
yet favored the smelly, unpretentious little shuls my father
frequented, over the large, neat, impersonal temples of the
German Jews on Madison and Fifth Avenues. And much as I
detested the sound of a *Galicianer* nasally and noisily mispro-
nouncing *Ich* as *Yach,* I preferred it to the German Jews'
elegant and rather self-conscious, exaggerated *Eesch.* At any
rate, in Madame Franko's social hierarchy, the Russian Jews
occupied the unenviable position of the *Galicianer* with us.
This I deeply resented.

About my probable benefactress, Miss Lilienwald, I had conflicting emotions. Though she symbolized "the enemy," I could
not deny the attraction of her wealth and power. At the same

time I resented the accident of birth that gave them to her. However generous to talented young people Miss Lilienwald might be, she could not possibly be as generous and tender-hearted as my sister Hannah, whose existence as a girl, and now as a married woman with children, was a constant struggle with poverty. How much more deserving Hannah was of the happy accident of birth that fell to the lot of Miss Lilienwald! I envied Miss Lilienwald, and despised her. And Madame Franko, unaware of the duality of my feeling for her wealthy friend, continued to exalt Miss Lilienwald, and to prepare me for the day of our meeting.

Each week Madame Franko reverted to the subject of my untidy appearance, my habit of biting my nails and my propensity, when walking, to raise one shoulder above the other. But above everything it was my want of respect for the advice and opinions of "older and more experienced people" that disturbed her. I realized grudgingly the validity of the changes Madame Franko desired to make in me, though I did once, in a moment of anger, remind her that Beethoven, too, had been negligent about his dress and deportment, and had shown no respect at all for the "older and more experienced people" around him. Yet Madame Franko's suggestions did not go altogether unheeded. I tried not to bite my nails, and I did my best to bring my shoulders into alignment when I walked. But on the subject of altering my opinions to win Miss Lilienwald's or anyone else's favor, I remained adamant.

One day Madame Franko greeted me smilingly and told me that she had finally induced Miss Lilienwald to present me in a musicale at her house. Miss Lilienwald occupied an *entire* house on Central Park West, and her parlor was as big as the stage of Carnegie Hall. It could easily accommodate all the wealthy patrons of music known to her and Madame Franko.

As was the custom at "privates"—Madame Franko's graphic name for musicales—my recital would be followed by a lavish supper catered from a well-known restaurant, and served on many little tables rented for the occasion. Rented, too, would be flocks of elegant little gilt chairs for the guests to sit on. (I had once seen such chairs at a polite Christian funeral.)

Madame Franko briefed me on the proper behavior of a soloist at a "private." This differed in some respects from a soloist's demeanor at a public concert. At Miss Lilienwald's I would be in close proximity to my audience. It was important for me to establish at the outset an intimacy with, at least, the first two rows of gilt chairs in front of the piano. To do this I must take care to smile at each patron in the first two rows, before and after every number on my program; or if there was not enough time, I must at once establish an intimacy at least with the ladies in the first row.

The recital itself, important though it was, would be, however, only a warming up, a preparation, for the even more important *social* performance at the supper. For I learned that it was actually the supper that would decide my destiny. Sitting right next to the hostess, I must bring into play my charm (the attribution was startling, since it was Madame Franko's very first nonmusical compliment to me), yet I must be careful not to overstep the limits of civilized "give and take." I must be "easy," and at the same time deferential; worldly, but not cynical. I must avoid all controversial subjects (I was so young, and people just hated to argue) like politics, labor unions (of which Madame Franko well knew I was in favor), the music of Strauss and Debussy and perhaps even that of the later Wagner. Madame Franko would be close at hand to help steer me through any crisis that might arise.

These preparations, briefings and manipulations, conceived

and carried out with exactitude and persistence, leaving nothing to chance, engendered an antagonism in me, the bitterness of which was augmented by the necessity to conceal it, at least until after the success or failure of the "private." I listened and said nothing, and practiced hard on a program designed to exhibit the salient characteristic of my talent, which, Madame Franko claimed, was an ability to communicate emotion. My technique had improved a lot under her guidance, but it was quite clear that I was definitely not the virtuoso type of pianist, and she believed in playing up one's strength.

With that end in view, Madame Franko gave the greatest consideration to the program for the musicale. After many preliminary drafts she settled on Liszt's transcription of Bach's Toccata and Fugue in A Minor (it was inconceivable not to start off with Bach—it just wasn't done); Beethoven's "Moonlight" Sonata; a waltz, a prelude and an étude of Chopin; and, for a finish, the Brassin arrangement of the "Magic Fire Scene" from *Die Walküre*. Since I was not permitted to have a voice in the choice of my program, the Wagner piece was, I could see, in the nature of a sop to my unpredictable sensibilities. The encores, however, were all to be, like the bulk of the program, "regular," chosen from composers like Mendelssohn, Schubert, Schumann and Henselt. Henselt's "Si j'étais oiseau" ("If I Were a Bird") was a popular encore at that time, even at concerts in Mendelssohn and Carnegie Halls.

About a fortnight before the date of Miss Lilienwald's "private," I happened to be in Malkin's bookshop on East Broadway having a look around. (It wasn't necessary to buy anything at Malkin's. The old man was glad to see people browsing in his shop and reading whole chapters. I could finish an entire book in nine or ten visits.) My eye was caught by Jack London's latest book, *The People of the Abyss*. I took it down and began reading. By dint of skipping around, I soon grasped the intent of the author. The "abyss" was the vast, dreadful chasm of poverty into which Jack London and, by inference, the great majority of the people of the world were born. It was from this abyss that Jack London had painfully risen; but neither his present fame nor his affluence had caused him to forget it. His heart was still with the poor and against "the system" which created and forcibly maintained the "abyss." Reading his impassioned, unselfish plea for the abolition of poverty, I thought with renewed bitterness about Miss Lilienwald and the power she commanded. I wondered how Jack London would regard my toadying to the creators and beneficiaries of that horrid "abyss" in which I was being coached by my well-meaning but misguided piano teacher.

It was in such a rebellious state of mind that I went, next day, to take my piano lesson; and when it was over listened once more to Madame Franko's stratagems for the great evening at Miss Lilienwald's. Passages from Jack London's book kept running through my head. I must have looked distraught, for Madame Franko commented on my lack of interest in my own future. Then she touched on a subject which at that particular moment deepened my unhappiness and drove me, at last, to open defiance. "We must rent you evening clothes for the concert," Madame Franko announced. I knew perfectly well that artists wore "tails" at "privates," as they did at public concerts in the evening. But "tails" at a public concert was the artist's uniform, having no more significance than the uniform of an admiral or the costumes of an actor. In the case of a "private," it was distinctly a social symbol, the dress of all the "gentlemen" there, the uniform, in short, of "the enemy." The picture of myself clad thus rose accusingly before me. Had Jack London ever compromised his beliefs by wearing "tails"? I could not believe that he had. I would consent to appear at Miss Lilienwald's "private," but never in tails!

I blurted out as much to Madame Franko, who stared at me in amazement, the image of incredulity. When she at last found her voice, she upbraided me for an ungrateful, stupid, uncivilized *Russian Jew,* declaring that she had suffered much from my stubbornness and intractability, but that this was the last straw. If I persisted in refusing to wear "tails" at Miss Lilienwald's musicale, she would be through with me forever. Outraged by her threat, I reiterated my refusal angrily. Madame Franko strode to the door and flung it open. I ran out of the house, resolved never to return.

Of course, I expected Mr. Franko to side with his sister, and to replace me with another pianist at the Educational Alliance. But if he heard about our quarrel, he never mentioned it, and I remained the orchestra's official pianist. On the contrary, he began to show me unusual civility at the rehearsals, sometimes going out of his way to comment on my good taste in phrasing a melody, or in subduing the piano part for the benefit of the over-all orchestral effect. And one night, after a rehearsal, when some of us accompanied him to the Third Avenue Elevated station, he unexpectedly asked me to ride home with him. He had never before invited any one of us to pay him a visit. What with his sister's continued animosity (I had not heard from her since the dreadful scene at her house) and this extraordinary mark of friendliness on his part, I was obliged to conclude that Mr. Franko quite disapproved of his sister's treatment of me, and wished me to know it. During the ride on the elevated, he asked me about my family and my life at home. But he made no reference to my musical studies or my need of a teacher.

His apartment, on the fourth floor of a brownstone house on Sixty-second Street near the corner of Madison Avenue, ran the

entire length of the house, and contained a bathroom and toilet
for his sole use. His living room had a grand piano and many
cabinets filled with music books. I had not seen so much music
outside of Katz's store on East Broadway.

Mr. Franko said I might want to use his bathroom. I did not
need to at the moment, but I thought it best not to offend him
and I used it. When I came into the living room, he produced
two bottles of beer, a large piece of Swiss cheese and some
crackers. We ate and drank and conversed, exactly like two
equals. Before I left, he took me into his bedroom and opened
the door of a closet. There, ranged symmetrically on a rack,
stood no less than half a dozen pairs of shoes, all of them filled
out with shoe trees—the first I had ever seen. I could not
imagine what he wanted with so many pairs of shoes. He took
a pair from the rack and bade me, "for fun," try them on. They
fitted me exactly. He said he was glad that they did, as they were
too small for him. I saw through his ruse, and I bridled and said
my own shoes were practically new, and that I couldn't think
of wearing other people's things. I knew all the time that he
meant well and wished to be kind. But his magnanimous gesture, coming so soon after my humiliation by his sister, reminded me of my poverty and dependence, and shattered that
equality he had earlier established between us. I said good night
abruptly, and left him looking puzzled, the offending pair of
shoes in his hands. I was glad I had had the courage to refuse
him. The shoes looked expensive and beautiful, and the temptation to accept them had been great.

THE KOVNERS AND
THE LESSERS

When the Educational Alliance Orchestra was formed, its cello section consisted of my friend Mike Dorf alone. A year later the section was augmented and strengthened by a newcomer, a girl of fifteen or sixteen named Elena Kovner. She had blue eyes, and her hair was copper-colored, like the hair of the lovely, pensive maidens in the paintings of the Pre-Raphaelites I went to see on free days in the Metropolitan Museum of Art. Her skin was delicate, her face freckled. She was a pupil of the first cellist of the Metropolitan Opera House, who was a friend of Mr. Sam Franko. Mr. Franko heard her play and was impressed by her talent, and it was at his suggestion that she joined the Educational Alliance Orchestra. It was Mr. Franko's belief that even a soloist could profit from the discipline of playing in an orchestra.

Every Wednesday evening Elena, accompanied by her father or mother, made the long trip from a far section of Brooklyn, where she lived, to the Educational Alliance. She was the only girl in the orchestra, though occasionally a tall, handsome Christian lady-pupil of Mr. Franko's came down to play in our second-violin section. We commented among ourselves on Elena's reticence and self-consciousness. She was shy and self-deprecatory when anyone praised her playing. But she gave one the feeling that she was fastidious and, perhaps, unapproachable. I felt this unmistakably at her first rehearsal with the orchestra. A piece of rosin she was applying to the hair of her bow slipped out of her hand and rolled over to the piano, where I sat. I picked it up and returned it to her. Our fingers touched. I would hardly have been aware of it had not Elena jerked her arm away as if she had suffered an electrical shock, and turned her face from me. A moment which would ordinarily have passed unnoticed suddenly assumed significance.

There were many differences between Elena and the girls in the neighborhood I knew. Redheads were common on the East Side, but Elena's hair was different from the others'. It was unobtrusively auburn, yet it was dimly alive and glowed faintly, and on sunny days I noticed additional subtly complementary hues, like overtones that faintly materialized when one struck a single note on the piano and held it with the sustaining pedal. Elena arranged her hair in several ways: in two braids, which made her look like a little girl, or plaited in a circle around her head, which gave her an unnaturally mature look and made me think of the colored print of the "Mona Lisa" which hung framed in Malkin's bookstore. Elena's arms were long and thin, even scrawny. Yet when she played they appeared strong and looked graceful. Indeed, the picture of Elena playing, her eyes closed, her head bent low over the strings, her right arm drawing the bow in a long, sustained line, her left hand insistently pressing the strings, was beautifully plastic. When she was not playing, her movements were angular and gawky. She spoke either hesitantly or explosively. Even her laugh was self-conscious and faintly hysterical, as if she considered natural and uninhibited laughter indecorous.

All this I might never have noted so carefully or speculated upon, but for Elena's sharp reaction to the touch of my hand at our first meeting. Her involuntary recoil was a blow to my self-esteem, and set me to wondering anxiously where there could be something physically wrong with me. Conversely, her gesture somehow established her own physical purity, which in turn justified her fear of contamination. All the same, I had seen her shrink from unpremeditated, accidental and wholly innocent contact with me, and I found it hard to bear. And the more unworthy I came to feel, the more desirable did she become, and the more unattainable.

After a rehearsal one night I fell into conversation with her father, whose turn it was to accompany her to New York. Mr. Kovner was a tall, loosely built, round-shouldered, balding man, with an aquiline nose and a face and brow deeply lined. He told me he had happened to hear me at my debut with the Educational Alliance Orchestra. He complimented me on the showing I made, and invited me to come to Brooklyn and play sonatas with his daughter. I was overjoyed at the invitation. My visit to Brooklyn would perhaps give me the chance to erase the unfavorable impression I felt I had made on Elena. However, before accepting, I waited for Elena to second her father. Mr. Kovner saw my hesitation and said sharply, "Lena, wouldn't you like to play sonatas with Chotzinoff?" Elena looked embarrassed, and the freckles on her face seemed more numerous than they were a moment before. "Yes," she replied hesitantly, avoiding my gaze and looking at her father, "if Chotzinoff can find the time." It was settled that I should come out the following Saturday early and spend the day.

We left the Educational Alliance together. Elena and her
father were walking to the Brooklyn Bridge to take a streetcar,
and I offered to accompany them. At the end of East Broadway
we came into the Bowery. I had been walking on Mr. Kovner's
right, Elena on the inside. But now Mr. Kovner took the
inside with the obvious purpose of shielding his daughter from
the drunks and derelicts who wandered out or were ejected
from the saloons that lined the street. Mr. Kovner talked all the
way. He spoke didactically, in a half-serious, sometimes banter-
ing way, and with a strong Russian-Jewish accent. I was impressed by the scope of his knowledge and the positiveness of
his views. "There goes Mr. Poverty," he said, pointing to a
bedraggled, unsteady figure who had lurched through the
swinging doors of a saloon we were passing. "Mr. Poverty in
person," he iterated sarcastically. "A little *schicker*"—drunk—
"too. But don't waste your sympathy on him. He looks quite
happy. When he gets home he'll be even happier beating up
his wife and children. Reform? He doesn't want to reform. He
wants beer. Yet for the cost of one battleship we could abolish
him—we could abolish this whole stinking Bowery. . . ." Mr.
Kovner laughed sardonically at the improbability of such a
thing ever happening. "I'm talking foolishness," he said. "A
battleship is important. This poor *schlemiel* is not." I asked
Mr. Kovner deferentially if he was a socialist. "I don't like
labels," he answered defiantly. "I am a *nothing*. But if you must
call me something, call me a common-senser. Common sense,
not theories, is what the world needs."

Later, through friends of the Kovners, I learned enough
about Elena's father to understand his skepticism about political
parties and social panaceas. He had been a nihilist in Russia, and
had been active in the revolutionary movement. The failure of
that movement, which he attributed to the inertia and, indeed,

the hostility of the peasants and workers, left him disillusioned and embittered. He came to America, where, after undergoing a long period of hardship, he managed to buy a small, hitherto unprofitable stationery store in Brooklyn. Mr. Kovner's industry soon turned the store into a moderately profitable business. He took pride in his store, and without relinquishing his humanitarian philosophy, he began to extol the virtues of private enterprise. The vacuum left by his loss of faith in the various economic ideologies he had embraced in his youth and early manhood he now filled with a passion for all things Jewish, and a secret belief in the musical destiny of his daughter.

The Kovners had four children. Elena, an only daughter, was the oldest. They were all named after their parents' favorite persons in life and fiction: Elena after the heroine of Turgenev's novel *On the Eve,* the boys, Leo, Theodore and Victor, after Tolstoi, Herzl (the founder of the Zionist movement) and Hugo, respectively. I considered Elena's name a fortunate choice, though I couldn't imagine Elena Kovner declaring her passion to her lover first, as the fictional Elena had done. But I found a similarity between the two in beauty, character and dedication to an ideal (music with the real Elena, revolution in the case of Turgenev's Elena).

I was so eager to visit the Kovners that I arrived at their stationery store in Brooklyn on Saturday very much earlier than I was expected. Elena was behind the counter dispensing cigars and cigarettes to customers. She was embarrassed when she saw me, and her greeting was self-conscious. Her father came in from a back room, welcomed me brusquely, and told Elena to take me upstairs to their apartment. This was a large flat on the second floor, directly over the store. It was comfortably furnished. Off the living room there was a kind of alcove with shelves lined with books, a couch and a morris chair. I looked

at the morris chair with admiration. I knew about William
Morris' efforts to beautify the homes of the poor with severe,
un-Victorian furniture. Someday I hoped to be able to afford a
morris chair. Elena had a room all to herself, facing the avenue.
I had never known anyone in a family having sole possession of
a room.

Mrs. Kovner came in from the kitchen, wearing a gay
flowered apron. After wiping her hands on it, she shook my
hand and expressed her pleasure at my visit. I had seen Mrs.
Kovner at several rehearsals and had been attracted by her
geniality and charm of manner. She was small and well filled
out, and she moved with a natural grace that made her look
younger than she was. Her way of speaking, and the musical
quality of her voice, hinted, ever so indefinitely, at coquetry.
The contrast between her warmth and naturalness and her
daughter's painful reserve and self-consciousness was startling.
(Nevertheless, I knew instinctively that Elena's reserve con-
cealed emotional depths that her mother lacked.)

"I am in the middle of baking a cake," Mrs. Kovner said,
with a smile that was like an embrace. "Come and see it." She
took me by the hand and led me into the kitchen. The cake was
a rich chocolate with many tiny round "button" candies, brown,
pink and white, embedded in its top. "You've seen Papa?"
Mrs. Kovner inquired, putting the finishing touches to the cake.
She, too, had a foreign accent. But, unlike her husband's, it was
soft, and it added a pleasant musical dimension to the sense of
her words. At that moment Mr. Kovner came into the kitchen.
"You are wasting precious time," he said to me mock-earnestly.
"Elena is waiting for you." I heard Elena tuning her cello in
the living room. As I left the kitchen, Mrs. Kovner called after
me pleasantly, "Look out for Papa. He's a slave driver."

We played several antique sonatas. Once, when we paused

to rest and chat, Mr. Kovner came in and asked Elena to play the Schumann concerto with me. Elena suggested that I might be tired and hungry. "At his age," her father said banteringly, "a man should never be tired. And if he is hungry," he added, "it should be for more music." We played the concerto and Mrs. Kovner came to the doorway and listened. At the finish, before Mr. Kovner could ask us to play again, she summoned us to lunch. Mr. Kovner looked disappointed, and murmured something about its being too early to eat. But Mrs. Kovner shooed us into the dining room with her apron, like a farmer's wife rounding up a flock of geese. The three boys now appeared, and we were introduced and shook hands. They were nice, good-looking boys, as yet too young to exhibit traces of the talents implicit in their exalted names.

During lunch Mr. Kovner had much to say, both seriously and jestingly. Mrs. Kovner did not hesitate to interrupt him, sometimes even at the climax of an anecdote or peroration, with some irreverent remark, laughing musically, and looking at him with affection. Mr. Kovner would cease talking, and frown at her, and she would pretend alarm and cry, "Oh, excuse me, Papa . . . excuse me. I only wanted to ask Chotzinoff if he'd like another piece of cake. . . . Chotzinoff, have another piece!" Mr. Kovner, still looking resentful, resumed his discourse, which happened to be a homily on the poverty of language. "The way people talk around here is really ridiculous. They have one word to describe everything . . . well, maybe two words. I asked a customer this morning how she was feeling. 'Gorgeous,' she said. Imagine! She felt *gorgeous!* If she hadn't been feeling 'gorgeous' she would be feeling 'rotten.' " Mr. Kovner's indignation grew as he continued. "Don't get so excited, Papa," Mrs. Kovner interjected, beaming at her husband as she spoke. "Eat your cake." Mr. Kovner looked sternly at his wife, perversely put his fork down and pushed away his plate. "The other day," he continued, "I heard young Sweeny—old Sweeny is a district judge around here—I heard young Sweeny say to another kid, 'My father is *it* around here.' Imagine! His father is *it*!" Mrs. Kovner laughed a long, silvery peal and said, "Well, isn't he?" Mr. Kovner gave her an angry look and was about to reply. But a bell rang in the hall, signifying the presence of a customer in the store, and he hastily went downstairs.

After lunch Mr. Kovner urged us to play again. But Mrs. Kovner intervened, saying we mustn't mind him, and suggested that I take Elena for a walk in nearby Prospect Park. The idea of being alone with Elena for a while gave me a pleasurable feeling. But as we were starting out, Elena asked her youngest brother, Victor, to accompany us. On our walk Victor exhibited a delightful propensity to wander off by himself. His absences were, however, remarked by his sister, who retrieved him from side streets and once, in the park, from behind trees and bushes.

Nevertheless, I enjoyed the walk, even though I saw that Elena deliberately maintained a certain distance between us. When she was not looking for Victor, we talked about books. I was delighted to find that she shared my preferences among authors, and that she liked poetry. She had just finished reading *David Copperfield,* and I was eager to know who was her favorite character in the book. I expected her to say David or Agnes or even Ham, all exemplary people, likely to appeal to her moral sense. But when she said Steerforth, I was both shocked and delighted, for I sensed in her choice a secret yearning for the romantic, with little consideration for ethics or morals. I could not have imagined that Elena would take to the passionate, generous, wicked, kind, cruel and noble Steerforth. I was not presumptuous enough to compare myself with Steerforth. Yet Elena's confession held, I felt, vague promises for me in the future.

When we returned, Elena, at her father's bidding, played an unaccompanied Bach sonata. Mr. Kovner was very fond of Bach, especially of the C Minor Sonata. One of the movements, he said, reminded him of a service by a cantor and a choir. The sonata was new to me, and it affected me deeply. I sat on a footstool in a corner of the room and watched Elena narrowly, as with eyes closed she sang the noble melodies and wove the threads of the beautiful ornamentation. Elena's tone and phrasing were highly personal, and (in retrospect) probably sentimental. Her pent-up emotions were released by her fingers and bow; every note vibrated with nervous passion. Even the double stops and chords throbbed with emotion. I could not help wondering how musical purists would regard such unacademic, emotional interpretation. For me, the provocative face and figure of the player, the tenuous affinity between us, and the blandishments of the music itself were all fused in a single disturbing yet happy feeling which I had never known before. When I used to listen to Sol Rashkin's luscious tone on the violin I was always uncomfortably conscious of his coarseness as a man. With Elena all seemed in harmony—her face, figure, manner, artistry, even her family and surroundings.

Elena herself was visibly moved by her playing, and when she finished the sonata she went to her room without a word. She came back ten minutes later, exhibiting her usual *nervous* composure. When I complimented her on her performance, she rewarded me with an awkward smile, and quickly spoke of something else. Her father said what a wonderful composer Bach was, and how universal the religiosity of his music was; that he could just as well have been a cantor in a synagogue in

Minsk as in a Lutheran church in Leipzig. "And how beautifully you played the sonata, Lena!" (I disliked his calling her
Lena; it sounded so prosaic.) "But now that Chotzinoff has had
a good rest, why don't you play something with him! It's kind
of foolish not to take advantage of his being here, don't you
think?" We played the Saint-Saëns concerto.

After supper we played again, and around eleven o'clock
Elena and I went downstairs, and sat and talked in a kind of
utility room in back of the store. At midnight Mr. Kovner shut
up shop and we all had tea. Mr. Kovner then said—pointedly, I
thought—that it was getting late, and summoning his wife to
bed, he said good night and went upstairs. Mrs. Kovner lingered
on a moment. And when her husband was out of earshot she
called him a bear, and said I was not to take him seriously, and
that I might stay awhile if I liked. She hoped I would feel at
home there, and that I would come as often as I pleased. "And
you don't *have* to play," she added, laughing, and left us alone.

The day had passed in a kind of enchantment. I had never
known a family like the Kovners. Music was actually a part of
their lives—indeed, the most important part. The peculiar charm
of the mother and the aggressive intellectualism of the father
were alike endearing. Elena herself was the ideal of girlhood I
had dreamed about for years, a combination of fragility, reserve
(too much reserve, alas, in Elena), intellectual curiosity and
musical talent. Her strange fear of physical contact with men—
I assumed, of course, she kept not only me, but all men at a
distance—enhanced her attractiveness. Her brothers looked up
to her, her parents adored her. It was a family of one's dreams.

I took Mrs. Kovner at her word and became a frequent
visitor in Brooklyn. I got to know Mr. Kovner well. When he
was not surfeited with music—this happened perhaps for only
an hour or so during waking hours—he talked about Jewish

folklore and Jewish literature. An atheist, he nevertheless found pleasure in memories of the Jewish ritualistic observances of his childhood in Russia. He introduced me to the stories of Peretz, which he read aloud in Yiddish, stopping frequently to comment on the author's understanding of the many Jewish types in the towns and villages within the Russian pale. I was surprised to find that there was a serious Jewish literature. Hitherto I had known only the cruder kind my parents devoured in the conservative Jewish newspapers, that which concerned itself with sentimental stereotypes. I had been taught in my childhood that the Jews were a superior race, vastly superior to the Christians. But their superiority, it was made clear to me, resided in their *cleverness.* The difference between a *Yiddishe kopf* (Jewish head) and a *goyishe kopf* was the difference between shrewdness and stupidity. I never thought of the Jew as a poetic figure. Yet in the stories of Peretz and Sholem Aleichem the Jew *was* a poetic figure, poetic in his cleverness, his wit, his humor, his religiosity, his naïveté and his unworldliness (except for an insignificant number of rich Jews—the *balabatim*—who felt important and were pompous). As Mr. Kovner read the stories, I felt my heart contract with sympathy for characters which I recognized as having lived all around me in my childhood and youth, in Russia and America. Now, for the first time, I felt the *poetry* of their humor, their pathetic nobility of character, their other-worldliness (even the money grubbers among them *changed* into other-worldliness on the Sabbath).

Tears filled my eyes as I listened, and Mr. Kovner, noticing them, looked up from his book and said, "Don't be ashamed of your feelings, Chotzinoff. No matter what we may think we are, we are, at bottom, Jews." I felt he was speaking the truth. Else why should I feel such kinship with the lowly people in the Peretz tales! Why should I understand the heroism of the impoverished, simple, unlettered porter in one of the stories, who, learning that in the Hereafter, in Heaven, his wife, being a woman, would be ineligible to join him there as an equal and could only serve as his footstool, renounces Heaven in protest! And why should I, a disbeliever like Mr. Kovner, identify myself with the old rabbi of another tale, who leaves his house before sunrise each morning and is held by the neighbors to ascend to Heaven; until a scoffer, determined to discover the truth about the rabbi's disappearances, follows him at a distance and sees him enter a forest, where, stooping painfully, he collects an armful of wood which he then carries, sighing and groaning as he walks, to the house of a poor bedridden widow, some miles out of town. "It is true!" the contrite skeptic later reports to his neighbors in the town. "The rabbi *does* ascend to Heaven. I saw him *myself!*"

Mr. Kovner's preoccupation with Judaism, with erudition, with ethics and with making a decent living was constant. But his absorbing passion was his daughter. He was determined that Elena should be a great artist. She was also to be an educated woman, for Education had been the lodestar of Mr. Kovner's impoverished youth. Mr. Kovner found me fertile ground for his theories and enthusiasms. But it was obvious that he regarded me chiefly as an aid to his daughter's musical progress. I was there to accompany her on the piano, and to spur her on to practice. And my general knowledge of music would widen her rather narrow musical horizon. On all counts I was *good* for Elena.

From Mr. Kovner's point of view I was better for Elena than Philip Diamond. Philip Diamond was a young piano student who lived nearby. Not that Philip did not have his uses. He practiced hard, and that in itself constituted for Mr. Kovner a good influence. Philip's technique was better than mine. I envied him his clean, brittle dexterity in scales, octaves and arpeggios. But for Mr. Kovner Philip was too keen on having a career of his own to be of any considerable benefit to his daughter. Furthermore he was, unlike me, a poor sight reader. He could play only what he had studied, and he certainly knew nothing of the general literature of music. Mr. Kovner encouraged both Philip and me to come often; but I felt I was the more favored. And when Philip sat too long at the piano, showing off his technique, Mr. Kovner, frowning, retired to his morris chair in the library alcove and lost himself in some Jewish literary work.

Philip's mother, a tall, dark-haired, handsome woman, came often to the Kovners'. She was as positive as Mr. Kovner was in her determination to make her child into a great artist. She herself weighed the merits of celebrated piano teachers and alone decided which one to choose for Philip. She knew the history of all concert pianists and their present standing with the public. Like Madame Franko, she sought out the "right" people. She took Philip to the parties that friends and neighbors were always giving, and managed to have Philip asked to play. I was sometimes tempted to envy Philip his mother. Compared with his, mine was ignorant and ineffectual. Yet after one of Mrs. Diamond's noisy visits to the Kovners', I thought that perhaps both Philip and I had the kind of mother best suited to our temperaments. "Phil is in the middle of 'Gradusesspennasses,'" Mrs. Diamond once announced loudly, with a careless disregard for the correct pronunciation of Clementi's book of technical studies and, obviously, with no idea of its meaning. "Play the one with the big skips." And Philip dutifully sat down at the piano and played very correctly and impersonally one of the most difficult études in the *Gradus ad Parnassum*.

The Diamonds owned a dry-cleaning establishment near the
Kovners' stationery store. Phil's father, a small, mild-mannered
man, worked long hours and was hardly ever seen. But his
industry enabled Mrs. Diamond to devote all her time to her
son. There was hardly a day when she did not drop in at
Kovner's store to tell about some new "connection" she had
made for Phil, to ask how Elena was progressing, and to offer
suggestions for the furtherance of Elena's career. As for me, Mrs.
Diamond implied that I was in no sense a rival of Philip's,
though I had my place (a modest one) in the world of music.
She talked to me about the difficulties of becoming a "virchee-
ozo," as against the ease with which one might become an accompanist, a teacher, a musicologist or music critic. When Mrs.
Diamond held forth on the subject of musical careers, Mr.
Kovner, pretending not to listen, paid heed, though he thought
her a silly, talkative woman. For Mrs. Diamond frankly avowed
an ambition that he secretly cherished. Mrs. Kovner, on the
other hand, entered wholeheartedly into her neighbor's problems and plans, and smilingly praised her foresight and
ingenuity. When Mrs. Diamond left, Mr. Kovner chided his
wife for being hypocritical. "I can't understand you," he burst
out, "listening to that foolishness. Besides, you know very well
Philip will never have a career. He plays without heart." Here
Mr. Kovner gave me a knowing look. Mrs. Kovner acknowledged her hypocrisy, but defended it. "Why shouldn't I make
her happy? Nobody likes to talk to the wall! Papa doesn't know
when he hurts people's feelings," she said, turning to me. Then
teasingly to her husband, "Don't you enjoy it when people talk
about Lena's playing?" Mr. Kovner, unable to cope with his
wife's raillery, abruptly left the room. "Poor Papa!" Mrs.
Kovner said softly, her eyes glowing with tenderness. "He tries
to be honest, even if it hurts people."

Once, when I happened to be alone with Mrs. Kovner, she told me about "Papa's" early struggles in America, and how hard he had to work to gain the comparative ease they were now enjoying. I said it must have been pretty hard on her too. "Oh!" she exclaimed, "I can stand more than he can. Besides, the children were a pleasure. I tell you, Chotzinoff, I couldn't keep my hands off them. I can't even now that they're grown up. All day long I played with them. I hugged and kissed them all day long. You won't believe me, Chotzinoff, but I used to be afraid that I would do them harm—sometimes they would be black and blue from my pinching. I would forget to make dinner for Papa, I was so busy with them, tending them, feeding them, washing and dressing them, and making them laugh. Oh, how we used to laugh, the children and I! Papa would come home and find no dinner, and he got angry and gave me a lecture. You know how he is even now. The house wasn't clean, he had to go out and buy delicatessen. . . . But he loved the children too, and worried as much as I did when they got sick. Oh, Chotzinoff! What happy times they were! But don't think I'm not happy now. I'm very happy. But the children are big now. They don't belong to me the way they used to. I can't hug and kiss them the way I used to—how would it look!" She laughed at the very idea, but she looked at me inquiringly, as if she hoped I would tell her that it would look good even now.

§ II

I began to spend more time at the Kovners' than at home. I now went to Brooklyn on weekdays as well as on Saturdays and Sundays, arriving in the late afternoon about the time Elena came home from high school. After Elena had her glass of milk, Mr. Kovner would show signs of impatience for us to begin playing. We generally played until suppertime. After supper Elena's brother Leo relieved his father at the store. Mr.

Kovner ensconced himself in the morris chair, lit his pipe, and asked us to play something especially for him. He cannily suggested some piece which Elena was studying at the moment; in playing it Elena would really be practicing, since she would be obliged to repeat passages that hadn't gone well the first time. Toward midnight he would say meaningfully, "Well it's time for all good Jews to be in bed. Come to bed, Sonia," he called to his wife. The couple retired and I would linger on, often on the pretext of playing some more. So long as we played, there was no protest from Mr. Kovner's bedroom. But when the music ceased for any length of time, Mr. Kovner's voice would reach us, loud and impatient: "Elena, it's late, you have school tomorrow . . ." and I would reluctantly leave.

On Sundays the Kovners kept open house, entertaining relatives and friends from morning to night. The Sklars, father, mother, son and daughter, came from Yonkers. Mr. and Mrs. Sklar had known the Kovners in the old country, and felt bound to them by nostalgia for their youthful liberalism and revolutionary ardor. Mary, the daughter, was about Elena's age. She was a vivid, pretty girl with large, liquid, coal-black eyes and dark hair, and a skin with the tawny, velvety texture of an early-ripening peach. Dr. Isidor Lesser and his wife, Mollie, came from the Lower East Side. Mrs. Lesser was considerably younger than her husband. She was small and quite thin. Her face, too, was small, almost miniature, and her skin, tightly stretched, glowed with a delicate fire which I thought beautiful until I learned that it was the outward reflection of an advanced state of tuberculosis. Mrs. Kovner told me the history of this couple. Like Mr. Kovner, Dr. Lesser had started out with a newspaper stand. He had managed, under the most trying conditions, to pay for evening courses in dentistry. He now enjoyed a fine practice, and was reputed to be rich. The Lessers had two children, a boy of six and a girl of eight. But Dr. Lesser's happiness was overshadowed by his wife's illness. The doctor, Mrs. Kovner said, treated Mrs. Lesser like a baby, carrying her from room to room when she had her relapses, and waiting on her hand and foot. He had sent her, the preceding year, to Colorado, at great expense. There the disease had been temporarily arrested. But he lived in daily fear of a recurrence. Mrs. Lesser, on the other hand, was gay and voluble, behaving like one who is not aware of the seriousness of her malady. Yet she was aware of it. According to Mrs. Kovner, gaiety and optimism were characteristic of all consumptives.

At first I was inclined to look down on Dr. Lesser simply because he was a dentist. Dentists, at the time, were the objects of ridicule, and the butt of jokes among us. They were considered ignorant opportunists who took advantage of the lenient requirements of the State Board and took the shortest possible cut to a profession that was second only to medicine in desirability. Dentists were springing up like mushrooms. They gave themselves the airs of physicians and even surgeons, and their wives referred to them ostentatiously as "my husband, the doctor." In addition, Dr. Lesser was rather unprepossessing physically. He was large and stoutish, with a round, rosy, homely face, sparse curly hair and a small, bulbous nose with a few small hairs sprouting from its tip. I couldn't at first imagine what could have attracted the fragile, neat and delicate Mrs. Lesser to him. But on further acquaintance I found in him an engaging forthrightness and honesty. He was also well read in subjects like economics and politics, and well versed in Jewish lore. In one respect he was unique: he paid cash for everything, and owed nobody anything! This I saw with my own eyes when I became a frequenter of his office-flat on Avenue B and Ninth Street, which I soon did, both as patient and friend. I was dumfounded by his fanatical addiction to settling money matters on the spot. He sent no bills. He obliged all his patients (except me) to pay in cash after each visit. Or, in the case of a prolonged dental "job," he exacted part payments large enough to cover the work he had done, in the event that the patient failed to appear. For his part, the doctor always carried a large roll of bills, from which he peeled off singles, twos, fives and even tens to pay for the dental appliances and medicaments itinerant salesmen brought to his office. Each morning he gave his wife her allowance in cash. He had no checking account, but every Friday he deposited money in a savings bank. I envied the Lessers for being so absolutely free of economic irritations. I did think, however, that Dr. Lesser was perhaps too money-conscious. It seemed to me that he could afford to live better than he did. The Lessers had only a single maid, who did all the work for both office and living quarters, and who never appeared to have a moment to herself. Well-to-do dentists usually lived in spacious quarters separate from their offices, on an upper floor of the same house, and had a trained nurse in a white cap and dress in attendance downstairs. The Lessers' apartment was actually one with the office and waiting room. The living quarters consisted of a single bedroom, a parlor, kitchen and bath. The children occupied the bedroom. The doctor and his wife slept on a divan in the parlor. And there was no nurse in white in the waiting room to call out, "Next patient," and to help the doctor administer gas for a difficult extraction.

One day the doctor asked me point-blank, in front of the Kovners, too, what my fee for teaching his two children the piano would be! I was embarrassed at his indelicacy, and Mrs. Lesser blushed with shame. She murmured "Isidor!" reprovingly. The doctor flared up. "I don't see what's wrong, Mollie, my asking him what he charges," he said, and he looked at everyone in turn as if for help against his wife's unjust, unspoken accusation. "I don't mind when patients ask *me* what I charge. I expect them to ask. Perhaps Chotzinoff is too expensive for me," he added seriously; but instantly sensing the humor of his remark, he added, "or too cheap." He looked appealingly at his wife, who turned away in scorn. "Well," he exclaimed, greatly annoyed, "you mean I should leave things up in the air . . . like this . . ." and he trailed off into indistinctness, altogether at a loss to convey the gravity, for him, of monetary disorder.

A week later Dr. Lesser asked me (this time we were alone) if a dollar a lesson would be agreeable to me. I was dumfounded by his generosity. My fee had never exceeded fifty cents. I suspected Mrs. Lesser's hand in this offer, not without reason; but I accepted it with gratitude, and set off to look for a second-hand piano for the Lessers. I found a good one at Spector's on Grand Street for a hundred dollars. Dr. Lesser, who accompanied me, peeled off ten ten-dollar bills from the great wad he always carried in a large leather wallet in the back pocket of his pants, and gave it then and there to Mr. Spector. Mr. Spector's business rested entirely on the credit system. He was quite taken aback by this unusual cash transaction, and he looked at Dr. Lesser as at some strange customer from another planet. The doctor asked for a receipt, and Mr. Spector, beckoning me to follow him, retreated into his office. He shut the door and held up one of the ten-dollar bills he had received. "Are you a teacher?" he asked. I said I was. "Ten per cent commission on teachers' sales," he said. "You got a card?" I blushed. I had no card. "A teacher and no card?" he said skeptically. I told him Dr. Lesser would vouch for me, and he laughed derisively, and said *that* was an old game he was

on to, a ruse to get a teacher's commission, which is then returned to the purchaser. But when I told him my name and
referred him to Katz's music store, he remembered my debut
at the Educational Alliance and asked to be excused for not
having recognized me. "In this business there are so many
ganovim"—thieves—he explained genially, "that a man has
to be careful." He gave me the bill, and hoped we would continue to do business together. And as we shook hands, he said,
"This friend of yours, does he always pay cash?" And when I
said he did, Mr. Spector looked puzzled and shrugged his
shoulders. "It takes all kinds!" he commented, opening the door
for me.

The Since the Lessers were by now my friends, I thought I was
morally bound to hand over my commission to them. But that
was the very practice Mr. Spector found so abhorrent. Still,
the commission represented a sizable sum for me, but not for
the doctor, who always had a great number of ten-dollar bills,
and one more or less could hardly affect his mode of living. I
could buy things needed in the house, give it to my mother
to pay bills, or, recklessly ignoring my obligations at home,
squander it on music and books. Torn between cupidity and
friendship, and unable to arrive at a decision, I decided to confide in Mrs. Lesser, and let her determine what I should do.
To my relief, Mrs. Lesser advised me to keep the money, which
she thought I had earned honestly. "And don't mention it to
the doctor," she advised, "though I'm sure he'd agree with
me."

The piano arrived the next day, and I began giving the
children lessons. They showed no talent for the instrument,
and after a month or so I said as much to Mrs. Lesser. I told
her she was throwing out her money (it came to four dollars
a week!) and advised her to stop the lessons and, perhaps, sell

the piano. Mrs. Lesser said I was silly, that neither she nor the doctor had ever expected their children to become artists, and that they would be satisfied with whatever I could teach them. Again she cautioned me not to say anything about the matter to the doctor. Having once more obeyed the dictates of friendship, I could now continue the lessons with a clear conscience. I also enjoyed being with the Lessers. After the lessons I was always urged to stay on. I read stories to the children while Mrs. Lesser, looking dainty and neat in a blue skirt and an immaculate white blouse with a starched collar, lay on the divan and knitted or sewed. Between patients the doctor darted in and out of the living room to speak tenderly to his wife ("and how is my little wifey today?"), or hear me play the piano, which I now did frequently. The doctor knew little about orchestral and instrumental music, but he hummed the leading arias of a few standard operas he witnessed year after year at the Metropolitan. When it came to the Metropolitan he did not stint himself. He and his wife sat in the balcony in two-dollar seats. One day when we were alone for a while he spoke of his partiality for *La Bohème*. Suddenly his eyes filled with tears, and he told me that he could no longer bear to see it. "Mollie will soon die, like Mimi," he said pathetically. "I don't know how I will be able to bear it."

But Mollie always weathered the frequent attacks of coughing and spitting blood. Some afternoons when I arrived at the Lessers', I would find her propped up with pillows on the divan, looking feverish, her little face full of red patches, her eyes overbrilliant, her small bosom heaving in pain and making rasping sounds with each breath. Between coughing spells she would murmur, "Chotzinoff . . . I can't . . . I *can't* . . ." as if she was being forced to do something against her will. Dr. Lesser was at her side as often as he could leave his office, fixing her pillows, wiping the perspiration from her brow, and giving her medicines to drink. He was cheerful in her presence, making light of her condition and constantly reminding her of her unusual recuperative powers ("Now be a good little wifey, swallow this. . . . You always get better"). When he went back to work I sat on a chair close to her and tried to divert her mind with talk of friends or of music and books, in a low voice, over the faint, insistent hum of the doctor's drill which came from his office, separated from us only by the small waiting room. To ensure quiet for his wife, the doctor sent the children to play in the streets. But when I offered to leave, both he and Mrs. Lesser begged me to stay.

When I was not at the Kovners' in Brooklyn, I was at the Lessers' on Avenue B. The Kovners, for me, represented culture and romance; the Lessers flattered my vanity and made me feel important. In their eyes, as in the eyes of my family, I was already a great pianist and a man of limitless culture. I played them the scores of operas they knew and of some (*Pelléas et Mélisande,* for example) they hadn't even heard of. I read them poetry I admired and novels I loved. I took them to concerts, or rather they took me, for when we arrived at Carnegie or Mendelssohn Hall, Mrs. Lesser whispered to her husband, and the doctor ran ahead of us to the box office to purchase seats in the balcony, or standing room in the orchestra. When the doctor worked late in the evening, Mrs. Lesser and I went to hear music by ourselves. And on returning we found the doctor in the living room catching up on the *Jewish Daily Forward.* We would have tea and cake. Between midnight and 1 A.M., the doctor would say, "Well, wifey, it's time . . ." and he would pull out the under section of the divan, which then became a double bed. This was my signal to leave, even though Mrs. Lesser protested, and claimed it was early and she was feeling quite well and wanted to stay up a while longer. Sometimes the doctor walked me home and talked about his fears for his wife. On all other subjects he was optimistic.

I became, in fact, one of the family, and came and went at my pleasure. One evening when the doctor pulled out the divan, Mrs. Lesser said it was too late to go home, and suggested that I should spend the night. I could share the couch with the doctor and she would make up a bed for herself on chairs. The doctor looked annoyed, and I quickly said that my mother would be waiting up for me and would worry at my absence. (This was indeed true; yet I frequently spent the night at the Kovners' without giving her notice.) That night I went home, much to the doctor's relief. But Mrs. Lesser repeated her invitations, and one night the doctor himself surprisingly seconded her plea. I gave in. And thereafter, when it grew too late to go home, I slept on the divan with the doctor, and Mrs. Lesser slept on a featherbed on chairs in a corner of the same room. To observe the proprieties, Mrs. Lesser went into the children's bedroom to change into nightclothes and give her husband and me a chance to slip into bed in our underwear; and in the morning she would disappear, to enable us to dress. The living room had a sink which the doctor and I used for our ablutions. Mrs. Lesser and the children used the bathroom. This had a porcelain bathtub, which I used occasionally, especially in the summer. The doctor went regularly to a Russian bath on Avenue B each Thursday night, and returned several hours later, in good humor and red as a beet from the hot, stifling vapors of the steam room.

My mother wished to meet the couple with whom I spent so much time. I invited the Lessers to supper one night. The doctor was very genial and quite hit it off with my father. They talked about the Talmud and other religious matters, and after drinking a good deal of schnapps (whiskey) out of my father's highly treasured silver goblets, they exchanged humorous anecdotes about the foibles and weaknesses of rabbis in the old country (Russia). My father surprised me by telling an off-color story about a peripatetic rabbi whose wife never ceased being pregnant, a phenomenon which baffled the townspeople, for the rabbi would come home on Friday in time to go to shul and depart Saturday night at sundown. Everybody wondered at the *rabbitsin's* (rabbi's wife) extraordinary fecundity. They had forgotten, my father said (this was the cream of the jest), the time-honored customary nap taken by all good Jews and their wives in the interval between the Saturday *cholent* (midday meal) and *salasudis* (Saturday-afternoon light repast). My father did not have to elaborate. Everybody, even I, understood the salacious implication, and there was general laughter. I did not, in my younger days, care for such anecdotes. But Mr. Kovner had infected me with his passion for Jewish folklore, and my father's story seemed to fall into that category. I enjoyed it with the others at the table. My father was also impressed with the doctor's reputed affluence and the large amount of cash he always carried about. When the Lessers left, my mother said she thought they were a nice couple, admirably suited to each other. However, in her opinion, *"ess passt nit"* (it wasn't proper) for me to spend so much of my time at their house, let alone to sleep there. I was displeased at the insinuation, and told her her suspicions were groundless, that Mrs. Lesser was devoted to her husband. Besides, she was ten years older than me. She had told me so herself. "Oh, she's more," my mother retorted, as she went into the kitchen to wash the dishes.

Dr. Lesser had many friends in the dental profession, and on Friday, the traditional free day of the week for dentists, they came to visit in Avenue B, arriving in the early afternoon, and remaining for dinner and a game of pinochle. They played for money, and the winners were pledged to spend a percentage of their winnings on ice cream for the company. Mrs. Lesser, when she was well enough, took part in the game. She was a lucky player, hardly ever losing. Though I did not know the game, she made me her partner and divided her winnings with me. She made me sit beside her, and she frequently asked my advice in jest. "Don't you think we should play this card now?" She generally played against her husband, and took unconcealed pleasure in winning from him. "We've won, we've won!" she would shout triumphantly. "Pay up, Isidor, pay up." Some weeks my share of her winnings added up to as much as a dollar and a half. I considered such money outside the jurisdiction of my family, and I spent it wholly on myself, buying second-hand books, and making payments on account at Katz's music store.

Most of the books I bought were classics. But sometimes my interest was engaged by some unknown, provocative title. One such book was the *Diary of a Lost One,* from the German, by an author whose name I can't recall. I read a few pages of the *Diary of a Lost One* in a second-hand bookshop, found them fascinating, bought the book and rushed home to finish it. The "Lost One" was a beautiful girl, forced by an early seduction and by poverty into prostitution, but craving, to the end of her short, tragic life, true love. To satisfy this womanly hunger, she went from man to man, believing each time she would find the true love she was seeking. At the end she fell in love and "gave" herself to an impecunious Russian aristocrat whose name ended in two f's. The poor creature was beguiled by the gentility and the noble breeding implicit in the two f's, as well as by the Russian's long, white tapering fingers. She adored

this idle, fastidious creature, and gave him all her earnings. His
inevitable desertion drove her to suicide. But she left her diary
(if I remember) as a warning to young girls to treasure their
virginity at all costs. I read the book in great agitation. It gave
me disturbing, yet pleasurable sensations. I could not explain
why, since the "Lost One" was as noble a character as I had
ever encountered in literature. I took the book with me to
Brooklyn to read aloud to Elena on a park bench in Prospect
Park. As I had hoped, Elena, too, was shaken by it, often turning away from me to conceal her emotion. I felt rather daring
in bringing such a book to Elena's notice, and I took care to
conceal it from her father.

George Moore's *Evelyn Innes* was another acquisition I
owed to Mrs. Lesser's luck at pinochle. I had read somewhere
that *Evelyn Innes* was the story of a gifted vocalist who became
a great soprano and a notable exponent of all the Wagnerian
heroines, from Elsa to Brünnhilde. Unlike the *Diary of Lost
One, Evelyn Innes* was a book I could openly give to Elena. I
bought it second-hand for fifty cents, and without pausing to
read in it, I took it to Brooklyn forthwith, and gave it to Elena
with the comment that I thought she resembled the heroine of
Moore's novel in several important respects. Elena was, of
course, impatient to read the book. As a result of my proselyt-
ing she was now almost as ardent a Wagnerite as I was. (Mrs.
Kovner told me, in confidence, that she had surprised Elena in
her room late one night, standing on a chair, flourishing a
yardstick and shouting "Hoy-yo-to-ho, ho!") Such physical
and emotional abandonment on the part of a girl so self-conscious and shy as Elena opened up possibilities for a closer
relationship between us. Now I saw in *Evelyn Innes* a book
that might draw us together or, at the very least, strengthen
Elena's devotion to Wagner. When I told Elena that she re-

minded me of Evelyn Innes, I permitted myself the fabrication of having read the book on the assumption that the author had made his heroine as pure and noble as the great Wagnerian women were. Of course, I intended to read the book at the earliest opportunity. "Yes," I reiterated with confidence, "you are very much like Evelyn. I saw the resemblance all through the book. I am sure you will see it too."

That night as I lay in bed, misgivings assailed me, and I regretted my rashness in lying to Elena so boldly. In the morning I got *Evelyn Innes* from the public library. To my horror, I found, as the story began to unfold, that Evelyn Innes had been endowed by the author with little of the purity and nobility of an Elsa or an Elizabeth. She was, in fact, the very opposite of these virtuous ladies. I shuddered to think what Elena must by now think of me as she followed Innes from one unholy love affair to another. Between blaming myself for my stupidity, and George Moore for his insensitiveness to the *moral* demands of Wagner, I spent a restless and miserable day. It was not until evening that I summoned courage to go to Brooklyn and face Elena. I expected her to overwhelm me with reproaches for comparing her "in several important respects"—the phrase haunted me—with the lewd Evelyn (how could George Moore make a lewd woman into a great artist!). But Elena's reaction was not at all what I thought it would be. Before I could even attempt some improbable explanation of my rash comment of the day before, she told me how pleased she was with the book, and how fascinating Evelyn Innes was. Had she forgotten my outrageous comparison? I believed she had. So, much relieved, I let the matter rest, and vowed to keep a closer watch over my tongue.

HAROLD L. GREENE

C&⁀Ɔ The year is 1907. I am eighteen years of age. We have moved from Rivington Street to Henry Street for no valid reason, except that people on the East Side were expected to move frequently. But I am now closer to the Educational Alliance and Katz's music store, for me the cultural centers of the East Side, both of them on East Broadway, a block or so away from our new quarters.

My sister Molly has married an immigrant cousin, a house painter, and the couple have gone to live in Waterbury, where jobs are easier to find than in New York. I am now the economic head of our house, tacitly acknowledged as such by my father, whose earnings from his profession as mohel (circumciser), officiator at weddings, and from the sale of matzoth and wines on Passover, are sporadic, and actually negligible. My own earnings are sporadic too, but not negligible. I have lean weeks when my piano pupils take sick, or find some other excuse for not coming, and my mother borrows small sums to tide us over. But I can count on four pupils who, during nine months of the year, take their lessons regularly. They are hardly ever subject to the ills that attack my less responsible pupils. They are, in fact, so devoted to me that I can keep them waiting for hours at a time, when I am visiting the Kovners or the Lessers, and I am loath to go home. My most basic pupils are the two Lesser children. They bring in regularly four dollars a week. A young accountant and his friend, also an accountant, bring me two dollars a week. Once a week I go to Jersey Heights to teach a boy of thirteen, the son of a Christian couple whose acquaintance I made the preceding summer at a Lake Hopatcong hotel, where I played the piano. Because it takes me four hours to go to Jersey Heights and return, Mrs. Courville, the Christian lady, pays me two dollars, and gives me a lunch of fried eggs and bacon (I now eat bacon, ham and all manner of Christian food without fear of divine retribution, though at home our table is strictly kosher). I have some pupils at fifty cents a lesson, and through Mr. Katz's influence I play occasional solos, or accompany singers and violinists at concerts and balls at Pythagoras and the new Clinton Hall. Summers are financially precarious. Although, since my disastrous fortnight at Kiamesha Lake with the sadistic Sol Rashkin I have become an experienced sight reader and never fail to get a job at a seaside or mountain resort, the pay is usually small and erratically doled out. Yet all in all our family is in a relatively strong position financially, the strongest I can remember since the old Connecticut days. My father's once intransigent temperament has realistically subsided into a mild individuality more in keeping with his diminished importance in the household. We are a small family of four (except for the constant and long visits of relations and friends). My half sisters and half brothers are all married, and my parents no longer have occasion to wrangle about them, and accuse each other of cruelty and injustice to "my" children.

There are only "our" children left—my younger sister and I.
My mother still loves me fanatically (I presume she is fond of
my young sister too, but I am certain her love for me takes
precedence over everything) and my father shows me a kind
of sheepish affection. I have no fear of him at all, and do as I
please, playing the piano at all hours, and filling the house with
my friends. He no longer complains about music as "noise"
that makes his head ache. Nor does he speak constantly, as he
used to, about the sons of his friend Zalman Reich, those
paragons of male progeny whose benefactions to their father
never ceased. The Reichs had moved uptown, and my father
now saw them infrequently. After a long absence, Zalman
Reich called on us one day with his little grandson of three,
the very one my father had circumcised. I suspect the true
object of the visit was to show off this remarkable child, whose
memory, his grandfather claimed, was as phenomenal as that
of the Vilna Cohen. Spurred on by my mother's promise of a
large piece of sponge cake as a reward, the boy planted himself
in the middle of the room, feet wide apart, and began cal-
culating rapidly, in an oratorical tone of voice, "two and two
is four; four and four, eight; eight and eight, sixteen; sixteen
and sixteen, thirty-two . . ." etc., etc. In this wise he went on
for a long time without pause, until the additions became
astronomical, and their accuracy had to be taken on faith by
his admiring audience. When he could read the complete
success of the demonstration on our incredulous faces, Zalman
Reich cut his grandson short in the middle of a computation
that was about to run into fifteen figures. "That's enough!" he
cried, and the child ceased abruptly and made a grab for the
piece of sponge cake which my mother held in her hand. That
was the last time I remember seeing Zalman Reich.

I made some new friends, most of whom I met at Katz's

music store, or through friends I had first met there. Not all of my new friends were musicians. Some were poets, some painters. Harold L. Greene was a student of literature with a passion for music. He was a heavy-set, tall youth whom I had seen often at Katz's buying music. He would come in dressed in a double-breasted dark-blue suit, stiff collar and large flowing tie, on his head a large fedora. He had a superior, forbidding manner, which was heightened by the rigid, lusterless stare of a wall-eye that always ran a little, and at which he kept dabbing with a handkerchief. Mr. Katz told me what he knew about H. L. Greene. Greene's parents ("Greene!" Mr. Katz said sarcastically. "Originally Greenberg, I suppose. And Harry," he added, "wasn't good enough for him. No. He had to change it to Harold. Don't ask me what the L. stands for") kept a fish store on Hester Street. H. L. was a student at City College and played the violin. How well he played Mr. Katz couldn't say, never having heard him. But judging by the didactic way in which H. L. spoke about the violin, and music in general, he thought he should play very well indeed. There was something so haughty about Greene that I could not doubt that he had great literary and musical knowledge. I longed to know him. And one day as H. L. Greene was looking over a volume of Beethoven sonatas for violin and piano, Mr. Katz said, "I think you two gentlemen should know each other. Chotzinoff—Greene . . . Greene—Chotzinoff." H. L. Greene turned his baleful eye toward me and nodded his head. "Yes, I heard you at the Educational Alliance," he said with condescension. Then, turning his face to the music, "Do you play these?" I had played some of the sonatas and I told him which ones I knew. "Not the 'Kreutzer'?" said H. L. sharply. I felt I was falling in his esteem, and I hastened to say that I was planning to look at the "Kreutzer" in the near future. H. L.

Greene stared at me so hard that his bad eye began to tear
copiously, and he was obliged to apply his handkerchief to it.
"*Look* at it?" he said incredulously. "But one does not *look at*
the 'Kreutzer.' One *studies* it." I said hastily that after a first
casual reading I would buckle down to learn it in earnest.
"Well," said H. L. loftily, "if you have nothing better to do at
the moment, come over with me to my house and we can play
it through." I said I would be happy to go home with him and
play the "Kreutzer." H. L. put the volume of sonatas under
his arm, said, "Charge it!" imperiously to Mr. Katz, and we
left.

The Greenes lived in a tenement directly over their basement fish store. The stairs leading to it were dirty, and on the
landing I caught a glimpse of a toilet that was even more un-
savory. H. L. led me into a room which he said he had all to
himself. This was unusual, and helped to explain his air of
superiority. The room contained a cot, a table, several chairs
and two large bookcases full of books, the overflow from which
lay in heaps on the floor. It was hard to believe that one person owned so many books. On my inquiring how he came by
them, H. L. said with a certain affectation of nonchalance that
he had "picked them up." They certainly represented a fortune
in money. I was eager to examine them, but H. L. opened his
violin case and took out his violin, which was wrapped in a
large silk handkerchief. He preceded me into the parlor,
where a brown upright piano stood against a wall. I sounded
the A and H. L., placing the instrument under his chin and
pressing its neck against the piano, began to tune noisily, turning the pegs back and forth vehemently, causing them to give
out pinched, rasping sounds. After much effort he achieved a
tuning to his satisfaction, but not to mine, though I said
nothing. "I would like to warm up with Bach," he announced,

placing the A Minor Concerto on the piano. But when he began to play I could hardly believe my ears, for he played clumsily, like an ill-taught, ungifted pupil. His tone was harsh, his phrasing crude. He played doggedly, with a kind of reckless desperation, the intensity of his fingering and bowing throwing his body into ungainly postures and bringing grimaces to his face. The performance was so out of keeping with the confidence and assurance of his bearing at Katz's music store that I could not trust myself to say something polite to him. Stranger still, he himself seemed unaware of his musical shortcomings. "Ysaye," he commented, as he placed the piano part of the Beethoven sonatas over the Bach, "Ysaye takes the first movement too fast, don't you think?" I had never heard Ysaye, and I made no reply. But I envied H. L.'s assurance, even though I saw plainly that it rested on a questionable foundation.

The "Kreutzer" fared no better. I was reading it at sight, yet I was more at ease than H. L., who had studied it and played it often. I was happy to turn from music to literature, for it soon was evident that H. L. knew a great deal about books. Here too, as with music, he assumed an air of lofty condescension. But now I did not mind. We went back to his room, and I examined his books closely. There was a great collection of plays, from the early Elizabethans to D'Annunzio. There was a complete set of the works of Henrik Ibsen, about whose importance I knew, but whose plays I had never read or seen. "He's a great playwright," I said, hoping to impress my new friend with my knowledge. "The greatest," H. L. said with sharp finality. I was taken aback. "Greater than Shakespeare?" I asked hesitantly. "Certainly!" H. L. replied, focusing his damaged eye on me in surprise, as if I had knowingly asked a foolish question. He then gave me a résumé of Ibsen's plays, the circumstances of their composition, the ideas they incorporated, their what he called tight, foolproof structure. H. L. Greene talked down to me, like a teacher to a pupil. He made me conscious of the gulf between us on the subject of Ibsen, but I was grateful for the lecture, and I began to look forward to a profitable association with him.

H. L. now proposed a walk. Downstairs we stopped in for a moment at the fish store. It was a cold day, and the shop was unheated. His father, mother and younger brother, bundled up to their necks in several layers of clothes, stood behind the counter, selecting and wrapping up fish for customers, mostly women, also bundled up. As we entered, H. L.'s parents paused in their work and looked at him with respect and ad-miration. "I won't be home to dinner," H. L. announced in an important voice. "Can you let me have a dollar? This"— pointing a backward thumb at me—"is Chotzinoff—the pianist." This flat, succinct reference to me as a pianist caused a mild sensation, and everybody turned to look at me. I felt like a commoner who has been suddenly knighted. H. L.'s father and mother wiped their right hands on their soiled and bloodstained aprons and shook hands with me across the counter. The elder Greene then took a dollar bill from a till and gave it to his son. "You don't need more?" he inquired anxiously. "It's enough," H. L. said. "Don't wait up for me," he added in the direction of his mother, and he stalked out of the store. "They aren't bad at all," he said apologetically. "Thursday nights, if I'm not doing anything, I don't mind helping them out at the store. I act as cashier. 'Fancy that, Hedda!'" he said airily, quoting (as I learned afterward) from Ibsen's *Hedda Gabler*. I had to admit to myself that there was something incongruous in the idea of H. L. Greene pre-siding at the cash box in the smelly, sand-strewn basement fish store we had just left. At the same time I could not but admire the generous impulse of this cultured young man to help out his parents on the busiest night of the week.

We walked toward Jackson Street Park on the East River. We had much to talk about. While maintaining by his lofty tone and manner the intellectual distance between us, H. L. condescended to fill me in on his past attainments, his future plans and his relations with his family. I must not, he advised me, equate the character of his parents with their business of purveying fish. They had never had the chance to better themselves. But they knew the value of culture and looked up to him, as I must have myself observed. Someday soon he, H. L., would be in a position to allow them to sell or give up their shop and live out their days in comfortable idleness. As soon as he was through with City College, H. L. was going abroad, to the University of Berlin, there to take postgraduate courses and receive the degree of Doctor of Letters. An appointment as professor of literature in some important American university would soon follow. With his substantial salary from the university and the royalties from a couple of critical works he had in mind to write (a critique of Ibsen was one), he looked forward to the future with an easy mind. In the meantime the fish store was doing well enough to see him through college and the University of Berlin, and to take care of necessities like books, theater, operas, concerts, music lessons, music and some pocket money besides. I appreciated H. L.'s confidence in me as he talked so openly about his private life. Though my own prospects were as vague as his were vivid, I would gladly have reciprocated by telling him about myself. But when I began to speak I saw that his attention wandered, and I hastily returned to the subjects that interested him more.

After a few hours of talk and walking about, H. L. said he felt the need of some refreshment. He took me to a restau-

rant known to him, on Grand Street near the river, and ordered
a nickel's worth of French fried potatoes from the man at the
counter. I had never eaten or even heard of French fried
potatoes, but they seemed to be no novelty to H. L., who called
them familiarly "French fries." They soon appeared, salted
and piping hot, in an oil-stained paper bag. We walked back
to Jackson Street Park, eating the delicious, soggy, limp strips
as we walked. We exhausted the subject of literature and H. L.
turned the talk to music. Here I was on firm ground. I shed my
diffidence and tried to speak with confidence and authority.
But while H. L. paid attention to my opinions and ideas, he
boldly advanced opinions and beliefs of his own, in his
habitual superior manner. But now, at any rate, I did not
hesitate to argue and contradict.

My own ideas about music had, in the last year, broadened.
To educate the Lessers up to the music dramas of Wagner I
had been obliged to start off with the popular Italian and
French operas, some of which they had heard, and so work up
to *Fidelio, Don Giovanni* and *Tristan und Isolde.* I borrowed
from the library the scores of *Faust, Aïda* and *Madama Butterfly,* none of which I had seen or heard. I was prepared to
despise them as prostitutions of art or, at best, collections of
tunes over naïve harmonies, foisted on dramatic situations of
which they were altogether independent. Yet when I played
and sang them I was unable to resist their spell. I was forced
to admit to myself that their harmonies were fresh, sometimes
startlingly beautiful, as in Amonasro's aria and in the Nile
scene of *Aïda.* (What extraordinary *Egyptian* color Verdi
managed in the oboe solo!) I was secretly ashamed to like
what the hordes of so-called music lovers who flocked to the
Metropolitan preferred over Wagner and Mozart. But in
playing and singing the popular operas for the Lessers, I
shamelessly succumbed to the blandishments of the music and

the stories, and my interpretations were emotional and sincere. So much so, that they affected me as genuinely as they did the Lessers, who listened entranced, as I could see from the concentrated expression of their faces. At last I gave up resisting them even secretly, and I decided, no matter how my friends at Katz's would regard my apostasy, to acknowledge openly their worth and standing as works of art, and add their names, though in lower-case letters, to the hallowed list whose supremacy I had hitherto so uncompromisingly upheld. Madama Butterfly (in the brand-new Puccini opera which, as interpreted by the young American soprano Geraldine Farrar, was the latest sensation at the Metropolitan) was not, as a woman, in a class with Isolde or Brünnhilde. Yet I could not restrain my tears over "Un bel di" or her final tragic farewell to life. I felt it would be unmoral for me to dissemble. I recalled the many admonitions of poets to acknowledge and, if need be, fight for one's convictions. Polonius had said to his son, "to thine own self be true,/And . . . thou canst not then be false to any man." (It was, of course, Shakespeare's own belief.) To be true to myself I knew I had to speak out about my new enthusiasms, not only to the Lessers, but to the musical skeptics I knew.

Munching the French fries, I confessed to H. L. Greene that it was now my considered opinion that Verdi, Gounod, Mascagni, Puccini and Leoncavallo had written worthy operas, notwithstanding the charge (true enough!) that their works were *melodious*. H. L. disdainfully rejected my claim and dared me to prove it. I accepted the challenge, and we adjourned to my house, where I had the scores of *Madama Butterfly* and *Pagliacci*. I played and sang my best, hoping to communicate my fervor to my new companion. I stopped often to explain the appositeness of a harmonic change, the effect of a modulation, the emotional truth of a melodic phrase. I knew my efforts were successful, and I could see that H. L. was trying to resist my onslaught on his emotions. He could not help acknowledging grudgingly the potency of some of the high points of the operas. But he capriciously refused to admit the works as a whole to the category of serious art. "Now play the 'Liebestod,' " he said cannily, after I had made an unmistakable impression with the end of *Madama Butterfly,* "and see the difference!" There was, of course, a difference. Only a year ago I had myself felt and spoken like H. L. But now I accused him of narrow-mindedness, and prophesied that in time he would, like me, take pleasure in the very difference he disapproved of.

We argued till nightfall, and then H. L. magnanimously offered to take me to dinner at a steak restaurant on Second Avenue. The place was a cozy cellar near Eighth Street. The steaks were twenty-five cents each, but French fries, fried onions, pickles, pickled tomatoes, a glass of tea and cake were included in the price. It was my first steak. Made hungry by the many miles we had walked, I left nothing of the steak but the bone, the while I kept up our heated discussion about music. H. L. paid the entire bill and left a nickel for a tip. I walked him home. But as I was about to bid him good night, we got into another argument about violinists and violin playing, H. L. contending that Sol Rashkin's exaggerated vibrato disqualified him from performing "pure" composers like Mozart and Beethoven. H. L. then walked me home. Our dispute not having been settled by the time we arrived, I walked him back. After disposing of Rashkin, we went on to other subjects, as if we were seeking pretexts for not going to bed. It was sunrise before we said good night. Tired and sleepy, but intellectually exhilarated, I went to bed on the floor of our front room. I could see that my mother was entertaining overnight visitors.

Bodies lay sprawled on the floor, looking in the raw morning light like disheveled corpses. I recognized Chaia-Riva Flayshig and her husband, Nochum, and the twins, and a distant male relation of my father's. My mother was asleep in a rocking chair in the kitchen, her usual bed when we had an overflow of guests. She had left a pillow and a quilt next to Nochum Flayshig for me. The air was fetid with a sickly sweet smell. It was the familiar odor of sleeping visitors, and I did not mind it. Indeed, I should not have been aware of it but for the sudden change from the cool morning air I had just left. It had been a provocative day and night, and as I lay down quietly next to Nochum, careful not to disturb him, I went over in my mind the arguments H. L. had opposed to mine, to to test their validity at leisure. But I was soon in a deep sleep, which was only once penetrated by the noise of people stirring about and moving chairs, and the sharp, faint sound of my mother's voice cautioning them to be quiet and to let me sleep.

H. L. Greene and I became fast friends. He remained conceited and overbearing, but less so with me than with my friends and acquaintances. I was obliged to explain him to them privately as a man of culture who had an unfortunate manner, but one who was basically kind and good. On the other hand, those who did not know him as well as I did thought his aristocratic mien ill became one whose parents kept a fish shop, the profits of which provided him with the independence which was, of course, the basis of his superiority. It was said that he was ashamed of his parents and of the business, and he was criticized for living off them. Among us it was unheard of that a man of eighteen was willing to live on the labor of his family. It was one thing to do so temporarily, to the legitimate extent of getting an education; it was quite another to get the education *and* a fabulous allowance

which put him in the category of a fashionable man about
town, able to buy the latest in clothes, to purchase books and
music, and to invite his friends to steak dinners on Second
Avenue.

The critics of H. L. Greene could not know what I soon
found out for myself, that H. L.'s father and mother (and his
younger brother) considered it a high privilege to provide
H. L. with everything he needed or wanted. One could hardly
blame H. L. for being conscious of it, or even for putting on
airs because of it. But he was fond of his family, and he proved
it by living at home and not renting a room of his own. If he
was ashamed of the shop—and I often attributed his outward
show of conceit and superiority to a secret unhappiness over
his parents' unglamorous business—he had the strength of
character not to divorce himself from it. That being so, his
officiating at the till of the shop on Thursday nights took on
the proportions of a heroic act, a sacrifice, a kind of penance
in full view of all who came into the store, or looked through
the plate-glass window. The fact that, while officiating, he
behaved like some prince of the blood, austere, aloof and dis-
concertingly condescending to the customers, could not mini-
mize the nobility of his gesture. The customers, most of whom
were aware of his attainments, looked upon H. L. as a model
son, a college boy about to seek the ultimate in education in
Berlin, who nevertheless was not ashamed to help out in the
store. His parents showed plainly their gratitude for his condescension. "Please pay my son Harold," his mother would
say to a customer, as she wrapped up a bundle of fish in pages
from back issues of *Der Tageblatt*. There was a conscious pride
in her voice as she said "my son Harold." Upstairs, before the
rest of the family and close friends, she called him Harry, and
when she quite forgot herself, Herschel.

I GO TO COLLEGE

᠀᠀᠀ Though we were about the same age, H. L. had already decided what his career was to be, and was following a well-thought-out plan toward its fulfillment. I, on the contrary, had no clear idea of my future. I had no fixed ambition, like H. L. One day I wanted to be a concert pianist, the next day a writer. Indeed, there was hardly an art that I did not, at one time or another, wish to pursue. I wanted to be a composer, a poet, a novelist, a teacher of literature, a musicologist. Or else, under the influence of some book I had read, I would repudiate all worldly ambition and decide to devote my life to some humanitarian cause. There were the lepers on Molokai Island who needed to be looked after. Reading about the devotion of Father Damien to these unfortunates, I felt I had been living a selfish life, engrossed in art, while the repellent, isolated lepers waited patiently for death. I located the island of Molokai on the map, and wondered how I could get to it. But then a moral obstacle presented itself: if I should go to Molokai Island, what would become of my family? I should be benefiting the lepers and leaving my mother, father and little sister

51

to starve. Reluctantly I gave up the idea of emulating Father Damien.

In Thoreau's *Walden* I encountered a way of life that seemed even more satisfying than Father Damien's. To divorce oneself from civilization, to live simply, devoting as little of one's time as possible to the rudimentary requirements of the body, thus leaving one free to contemplate and savor fully the glories of nature, seemed the only rational life. In the light of Thoreau's existence at Walden, all my former ambitions and desires appeared meaningless. Why should one long—as I did —to own a morris chair, when a rude three-legged stool made with his own hands was sufficient for Thoreau to sit on, as he shelled his peas for supper, or wrote down his thoughts in his journal? Could I live alone in the woods by the side of a lake as Thoreau had for three years? I was certain I could, though I had a secret fear of mice, and I could never, like Thoreau, feel brotherly about them. I could embark on such a life easily and without delay, since no obstacle so formidable as transportation to a Pacific isle stood in my way. For a dollar and a quarter I could take a train to Waterbury, and in a woods I had known as a child, build myself a rude shack and plant some vegetables for my needs. But, as in the case of the lepers, it would mean the abandonment of my family. Also there was Elena Kovner, without whom it seemed to me I could not live. Could I persuade Elena to give up her career, go with me into the woods and break her father's heart? Difficulties and barriers of one kind or another always barred the way to the realization of my ever-changing ideals for a soul-satisfying life.

No difficulties appeared to stand in H. L.'s way. Indeed, a forceful, self-confident nature such as his would never admit they existed. Though he loved art and planned to devote his life to it, it was obvious that H. L. accepted the world as it was. His only concern was his own position in it. To enjoy in ease and comfort that aspect of it which appealed to him—literature and music—was the career he envisioned. I envied him this solid, unwavering outlook on life, especially when some idealistic vision on which I had decided to base my future became altogether uncorporeal the moment I began, even in thought, to translate it into reality.

It was at such a baffling moment that I decided to base my life on something that I might successfully carry out. I decided to go to college and become later, like H. L., a professor of literature. I would not, of course, give up music. But music, as a profession, was uncertain. Even Elena Kovner, with her unusual talent, might fail to achieve the career she deserved. In that case, certainly, I would, as a professor of literature, provide a suitable home for her, a cultural setting in which she could move about as an amateur (in the noblest sense). The idea of Elena without a career was even pleasant to contemplate, for she would then be altogether dependent on me. In any case I was getting on in years (I was eighteen), and it was time for me to relinquish my daydreams and work toward an assured, lucrative profession. Upon inquiring, I learned that teachers in colleges were paid from one thousand to fifteen hundred dollars a year. The earnings of associate and full professors were, of course, even more substantial. Elena and I could do handsomely on the salary of any college teacher.

Two obstacles stood in the way of my studying at Columbia. One was the entrance examination, the other the tuition fee. The first was easier to solve than the second. I could prepare myself for the examination with the aid of textbooks and, perhaps, some private lessons in a difficult subject like mathematics. I bought second-hand textbooks in Latin, English,

English literature, German, and American history, and for a
dollar a week I joined a class in algebra and geometry at a
preparatory school on Clinton Street. After nine months of concentrated study of the required subjects, I felt prepared to take
the entrance examinations. But how and where to raise the great
sum of $150, the first year's tuition? My mother suggested Mr.
Beylinson, my father's old pupil and friend, who had in the
past "loaned" us money in the frequent financial crises that
confronted us. But Mr. Beylinson had married and had several
children, and the sentimental ties that once bound him to us
could no longer be invoked.

At a loss where to turn, I confided in Mrs. Lesser. To my
astonishment Mrs. Lesser had an immediate solution. This was
to have Dr. Lesser advance me the money against the piano
lessons I would give their children. The boldness and simplicity of this solution took my breath away. Yet I had misgivings
about asking the doctor to part with so much money at a
stroke. Mrs. Lesser saw nothing unfair in such a transaction—
I would only ask the doctor to do what Columbia was asking
me to do. In either case it was merely a demand for payment in
advance. Furthermore, Mrs. Lesser would relieve my mind
by speaking to the doctor herself. She was sure there would be
no difficulties on his part. And, indeed, there proved to be
none. The doctor gave me $150 in ten-dollar bills, and asked
for no receipt. In due course I took the examinations, which
I passed with fair marks (I recall mistakenly identifying
Hampton Roads as the approaches to Cardinal Wolsey's
palace), and paid out the $150 to the college bursar.

I found going to college exciting. Not since the old Waterbury days at the Webster Grammar School was I *obliged* to
study on schedule. Now I had to get up at a quarter to seven in
the morning in order to dress, wash, eat breakfast and brush

up on the day's studies which I might have neglected the night before by staying late at the Kovners', the Lessers', or walking till sunrise with H. L. along the waterfront and in Jackson Street Park discussing the arts. It took me a good half hour to walk from Henry Street to the Spring Street subway station, and another half hour on the subway to 116th Street and the college.

It felt good to sit once again in a schoolroom, and even better to know oneself as a grown man surrounded by grown-up colleagues. I went from room to room for the subjects I had elected or that were prescribed. The teachers and professors were all, I thought, remarkable. A youngish man, a Mr. Odell, pleasant and sandy-haired, taught us English composition. In music I knew by now a good deal about harmony, counterpoint and form, but I had never thought seriously about the components that go into a literary work, believing that once a writer knew the elements of grammar, he was then ready for the winds of inspiration, like an aeolian harp. Mr. Odell corrected this misapprehension, and writing became, as a consequence, more difficult for a while. But soon the restrictions he advocated seemed imperative, and the little essays he made us write began to reflect thought, design and discipline. At first I chose romantic or bizarre subjects for these five-to-six-hundred-word compositions. I wrote about "The Fall of the House of Usher," using the ominous, ever-widening crack in the house itself as a symbol of the progressive derangement of the ill-fated inhabitants. Mr. Odell marked my composition A, and read it aloud in class. But he thought we might better look around us for contemporary subjects, everyday things or scenes—for example, Grant's tomb, which we could glimpse from one of the schoolroom windows. The suggestion was of course taken up generally, and many compositions on Grant's

tomb were handed in. Most of them described a typical scene
at the shrine, the visitors looking down with emotion on the
marble crypt below. For myself, being at that time antimilita-
ristic like Mr. Kovner, I chose to describe the building itself. I
had often felt that there was something aesthetically wrong
with the shrine. Now I walked around it, and looked at it
from the perspective of a few blocks away. It came to me that
the cupola or superstructure was artistically wrong, and that
it ruined what would otherwise have been a lovely, simple
Greek temple. This rather drastic judgment sent me to the
article on Greek architecture in the *Encyclopaedia Britannica,*
which in turn gave me an interest in architecture in general.

I took a course in psychology with Professor Lord, a small,
thin old man, extraordinarily spry on his feet, and much given
to witty sallies. I was astonished to find that the mystery of
human behavior had been probed and charted to the extent
almost of a science. But it was *fun* to study because, like history,
it had to do with people and therefore could never really be
an exact science. William James's *Psychology,* one of our textbooks, was as exciting as a fine novel. And with it as a starter,
Professor Lord extended its principles into ordinary, everyday
life. I had the pleasure (and disappointment) of recognizing
impulses and emotions in my own behavior that Professor Lord
showed were common to everyone. And he illustrated his
points with wonderful anecdotes in his earthy, good-humored,
slightly ironic way. Everybody looked forward to Professor
Lord's psychology course.

But then all the courses were exciting. The History of
Europe Between—I've forgotten the exact dates—taught by
Carleton Hayes, a slim, bespectacled, youngish-looking man,
which took an hour and a half each Tuesday morning, seemed
no longer than a quarter of an hour. Mr. Hayes was lucid and

factual, yet he discoursed about great events and significant trends intimately, as if he himself had taken part in them, or had been a highly interested spectator, not altogether unbiased. It was rumored that Mr. Hayes was a Catholic. This I did not wish to believe. In the first place, he looked young. Not too young to have Catholicism thrust on him, nor old enough to embrace Catholicism of his own free will. He was in that maturity of youth when one must be (I thought) devoutly skeptical of religion, and believe nothing without proof. Mr. Hayes seemed very intelligent, and liberal in his sentiments, as he explored with us the political and economic changes in Europe between the years —— and ——. How, I wondered, could so rational a historian accept Catholicism? Or, for that matter, Judaism, Mohammedanism, Buddhism or any other religion! It was the inconsistency that troubled me, as the inconsistency of Balzac, being a monarchist while living in a republic, troubled me. It seemed to me that a man who had before him the entire panorama of history already knew too much to accept revealed religion. Even I was forced to reject all religion, simply because of the incongruity of the multiplicity of faiths. Who could know which, if any, was the true faith? As for Balzac, I wondered further how anyone, let alone a great writer, could be a monarchist *after* the French Revolution!

Nevertheless, I treasured Mr. Hayes, as I did Professor Lord. But the most stimulating of all my teachers was Professor John Erskine, two of whose courses in literature I had the good fortune to take. Ten years earlier, as a pupil nine years old at Public School Number 2 on Henry Street, I had completely fallen under the spell of my teacher Mr. Strassmeier. Mr. Strassmeier was an outspoken socialist, a champion of the poor (he was, alas, not always charitable to his pupils), a lover of literature and music. Now I saw in Professor Erskine a counterpart

of Mr. Strassmeier. I could find out nothing about Professor
Erskine's politics. But he, too, loved literature and music, and
his mature enthusiasm for both communicated itself to me as
directly as Mr. Strassmeier's had a decade before. Unlike Mr.
Strassmeier, Profesor Erskine was never patronizing. He was a
large, confident man, impressive as he strode across the campus,
book in hand. He had a lisp, and his speaking voice was reson-
antly soft. In his lectures he reduced everything to its simplest
terms. I remember his describing Thackeray's way of telling a
story as a leisurely relay race. His lectures on eighteenth-century
novelists were complete vignettes, made up mostly from passages
cleverly selected to build up their portraits. I was not too young
to notice in Professor Erskine the absence, in a negative sense,
of a critical faculty. He appreciated an author without reservations, much as one does the people one loves. If he called
attention to the sentimentality of the "good" people in Dickens,
it was not in reproof, but only to assure us that the sentimentality was genuine, and quite real to Dickens. He gave me the
feeling that great writers, like gift horses, were not to be examined for faults. Often I thought that I alone among his
students understood him. Though there were several brilliant
men among my classmates (there was Randolph Bourne, who
soon was contributing pieces to *The Atlantic Monthly*), I
couldn't believe that anyone but me possessed the sensitiveness
to *feel* literature in the way Professor Erskine did.

His course in poetry was, perhaps, even more exciting. In
poetry he was an authority, having published a little volume
on the Elizabethan sonnet. Our first assignment was Sir Philip
Sidney's sonnet sequence *Astrophel and Stella*. Reading it at
home, I found it obscure and mannered, though shot through
with beautiful and lofty images. But in class Professor Erskine
treated it as if it were a contemporary work. The first thing he

did was to expose its story line. The poem became a novel, each sonnet a chapter. He explained away the obscurities in revealing the story. And when he read the sonnets aloud, the Elizabethan formalism and the stylistic mannerisms somehow appeared natural and right. I accepted them as I accepted the conventions of Elizabethan dress, and the rigid convention of the sonnet form itself. When Professor Erskine had finished talking and reading, nothing stood in the way of the love story of Philip Sidney and Lady Rich. After we were given the clue to *Astrophel and Stella,* our ensuing assignments offered no difficulties. The Shakespeare sonnets were beautifully simple. Professor Erskine would not permit us to waste time on the identity of Mr. W. H., the "onlie begetter," but made us concentrate on the "dark lady," who, he maintained, was the first real flesh-and-blood woman in English poetry (with the exception of the ladies in Chaucer, he was careful to add). We read *The Faerie Queene,* and Professor Erskine made chivalry come alive and seem immediate. And in *Prothalamion* and *Epithalamion* he savored for us the sweetness of Edmund Spenser on the subject of love and marriage, pointing out obliquely how this great artist, though tender and romantic in his approach, gave the physical side of love its due place (but its *due* place only), ennobling it by not isolating it, but showing it, one might say, as the excess of love. For myself, I understood both Professor Erskine and Edmund Spenser quite clearly, and I took to heart the tremendous effect of proportion and understatement in Spenser's great marriage hymn. Though Professor Erskine only hinted at these effects, I felt keenly the beautiful implication of the line "And tymely sleep, when it is tyme to sleepe. . . ." For here in a line was love in its proper relation to life.

I was able to get the measure of Spenser's greatness not alone through Professor Erskine's illuminating interpretations. Con-

current with his course in Elizabethan poetry I attended Professor Ayres's course in early English poetry; and in Chaucer's
Troilus and Criseyde I found the very contrast to Spenser's
Epithalamion. Love was the subject of both, but how different
one was from the other! The love of Troilus set my brain on
fire. It was hardly to be borne, it was so real, so violent, so exclusive. Troilus, too, could hardly bear it. "And down he fel al
sodeynly a-swowne." For such consuming, physical love there
can never be a "time to sleep." So I thought as I read *Troilus
and Criseyde,* my face flushed, my senses overcome by the
searing words of the poet. There was no doubt in my mind
which was the greater poet. Chaucer was the veracious reporter
of the senses in their stark exigency. Spenser celebrated the
senses too, but only in their proper relation to the whole of life.
Chaucer was actually cynical, though he took a sensuous delight
in the loveliness of nature. Cynicism was exciting and made one
feel adult. Yet, though I reveled in Chaucer's worldliness, it
was not satisfying. Spenser also delighted in nature, but even
his delight was well tempered. He made me feel that nature
was to be apprehended not by the senses alone, but equally by
the spirit, of which it was a symbol. Nature and man were one
for Spenser. I felt this interrelation in the last lines of each
stanza in the two great love hymns: "Sweete Themmes runne
softly, till I end my Song" in *Prothalamion,* and "That all the
woods may answere, and your eccho ring" in *Epithalamion*.
Chaucer threw me into a turmoil. Spenser with a line placed
the passion of love—indeed, all passion—in perspective. He
calmed and ennobled my senses without denying them, made
them seem natural and beautiful, and brought them into relation with all of life. For him love culminated in a mysterious,
noble, secret rite properly veiled from all scrutiny. I marveled
at the delicacy of his treatment of the bridal night in *Epitha-*

lamion. When the lovers retire to their chamber, he calls on night to "Spread thy broad wing over my love and me,/That no man may us see," and we gravely avert our gaze.

Now I had before me three violently different poetic treatments of love in *Troilus and Criseyde, Epithalamion* and Shelley's *Epipsychidion.* All three illuminated my love for Elena Kovner, all three were expressions of it. But Spenser's poem alone gave me back the essense, the distillation of my many-sided love, and pointed to a vista of a future, high-flown and poetic, yet in beautiful harmony with all of nature and life.

In my classes at Columbia, or hurrying from one class to another, I was also always conscious of a deep harmony between me and the spirit of the place. I should have liked to give myself up entirely to college life and live in Hartley Hall, and from a window of my room look down on the campus and watch the students practicing football—I had no time or inclination for sports, and grudged even the few hours a week at the gym—and, looking up from my studies, gaze poetically at the Hudson River in the distance. Residence in college was, of course, out of the question for me. But I consciously breathed in the academic atmosphere of the place, which was so aptly symbolized by the Alma Mater, the serene, ample figure in stone, her head crowned with bay leaves, that sits halfway up the great staircase that leads to the domed library. For lunch I would hastily eat two egg sandwiches my mother wrapped for me each morning, and then I would repair to Earl Hall, where there was a piano in the lounge. Students would drift in as I played, and sit awhile and listen. One of them took an unusual interest in what I played and introduced himself as a music lover. His name was Alfred Knopf—later the founder of the publishing house bearing his name—and I saw by his familiarity with the operatic and symphonic scores I played that he was indeed what he said he was. He came often to Earl Hall during lunchtime, and after I played we had interesting discussions about music and musicians.

I sat and read in the great circular room of the library, enjoying the studious silence around me as much as I did my book. I attended lecture series given by celebrated literary and scientific personages from other American and British universities; and as I sat in the balcony of the McMillin Theater I was conscious of the privilege of being there. Many lectures I did not understand, for they were on special subjects about which I had only the haziest notions. But I *enjoyed* them just same, if only for the consciousness of sitting at the feet of notable men. Every Saturday I read the book section of the *Evening Post* greedily, and I learned a great deal about American and foreign writers in many fields. So when I attended a course of lectures by George Santayana I knew all about the Harvard philosopher, though I could make little sense of his philosophy. When I first saw him come out on the stage his appearance jarred my sense of fitness. He looked anything but the philosopher. And as I noted his well-fitting, recently pressed, indeed fashionable suit of clothes, his high starched collar and elegant cuffs, even his absolutely bald head glowing as if it had that morning been polished, I found it hard to reconcile my preconceived idea of a philosopher as a carelessly attired, unworldly person, with the fashion plate before me. But when he began reading from a manuscript in a high-pitched voice I was reassured; for what he said *sounded* like philosophy, although I appreciated very little of it, except some striking images and poetic phrases.

LOVE

I was deeply in love with Elena Kovner. Though for a long time I had thought of her constantly, the certainty of my being in love overcame me suddenly. It was as if I had been wading and dallying on the seashore, and the sand under my feet had suddenly given way, and in an instant I was no longer of the land, but had become a creature of the water. The shock of the transformation was, however, momentary. Like a young swimmer who abandons himself to the greedy, riotous waves, I embraced the new element of sovereign love joyfully, and gave myself up to it recklessly. I sensed many dangers and foresaw many frustrations. But they were inherent in the new element, and I did not fear them.

I loved Elena exclusively. I loved her above my mother, my sisters, my friends. Indeed, I wondered if I *ever* had loved them, for the feeling I had for them had no resemblance at all to the love I now had for Elena. I even loved Elena's mother more than mine. Everything appertaining to Elena I accepted without reservation as good and treasurable. Certainly no one could be more charming and gracious than Mrs. Kovner, or more honest

and wise than Mr. Kovner. (He was, perhaps, overambitious for
Elena, but was that a fault?) Were there ever three boys so
pleasant and trusting as Elena's brothers! As for marital felicity,
where else but at the Kovners' was it to be seen in such strength
and perfection! For all her coquetry, Mrs. Kovner loved her
husband deeply and *tolerantly*. She allowed for his intellectual
intransigence, his gruffness, his outbursts of anger, his obsession
with his daughter's career. If, as my mother often said, "the
apple does not fall far from the tree," then Elena would be
just such a wife, just such an understanding, *unquestioning*
helpmate. And Elena would also be the Wagnerian ideal of a
woman, as exemplified in Senta and Elizabeth. I understood
now, as never before, the significance of poor Elsa von Brabant's
attempted intrusion into the secret life of her husband, Lohengrin. Every man has secrets which he canot reveal to anyone,
not even to his beloved. The ideal woman must, like Senta,
Elizabeth and Mrs. Kovner, take her beloved on trust. I myself
had felt and done things which I never could tell Elena. And
now I was certain that in *our* marriage Elena would be as
understanding and uninquisitive as her mother was in hers. Not
that Mrs. Kovner was averse to asking Mr. Kovner embarrassing
questions. But when she did ask them, it was always in fun. Had
she been in Elsa's place she would slyly and pleasantly have
intimated that she guessed that Lohengrin had secrets from
her, but that it really didn't matter, since her love was so
encompassing as to enable her to accept the entire man or (in
the case of Lohengrin) the entire half-god. (Here I had the
disturbing and impious thought that Wagner's compassionate
heroines lacked Mrs. Kovner's beneficent sense of humor.)

How completely happy I should be with Elena! I could see
our future life together in every detail. All during the day we
would, separately, practice and study music, meeting for the

first time at dinner. The rest of the evening we would devote to ensemble playing, or to books, which I would read aloud. Everybody said I read aloud beautifully and I, too, felt that I did. Frequent concert tours would take us to far countries, but they would always be joint tours. I even went so far as to outline what we would play. Each concert would begin with a group of solos by Elena and me, and end in a sonata for cello and piano. On this noble plane we would live out our lives together, secure in our love and in the love of our children.

Our children . . .! But here my musing struck a snag. Although I loved Elena completely—intellectually, romantically and passionately—I could not clearly envisage the ultimate physical relation between us. As yet I had never really touched her, never been close to her. Apart from an uncomfortable sense of my own unworthiness, which I found difficult to overcome, there was something so virginal about Elena that my mind stopped short at imagining her in close physical relationship with me, or with any other man. There was indeed something indelicate, even shameful, in the idea of Elena being possessed like ordinary women. Yet I ached to hold her close, and often pictured her, when she went to her room at night, making her toilette and getting into her narrow bed, and I gave myself up to sweet, disturbing thoughts of her physical purity and isolation. There was a line in Mark Twain's play *The Prince and the Pauper* (performed by the Educational Alliance Children's Theater, for which the Educational Alliance Orchestra, with myself at the piano, provided the overture and incidental music) which I could never hear without emotion. Espying the lovely heroine asleep in a sylvan clearing on the stage, the hero murmured ecstatically, "Who would not wish to lay his head next to so fair a one!" or words to that effect. I could be that hero, and Elena the sleeping beauty. Sometimes I was so preoccupied with imagining such a substitution that I missed playing the opening bars of the nocturne for which the breathtaking line was the cue.

For all her physical aloofness, I could not doubt that Elena loved me. She *had* to, dissemble as she might. For we were as one in all respects, in our passion for music, for books and poetry. We seemed to have been created to complement each other in temperament, in character, in aesthetic taste, even in the wonderful accident of our choice of different musical instruments. And how explain her fear of touching me except as fear of her own deeply emotional nature overstepping the bounds of reserve she had misguidedly (I thought) set for herself? She was simply afraid to trust herself with the man she loved! She had, it was true, never spoken a word of love to me. But, then, neither had I to her. Yet all my actions spoke of love, as did the frequency of my visits and the consequent neglect of my own affairs at home, my musical studies and even my pupils. My great interest in music for the cello and in compositions for cello and piano, my gifts of books, cannily selected for their romantic implications, the poetry I read to her when we were alone, all spoke eloquently of love. I could not look at her dispassionately, and I felt she was conscious of it.

I adored her openly, without saying so, for all to see. And I respected her reserve, and even found pleasure in doing so. As I could convince myself that this reserve was a secret manifestation of love, so I was able to interpret certain looks and gestures on her part as signals of acknowledgment of my love, and as a sign of her favor. When, after I stayed away for a few days, purposely, in the hope that she might say she had missed me, she said nothing, I read into her silence a secret rebuke. And when she failed to urge me to stay awhile after her father had bade me a pointed good night, I consoled myself with the thought that had by now become a fixation with me, her fear of herself.

Only in music did Elena give herself away. Her playing was a negation of the picture of herself she wished us to see. Her throbbing, sensuous tone, the boldness of her phrasing, the freedom of her interpretation, which often bordered on license, canceled her modesty, her aloofness, her self-consciousness and her fear of physical contacts. All the same I treasured that inhibited, outward picture. It too, in a sense, reflected Elena, and it gave poignance to the reality her playing disclosed. The two sides of the picture were only superficially contrasting. To me they were interdependent.

Like Neuvillette in *Cyrano de Bergerac,* I did not myself attempt to speak of my love to Elena. I conveyed my love obliquely through the works of great composers, great novelists and great poets. Sometimes I found the unique quality of my adoration even in the works of lesser men and women, and I would bring these to Elena with significant passages underlined. In Mrs. Browning's *Sonnets from the Portuguese* I drew a heavy ink line underneath:

"Guess now who holds thee?"—"Death," I said. But there, The silver answer rang: "Not Death, but Love."

Accidentally I came across a little-read novel, *Christie Johnstone,* by Charles Reade, in which the hero was diffident and tongue-tied, like myself, in relation to the heroine. I read Elena those passages which showed his reticence in declaring his love. Music offered a more direct approach, going straight to the heart, unimpeded either by the imprecision of words, or by their too precise suggestion of the mundane and prosaic. Playing the Prelude to *Tristan,* I made a shattering assault on Elena's emotions, as I could plainly see and feel, though the

room might be full of people quite unaware of the secret
current of feeling running between Elena and me. Indeed, their
unawareness heightened for me the ecstasy of our communica-
tion.

Yet there were certain words of great poets that equaled
and sometimes, though rarely, even transcended the aromatic,
heavy-laden, aching, unbearably insistent love music of *Tristan*.
Such a line, terse and simple, was "That day they read no
more," from Dante, leaving one to *imagine* the overwhelming
force of the love that overcame Paolo and Francesca as they sat
close together reading the guilty story of Lancelot and Guine-
vere. I felt that in this one line Dante conveyed everything that
Wagner spelled out at such great (though tremendously exciting) length. I read the canto to Elena as we sat on a bench
in Prospect Park. I spoke the great line calmly, as a tribute to
Elena's sensitiveness to nuances in art. And the effect on her,
as I expected, was unmistakable. She turned away from me, and
for a time sat unmoving. That day we, too, read no more. We
walked back to the house in self-conscious, eloquent silence.

An even greater poetic instrument for my purpose was
Shelley's *Epipsychidion,* the final part of which achieved in
words the great climax of the love duet in *Tristan*. Fortunately
for me, Elena had never read Shelley's poem. I was impatient
to read it to her, but I had to wait for the right moment. It
came one Sunday, late in the evening. All day we had played
sonatas and concertos in the parlor, while friends and neighbors
drifted in and out, and Mr. Kovner sat in his morris chair,
listening carefully and critically, and urging us on when we
showed signs of flagging. After supper we went downstairs and
sat in the room adjoining the store. Mr. Kovner read us a story
of Peretz, and then expatiated, as was his habit, on the subject
of Jews, reaching his usual dogmatic conclusion that in spite of

everything they were the salt of the earth. He discounted
the disadvantages of being a Jew as superficial. And speaking
for himself, he considered it a privilege to belong to a race so
hardy, so wise and so imbued with genius. "You cannot pooh-
pooh the Rambam, Spinoza, Moses Mendelssohn, his grandson
Felix"—let him be baptized a hundred times and given the
Frenchified name of Bartholdy, he would still be a Jew, and
his music would be Jewish!—"Goldmark, Bruch, Rubinstein
and many other great Jews," he shouted, as if he were the
opposing orator in a public debate. When I timidly mentioned
Bach, Beethoven and Wagner as the not inconsiderable products of the Christian faith, Mr. Kovner laughed scornfully.
First dismissing Wagner as a German noisemaker, not fit to
be mentioned in a breath with the other two, he said that in
the first place the Christian faith was based on the life and
teachings of a minor Jewish prophet and the Jews could, if they
liked, claim the credit for Bach. And in the second place he
would ask me to consider the numerical preponderance of
Christians over Jews, and to tell him whether we had not
produced great men out of all proportion to our numbers. This
challenge silenced me. Mr. Kovner, having triumphed, as he
always did over me, rose and said meaningfully that even a
superior people like the Jews were subject to the demands of
nature, that he was tired and was going to bed, and he hoped
"other" Jews would follow his example. Mrs. Kovner, sympathetic, as always, toward my ill-concealed desire to be alone
with Elena, before following her husband, created the excuse
I needed by telling her daughter to tidy up the room before
she went upstairs.

I had my volume of Shelley with me. And while Elena
washed and dried the cups and saucers, I told her about *Epipsychidion,* and how surprised I was to find in the poem the naked

expressiveness of certain pages in *Tristan*. "But you must hear
the poem from the very beginning," I said, "or you will miss the
marvelous building up of a crescendo to the great climax at
the end." And without waiting for permission, I began the
poem calmly, even prosaically. Elena listened as she went about
her chores. But at the words:

> There was a Being whom my spirit oft
> Met on its visioned wanderings, far aloft,
> In the clear golden prime of my youth's dawn . . .

she sat down, a plate and a dishcloth in her hands, bent forward and gave all her attention to me. I read on, myself
caught up in the ever-mounting passion of the verses. At the
start of the long *musical* crescendo, I daringly substituted the
name Elena for the "Emily" of the poem.

>   Elena,
> A ship is floating in the harbour now . . .
> Say, my heart's sister, wilt thou sail with me?

I was confessing my love, my hopes. I could not curb the
tremor in my voice. The tumultuous crescendo of felicities and
joys were like a never-ending succession of waves forming and
breaking and forming again. Elena's tenseness was palpable,
as the images fell over themselves in their haste. At the in-
supportable climax:

> One Heaven, one Hell, one immortality,
> And one annihilation. Woe is me!
> The wingèd words on which my soul would pierce
> Into the height of Love's rare Universe,
> Are chains of lead around its flight of fire—
> I pant, I sink, I tremble, I expire!

my voice broke. I knew the words by heart and I looked straight at Elena as I brought them out. For a trembling second Elena returned my gaze. Then she looked away, got up awkwardly and began tidying up the room. Still trembling with emotion, I shut the book without reading the concluding stanza.

Mrs. Kovner, in dressing gown, her hair in curl papers, came in from the hall to tell us that "Papa" was fretting and would not go to sleep until Elena was in bed. I left at once. Too excited and exalted to ride, I walked home as in a trance, reaching my house all too soon, though it was a two-hour journey on foot. My mother was sitting at an open window of our front room, looking in the direction from which I usually returned home. By the time I climbed the four flights of stairs to our flat, she was in bed. We had no guests spending the night, and the horsehair "lounge" in the front room was unoccupied. I undressed, and lying down on it, I abandoned myself to thoughts of one immortality and one annihilation for Elena Kovner and me.

A DINNER AND MUSICALE
ON HENRY STREET

CURVE My professor in music appreciation was Daniel Greg-
ory Mason. His appearance, like that of Santayana, was not
what I had expected. He was an ordinary-looking, bespectacled
man with a mild face, limpid eyes and graying hair slicked
down and very neatly parted on the side. He looked like a
small-town lawyer or a worker in a government office. Yet he
had written several important books on music, had studied
with Vincent d'Indy in Paris and had composed some chamber
music and songs. Furthermore, he was related to the celebrated
Mason family of Boston, which had produced in William
Mason one of the first American concert pianists to gain recognition abroad, and which was even then manufacturing, under
the name Mason & Hamlin, pianos that rivaled Steinways. On
learning that I was a pianist, Professor Mason invited me to
help him illustrate his course by playing four hands with him.
He would analyze for us a symphony by Haydn, Mozart or
Beethoven, playing the themes on the piano himself. Then, as
a finish, he and I performed the entire work. This, of course,
required preparation, and we would rehearse in the late after-

noon. Professor Mason often complimented me on my musicality, sometimes in front of the class, and I was pleased with the deference the other students showed me. Notwithstanding my acceptance (and admiration) of Italian and French opera, I was at that time firmly under the influence and at the mercy of Wagner, and I listened to Professor Mason's painstaking analyses of the symphonies with a kind of benevolent tolerance. I knew that without the symphonic works of Haydn, Mozart and Beethoven, Wagner could not have evolved his symphonic music dramas. These composers had been essential to Wagner's development. But they were only forerunners, and I thought Professor Mason was devoting too much time to them. Yet when he played these rather simple and naïve symphonies on the piano—I taking the more difficult treble parts—I brought to them the emotion, rhythm and drive I lavished on the music of Wagner. Then the simple compositions, with their prescribed first, second and subsidiary themes and their academic modulations and changes of key and development sections, sounded beautiful enough. They "came off" naturally, and even did not sound antiquated. As we played, though I knew what was to happen, I could not help a feeling of excitement. And it was only when we had finished that I felt a certain uneasiness and even shame for abandoning myself to so rigid and cut-and-dried a musical form. Sometimes at rehearsals I told Professor Mason my reservations about the classical composers. He heard me out patiently, smiling indulgently, and reminded me that my playing quite belied my words. He once shocked me by confessing that he preferred these classical works to the music dramas of Wagner; though he assured me he admired the latter very much. I liked Professor Mason, and respected him too much to regard this preference as a lack of sensitivity to Wagner's endless melody. Charitably I attributed his bias to the activities of Poe's universal "Imp of the Perverse," who often leads us on to think and do things against our inclinations and beliefs.

One memorable day Professor Mason asked me to come on the following afternoon to his house "to tea." The invitation threw me into a state of confusion. In novels I had read of people of the upper classes coming "to tea," but I had never gone "to tea" myself, and did not know personally anyone who had. "What time?" I asked, when I was able to catch my breath; and Professor Mason looked at me in surprise and said, "Why, the usual time—five o'clock or so." I sought out H. L. Greene as one who might be in a position to advise me on the proper behavior of a man at a tea. H. L. said he had had tea numerous times at certain homes. "It's very simple," he told me. "Watch what the others are doing, and do the same." The next day, after classes, I took the Broadway streetcar and got off at Fifty-sixth Street, where Professor Mason lived on a floor of a brownstone house next to a church. I rang his bell, and a maid in an apron let me in and led me through a hall into a pleasant room. Professor Mason, who had been reading a book at a large, desklike table on which were a student lamp, writing materials, some books and a stack of magazines, rose from a morris chair, greeted me in the most friendly fashion and introduced me to Mrs. Mason, a tall, middle-aged woman who was sitting on a sofa, also reading. Mrs. Mason looked older than her husband. I had heard from some of my classmates that she had left her first husband to marry the professor, and I had expected to find her a young and alluring woman. But she was pleasant enough, and talked to me like an equal, asking me if I had read the book she had just put down, a novel by an English author, Arnold Bennett. The book was called *The Old Wives' Tale,* and had only recently come out. I had not read the book, though I had heard of the author. The maid came in again, carrying a large tray full of cups and saucers, a china teapot, and biscuits and cakes. She placed the tray on a small, knee-high folding table in front of Mrs. Mason, and left. Mrs. Mason asked me how I liked my tea, and I said, "Very much." "How many lumps?" she then asked smilingly, and I said, "Three." "Did you say *three?*" Mrs. Mason asked again, and I nodded. She took from the tray an ornate silver instrument that looked like a pair of scissors, delicately trapped a lump of sugar from a bowl and dropped it into my cup. When the three lumps were in, she poured the tea and handed the cup, and a plate of biscuits and cakes with a fork, to Professor Mason, who in turn handed them to me. There was no table near me on which to place the cup and plate, so I sat with both hands full, and waited to see what Professor Mason would do for himself. Mrs. Mason, not consulting her husband, again lifted a lump of sugar with the silver pincers, and dropped it into a cup, while her husband stood by waiting. Receiving his cup and plate and fork, he sat down on a chair beside me. I watched him closely. In his left hand he held his cup. He deposited his plate on his right knee. When he was not raising his cup to his lips with his right hand, he used it to wield his fork on the cake. He did not seem at all disturbed or ill at ease, for he talked to me as he drank and ate. I did what he did, but not at all with ease. My right knee trembled a little, and it was some time before I was able to summon the courage to use my fork. I finally got the hang of the perilous operation, but I refused a second cup, and was glad at last to deposit the impedimenta on the large table. Tea over, Professor Mason showed me a manuscript of a piano quartet he had just composed, and I went over it with him on the grand piano (a Mason & Hamlin). It was a melodious work, but I did not find it especially interesting. I knew I was expected to say

something nice about it. So far I could not remember ever
having lied about music. But the genteelness of my surroundings, the sight of my first sugar tongs, the kindness of my hosts,
demanded some form of reciprocation. I hastily decided to say
I liked the quartet, but fearing that my eyes would give me
away, I fixed them on the music as I hesitantly told Professor
Mason that his composition was beautiful. "That is high praise,"
the Professor said smilingly to his wife. "You know, Chotzinoff
is very critical even of the classics." I turned away to hide my
blushes. Yet I was not sorry that I had lied. Something even
drove me to exaggerate and compound the lie. "I should like
to play it with the strings," I said quickly. "I know three
players who would love to play the quartet. Maybe you would
come down to my house some night and we'll play it for you?"
Professor Mason beamed and said it would make him very
happy, and Mrs. Mason asked if my invitation included her,
and I said of course it did. "In fact," I added recklessly, "we'll
have a nice evening, first supper and then music." Mrs. Mason
protested that it would be too much to have both, that they
would come after supper. But I said it was nothing, that my
mother didn't mind cooking, that our house was always full
of people. Mrs. Mason laughed and said that that must be
rather hard on my mother. But I said, "Not at all," and the
professor and his wife said that in that case they would be
delighted to come.

We sat and talked for some time. Mrs. Mason was interested
in my family and asked questions about them. Then the conversation seemed to die out, and there came intervals when no
one spoke. The clock over the fireplace pointed to half-past six,
and I thought perhaps I should take my leave. I had no idea as
to the proper duration of a "tea," and I had quite forgotten to
ask H. L. about it. Certainly an hour and a half was long

enough. But then the question of how one left a "tea" presented itself to me, and I sat for a while thinking about it. At
one point I rose half out of my seat, but I was gripped by a
fear that I should not know what to say, and I sank back. It
was suddenly a quarter to seven. I must get out of the house
somehow. Yet when I attempted to rise I felt glued to my chair.
Professor Mason spoke, and his words were like a reprieve,
though I knew them to be only a formality. "You're sure you
won't have another cup of tea?" he asked pleasantly, but impersonally, as if there could be no question that my answer
would be in the negative. I shook my head mournfully and
murmured, "No, thank you . . . it's enough." Silence fell again,
when all at once the clock began to give out premonitory
noises. I gave all my attention to the clock, which, having
wound itself up to the breaking point, now burst into deliberate and distinct strokes. The horrifying thought came to
me that even if I could get myself out of my chair, it might
now be too late to leave. But Mrs. Mason had risen and was
advancing toward me. "Good-bye," she said smilingly. "I'm so
sorry I can't ask you to stay to dinner," and she put out her
hand in farewell. I felt the blood rushing to my head. Was it
possible that Mrs. Mason thought I had lingered on till dinner
in the hope that I would be asked to stay! What did she take
me for! I got up quickly, but refused to take her outstretched
hand. "Dinner!" I retorted angrily. "I don't want your dinner!
I want to go home!" I ran from the room.

I walked for blocks, smarting under this affront, and I
swore at the Masons for a pair of rude, insensitive Christians.
What good was their education, their culture, their morris chair,
their student lamp, their maid in her flowered apron! Even my
father, in the old days when he had the upper hand in the
house and his tyranny knew no bounds, was never guilty of

such rudeness toward anyone who visited us. The Masons should have understood my plight and found a way to help me. And why *couldn't* they ask me to stay to dinner? In our house at dinnertime any relative or acquaintance or even stranger was asked to stay and eat. Why couldn't Mrs. Mason, like my mother, add some more water to the soup? Only Christians could be so unfeeling, I bitterly reflected. For all their book learning, their calmness, their veneer, they were at bottom cruel, even inhuman. I laughed to myself scornfully as I recalled Professor Mason's insistence, in his lectures, on the civilizing influence of art and music. My mother did not read the latest novel of Arnold Bennett; indeed, she hardly knew a word of anything but Yiddish. Yet she had infinite tact, and respected people's sensibilities. As for Professor Mason, while he was technically innocent of insulting me, he had refrained from admonishing his wife, or saying anything to me to alleviate the hurt to my pride.

I went directly to H. L.'s house and told him in detail about my disastrous visit to the Masons. To my surprise he blamed me for having placed *them* in an embarrassing situation. According to H. L., Mrs. Mason's social behavior had been correct. Social behavior, he said, is a game with clear-cut rules, and its language, though composed of words used in everyday life, is one that has to be learned. A simple sentence may mean quite the opposite of what it says, depending on the circumstance and situation at the moment. Thus, if at dinnertime Mrs. Mason had said, "Won't you stay to dinner?" what she really would have been saying was, "You have stayed too long. But I am obliged by my social code to ask you to remain to dinner, and by the same code you are obliged to say you would like nothing better, but unfortunately you had made another engagement." I asked H. L. how he happened to know so much about social matters, and he said he had often had tea and even dinner at the houses of his professors, and had listened carefully (as a student of the drama) and evaluated the conversation and behavior of the hosts and guests.

This threw a new light on the matter. Since the Masons had behaved according to a prevailing social code, I was obliged to absolve them of cruelty or even insensitiveness. And to prove to them that I harbored no ill feelings toward them, I made plans to entertain them at my house with supper and music, as I had promised. When I next saw Professor Mason, he appeared to have forgotten my anger and my precipitate flight from his house. He was genial, as usual, and he said he and Mrs. Mason had "so enjoyed" my visit, and they were looking forward to the performance of his quartet at my house. We arranged a date, one sufficiently distant to give me time to make the preparations I considered necessary for so important a visit. For not since the time Madame Franko had without warning called on us at Rivington Street had anyone remotely approaching the Masons in importance come to see us.

I examined our apartment critically with a view toward possible not-too-expensive improvements. Our two living-room windows had half curtains made of second-hand, coarse lace of an extravagant design my mother had picked up on a pushcart. But in Professor Mason's living room the windows had not only inside curtains but long draperies on the outside, which hung down in graceful folds. Feeling quite sure that Mrs. Mason would notice the absence of outside draperies from our windows, I purchased in a basement shop in Hester Street fifteen yards of green burlap at ten cents a yard. These I cut to the measurements of the two windows and secured to the window frames with carpet tacks. I had hoped to imitate the hang of the outer draperies at the Masons'. But I found to my dismay that because of its rather solid texture, the burlap resisted all efforts to shape it into folds. Yet, though they hung stiff and ungiving, the new curtains managed to lend a touch of elegance, even opulence, to the room.

I then remembered the sugar tongs I had seen at the Masons'. Mrs. Mason would certainly be astonished to see us handling sugar with our fingers. I described the instrument to my mother, who marveled at it, but questioned the need for it for people like the Masons, whose fingers were, presumably, generally clean. But I had already set my heart on a pair of sugar tongs, and she finally agreed that if we were to continue entertaining on a large scale people who might have an influence on my career, the thing might be an asset. I walked the length of Grand Street to find a pair of sugar tongs. Between the East River and the Bowery, Grand Street had about half a dozen jewelry stores, but none of them carried sugar tongs. Indeed, their proprietors and clerks had never heard of such a thing. I was obliged to make a trip to Siegel Cooper's, on Sixth Avenue and Eighteenth Street, to find one. But the only pair of tongs in the store formed a part of a beautiful nickel-plated sugar bowl with ten spoons hanging from ten little rings attached to the bowl's circular rim. The whole thing sold for two dollars, and looked magnificently ostentatious. I remembered that Mrs. Mason's sugar bowl was plain silver, and had no attachments whatsoever. This complex bowl would certainly impress her. The temptation to buy it was strong. And since the tongs were not to be sold without the bowl and spoons, I stifled my feeling of guilt at my extravagance and bought the entire thing.

The preparations for our supper and musicale were extensive and thorough. My mother washed the windows inside and out. When washing the outside, she sat on the windowsill and I clasped her knees for safety. In the evenings, my friends—Mike Dorf, cellist, Hymie Fink, violinist, a young viola player Hymie brought along—and I rehearsed Professor Mason's piano quartet. As the appointed day drew near I was seized with a fear that friends or relations might suddenly drop in, as they often did without warning, and expect to stay to supper and listen to the music. It wasn't that there would not be enough food. My mother was adept in an emergency at stretching a meal to any length. Nor would I mind the intrusion of grown-up friends or relations. What I feared was the behavior of their children, whose lack of manners would be noticed by the Masons. I went so far as to suggest that my mother should give out—of course, in the most casual way—that no one would be at home that day, that we had all been invited to friends in Newark. This she rejected as being suspicious in itself, and likely to induce people to test our veracity by unexpectedly showing up, probably just as we were sitting down to supper. We could do nothing, my mother said, but hope for the best. And with great misgivings I left it at that.

My fears were only too well founded. Around three o'clock on the afternoon of The Day—a very warm day in June—there was a knock on the door, and in came Chaia-Riva and Nochum Flayshig and their twins. I was speechless with dismay. My mother's face reddened, but she greeted the visitors in her usual voluble, hospitable manner, and after a moment of hesitation I, too, welcomed them, though rather lamely. I thought, wildly, of taking Chaia-Riva into my confidence, laying the matter before her and asking her to return with her family to Brooklyn. But when I looked at the perspiring faces of our unwelcome guests, my irritation gave way to a feeling of pity, and I determined to make the best of a situation that could not be changed. It was obvious that the Flayshigs had come for the day and were hoping to spend the night. Chaia-Riva, observing the burlap draperies and the unusual neatness all around, said the house looked as if we had prepared for a celebration. My mother then told her, not without a touch of pride, what was afoot, and Nochum asked jokingly whether they would be in the way. My mother pooh-poohed the idea, to the Flayshigs' great relief.

Around six o'clock I went out in the street to wait for the Masons. The stoop was full of tenants in various stages of undress who were trying to cool off. As I made my way down the steps between them I became aware of slightly disagreeable smells, both from the squatters and from the refuse in the open garbage cans on the street and in the gutters. They were familiar odors. But I could not recall ever being annoyed by them before. There were no such smells around the Masons' stoop. What would the Masons think? But the Masons had just then turned the corner. I ran up to them, greeted them and conducted them up the stoop. The Masons looked around them and smiled. The people on the stoop moved aside to let them pass, and gazed at them with curiosity. And the Masons, still smiling, asked their pardon and said, "So sorry" and "Thank you very much" in the pleasantest manner possible. I went ahead of them upstairs and led them into our tenement. My mother had by now put on a clean shirtwaist and had secured a handkerchief, neatly folded in the shape of a triangle, to her waist with a large safety pin. I introduced the Masons around. They said they were "charmed" to everyone, and they patted the heads of the twins. Indeed, their apparent delight in meeting my parents and the Flayshigs, and in being in our house, had the effect of dissipating all my fears and putting me at ease almost at once.

Supper was soon ready (the Masons called it *dinner!*). Our

round dining table had been enlarged by an extra board, and all of us, except my mother, who served and never sat down, grouped ourselves around it. H. L. Greene had advised me about the protocol of seating distinguished guests. I placed Professor and Mrs. Mason on either side of my father, who, in the Prince Albert which he wore at weddings and circumcisions, and a black silk yarmulke (skullcap) on his head, took the head of the table. I thought it prudent to sit at the opposite end, with Nochum on my left and Chaia-Riva and the twins on my right. In this way I would be in a position to keep Nochum's jocularities and Chaia-Riva's aphorisms within bounds, and to curb the notorious propensity of the twins for grabbing at food. H. L. Greene elected to sit on Mrs. Mason's right. He had heard that she was interested in the drama, and had written several plays which were at the moment going the rounds of theatrical managers. Mike, Hymie and the viola player sat anywhere.

My mother had placed the nickel-plated sugar bowl, filled to the brim with large pieces of sugar in the shape of dominoes, the tongs perched vividly on top, as the table's centerpiece. The bowl with the pendent spoons was indeed eye-filling, and I caught Mrs. Mason looking at it more than once. I was glad I had yielded to the temptation of buying it, for it was imposing enough to divert one's attention from the cutlery and the dishes, which were plain and ill-assorted.

The table became noisy almost at once. Snatches of Yiddish and English rose above the din, and then the two languages became fused, and emerged as a clamorous, high-pitched, quite incomprehensible tongue. I gave most of my attention to the Flayshigs, but I was also alive to the deportment of our other guests. Mrs. Mason seemed happy enough with H. L., who was discoursing about his favorite dramatist. "Now, in *Emperor*

and Galilean, Ibsen . . ." I heard him say above the general din,
but it was drowned out by a voice from across the table. Professor Mason, talking to my father, was saying ". . . a very intelligent boy, your son . . . so sensitive . . . so . . ." and my
father, understanding no English but gathering the gist of the
remark, murmured, "Yes, mine son . . . yes. . . ." My father,
looking very serious, as if sensible of the honor and importance
of the occasion, was carefully pouring wine, filling to the brim
our two little silver goblets, one of which he handed to Professor Mason and the other placed in front of himself. They
clinked goblets and drank. My father then refilled them several
times, and passed them to the other men around the table. My
mother brought in a large plate of chopped herring covered
with chopped egg as if with a yellow blanket, and placed it on
the table near me. Thereupon one of the twins, who had been
munching a slice of bread, suddenly stuck it in the platter.
Before I could make a move, he had withdrawn the piece of
bread, which was now entirely covered with herring, and
shoved it into his mouth. Mrs. Flayshig, red with shame and
anger, slapped her son loudly across the face and spoke sharp,
abusive words in Yiddish. I looked apprehensively at the
Masons. They either had not seen the incident, or pretended
they hadn't. Professor Mason kept on talking to my father, who
was not listening, and was glaring sternly in the direction of the
twins, while Mrs. Mason still had her face turned toward H. L.
There was considerable tension at my end of the table. But
Nochum Flayshig, seemingly not affected by his son's outrageous behavior, began a long, pointless anecdote in his easy,
good-natured tone of voice. "Leave him be," he interrupted
himself to say smilingly to his wife, who had risen and was
pushing the offending child away from the table. "How much
could he have taken, as the waiter said to the customer who

found a fly in his soup?" Then Nochum resumed his anecdote, speaking to no one in particular, for the attention of everyone, with the exception of the Masons, was focused on Mrs. Flayshig and her recalcitrant child.

There was no further disturbance to mar the dinner. The Masons were loud in praise of the chopped herring, though they partook of it sparingly. The soup, which always came last, was, out of deference to our Christian guests, served immediately after the herring, but not to my father, who could not reasonably be expected to change the habit of a lifetime. He ate his soup last, while we all were drinking our tea. This was the moment when our pièce de résistance and centerpiece came into full play. Bowl in hand, I walked around the table, inquiring of each guest, "How many lumps?" as I had heard Mrs. Mason say at her house. I dislodged a spoon from the rim of the bowl, placed it alongside the glass of tea, and taking up the tongs, I delicately pinched and drew forth the domino-shaped piece of sugar and dropped it into the glass. My mother came in from the kitchen to watch this ceremony, and she called out to Mrs. Mason with unconcealed pride, "You like?" Mrs. Mason smiled and said fervently, "Indeed I do. It's most interesting," and proceeded to examine the bowl carefully. I had arranged a signal with H. L. for leaving the table and going into the parlor. And after everyone had had tea and my father had finished his soup, H. L. murmured, as if to himself, "'Fancy that, Hedda!'" This was the signal agreed upon. Startled, Mrs. Mason turned inquiringly to her neighbor. But I said in a loud voice, "Now we'll have some music," and got up. There ensued a noise of chairs being moved and everybody spoke at once, and Mrs. Mason, quite forgetting H. L.'s cryptic remark, passed along with me and the others into our front room.

Although I saw Professor Mason frequently for some years after this dinner party and musicale in Henry Street, it was forty years later that I again saw Mrs. Mason. Professor Mason desired my assistance in getting his overture *Chanticleer* recorded by R.C.A. Victor, a company of which I was then the artistic director, and he invited me to tea to talk it over. The Masons now lived in a large, old-fashioned apartment house. As I rang their doorbell, I remembered with emotion my first invitation to tea at their house on West Fifty-sixth Street. Professor Mason opened the door and led me into the living room, where sat a little old lady on a sofa, book in hand. "You remember Chotzinoff?" the professor said. Mrs. Mason put out her hand. "Indeed I do," she murmured. Then, as if it had taken place only yesterday, she added, "What an excellent dinner you gave us!"

THEOSOPHY

⟨◯⟩ There were art classes among the many activities of the Educational Alliance. The large room in which Sam Franko's orchestra rehearsed in the evenings was in the daytime a studio where art students drew, painted and modeled with clay. The walls were hung with unframed paintings. Plaster copies of classic sculptures rested on tall wooden columns, and student copies of them, in green or mud-colored clay, stood, shrouded in damp cloths, in many stages of near completion, on a long table near a wall. Before and after our rehearsals and during intermissions, I used to examine the paintings and the sculpture with interest. The paintings were generally lavish in color. The portraits were mostly of East Side types I knew so well. The outdoor scenes pictured the streets of the neighborhood in their colorful squalor. There were figures of sad children, fat, shrewd-looking women, and young and old men of the Hasidic type, with curled earlocks and beards, their faces a bright, unhealthy hue, their eyes shining with a kind of rapture, as at some joyous tidings hidden from all but them.

Several times I took the Lexington Avenue subway, got off

at Eighty-sixth Street and walked to the Metropolitan Museum
of Art. I wanted to get to know certain masterpieces I had read
about in books, and also to compare them with the student
works at the Educational Alliance. At the beginning of the century there were many paintings at the Metropolitan which were
popular more for their subject matter than for their artistic
merits—huge canvases like "Washington Crossing the Delaware," "The Horse Fair" by Rosa Bonheur, "Military Scenes"
by Meissonier, portraits by Boldoni, bloody battle scenes by
the Russian Vereshchagin—most of them since discarded. Especially popular were sentimental genre pieces, poor little waifs
crying, child bootblacks shining shoes, etc. I was attracted to
these paintings, in particular to the larger canvases with their
epic overtones. I paid scant attention to the works of the Dutch
school (except landscapes with windmills, which I liked very
much) and the classic Italian, French and English painters. The
religious pictures, the crucifixions and annunciations, the saints
and their tribulations, made hardly any impression on me; and
I barely glanced into the salon devoted to the nineteenth-cen-
tury Impressionists. I had once read, as a child, about an artist
so realistic that the draperies he had painted into one of his
pictures looked so real that spectators tried to lift them up; I
had from that moment believed that realism was the ultimate
test of quality in painting and sculpture. For this reason I was
especially drawn to an artist like Meissonier. His pictures of
brightly colored soldiers, their uniforms and decorations meticu-
lously represented—even the buttons on their uniforms looked
real—seemed to me in the tradition of the ancient Greek painter.
Compared with such art, the work of the students of the Educational Alliance looked unfinished, though I admitted they might
be perhaps more thought- and emotion-provoking.

Pictures began to interest me more and more. I had, how-

ever, never met a painter in the flesh, not even a student at the
Educational Alliance. I was therefore delighted when I discovered that my friend Hymie Fink knew a young painter intimately. His name was David Olshinsky. Hymie had, in fact,
told him so much about me that Olshinsky was as eager to meet
me as I was to meet him. The meeting was arranged, and Hymie
took me to Olshinsky's house on Henry Street, very close to
mine. At first sight I was disappointed in Olshinsky's looks.
He was a tall, heavy, blond youth of about my own age, with
a round, pleasant face. I had expected him to be thin and ema-
ciated, with a faraway look in his eyes. I thought artists ought
to be shy and reticent, yet David was the very opposite—enthusiastic and outgoing. He told me openly that he had admired
me for a long time and had been dying to meet me. He showed
me some of his paintings, none of which he had cared to finish.
"I meant them to be impressions," he said in explanation. Like
the work of the students at the Educational Alliance, they were
portraits of Jews and scenes of the East Side. David talked about
art in a very professional way, using strange terms like "fore-
shortening" and "perspective," which he illustrated by holding
a pencil out at arm's length toward a canvas and shutting one
eye. I felt I was being initiated into the mysteries of the art
world. At last I should be able to add a knowledge of art to
music and literature, and be professionally conversant with the
trinity of arts that Wagner had fused in his music dramas. I
would, in turn, teach Olshinsky the elements of music. We
would thus be of mutual benefit to each other.

Over a vegetable luncheon which Olshinsky's mother had
prepared, we discussed art by itself in its relation to music. Mrs.
Olshinsky was a stoutish, voluble woman who, surprisingly,
spoke English. (Very few East Side mothers could speak English.) She was a Christian Scientist, and her son professed him-

self a vegetarian. "I hope you don't mind eating vegetables,"
he said. "I can't understand how anyone would want to eat
something that was once alive!" I had never thought about food
in that way. But now I felt he was right, and a feeling of guilt
for having eaten so many things that were once alive came over
me. I looked at the vegetables in front of me with a new interest.
I remembered, with a sense of horror, the slaughter of chickens
I had assisted at, as my father's aid in the old days. And as I
ate my pot cheese and lettuce, I stole glances at Mrs. Olshinsky.
I wondered how a Jewish woman could be a Christian Scientist
without becoming a Christian.

To prove I was not altogether an ignoramus on the subject
of art, I told David about my frequent visits to the Metropolitan
Museum and my preference for certain of the pictures there.
But when I praised Meissonier, David shook his head disap-
provingly and said I must be joking, for Meissonier painted
only "potboilers." I didn't dare ask what a potboiler was. From
David's contemptuous tone of voice I could see that it was something to be shunned. But I mentioned "realism" in a vague sort
of way, and David excitedly launched into a harangue about the
French Impressionists and a new American school that was following their principles. I saw I should be foolhardy to deceive
David further, so I confessed, though rather airily, that my
knowledge of painting, especially of the French Impressionists
and their American disciples, was scanty. Whereupon David
proposed to visit the Museum with me right away, and point out
some outstanding examples of the modern school.

When we arrived at the Museum, he led me into a room I
used to pass through hastily, and straight up to a tall painting
of a woman in a kind of long brown nightgown. On the outstretched forefinger of her right hand a parrot was perched.
The woman's face, her gown, the parrot and the general sur-

roundings were all of the same drab color, or perhaps many gradations of the same color. David went into ecstasies over the painting. He talked of color harmony, atmosphere ("the externals must express the soul," he said), etc. He next showed me a picture of a girl in a garden, by an American, and pointed out the "whiteness" of the girl's white muslin dress and the splashes of sunlight all over the picture. We went from one Impressionist painting to another. We inspected murky, gray, unsubstantial landscapes and wraithlike portraits by Whistler. David anticipated possible reservations on my part by "explaining" the beauty of Whistler's indefinite, pastel shades, and presently I caught his enthusiasm and began to see the pictures in a new light. Compared with these examples of Impressionism, the pictures I had formerly admired now seemed hardly to belong in the realm of art. I returned to look once more at the girl with the parrot. And this time I felt that what David had said about it was absolutely true. I saw no drabness now, but the most delicate gradation of subtle colors. And turning again to Whistler, I felt myself in the presence of a new world of meaningful fogs and vapors, and people with faces and figures to match. It reminded me of the vague world of Claude Debussy, which, when I first looked at the score of *Pelléas et Mélisande,* struck me as absolutely authentic, though quite strange. Only one thing troubled me. The realism I had admired had been exposed by David for what it was—the negation of art—and I was quite ready to throw Meissonier, Rosa Bonheur and the men who painted the pathetic little shoeblacks and "Washington Crossing the Delaware" overboard. But what about the celebrated classic Dutch, English and Italian painters? They too were realists. Their eye for detail was certainly as sharp as Meissonier's. The ladies and gentlemen who sat for Reynolds and Gainsborough wore the most elaborate clothes, which the artists had painted in with minutest care and in astonishing detail. Did this realism detract from their art? David assured me that it didn't, for the reason that the external details were never at the expense of the character of the sitters. "Take," said David, "the portrait of the Duchess of Devonshire by Gainsborough. The dress she wears and the fan she carries are realistic in every detail. But the face of the Duchess is that of a beautiful, living and breathing noblewoman. Whereas in the potboilers you used to admire, the faces count for nothing, the dress and surroundings for everything." That settled it. My conversion was now complete, and I felt the happiness of one who has acquired a rigid standard by which everything can be safely measured.

David had many young artist friends who shared his ideas. One day he took me to a tumbledown house in Canal Street to meet two painters he felt I should get to know intimately. The two men I would meet were not only talented painters, David said, they were also Theosophists. Before I could ask him what a Theosophist was, we had climbed four rickety flights of stairs and entered a back room in which two men sat painting at easels. They were copying a framed picture which rested on an easel between theirs. The framed picture was of that sentimental kind—a tattered child bootblack, in fact, seated on his little box, eating a banana—which belonged in David's potboiler classification. The young men put down their brushes and greeted David, who then introduced me. The older-looking man, whose name was Morris Mandell, pointed to a dozen copies of the little bootblack, which stood drying on the floor against the wall, and said that he and Sam Rubinstein, the man at the other easel, were filling an order for three dozen copies at a dollar and a half apiece, to be delivered not later than the end of the week. "So, if you don't mind," he added, "take a couple of chairs and visit with us while we work." They re-

sumed painting, talking the while. Mandell had red hair, limpid
eyes and a fleshy face. His lips were full and sensuous, but his
smile was pensive. He had the quiet air, the conscious serenity
of one who has some beautiful secret, some lonely faith, spiritual, yet strong enough to adjust to the hazards and misfortunes
of life, even to the bitter necessity of painting potboilers for a
living. His friend Sam seemed to have a jollier nature, for he
laughed and joked as he painted away, making fun of the little
bootblack and invoking, in a jocular way, the wrath of the gods
on the picture dealer who paid them to desecrate art. For this
he was mildly rebuked by his companion, who appeared to have
compassion for everybody and everything. "We are just as bad
for taking on the job," he said. "By the gods, you are right,
Mandell, as always," Sam apologized. "I hope you'll excuse
these outbursts, Chotzinoff," he said to me. "I get so tired of
these potboilers that sometimes I forget myself."

I felt drawn to both of them, but especially to Mandell, the
effect of whose unruffled patience and gentleness was heightened by his companion's outbursts of merriment or displeasure.
I was impressed with Mandell's quiet air of spiritual superiority, and I longed to know his secret. Was it Theosophy, whatever that might be? But Sam Rubinstein was a Theosophist too,
yet there was no intimation of a secret faith in Sam's behavior.
It was all very mysterious and provocative.

We talked about music, literature and painting. They were
both ardent Wagnerites, Sam less reverently so than Mandell.
The difference was that Sam regarded the personages in the
music dramas as people, whereas for Mandell they were sym-
bols of good or evil. Sam held that the passion of Tristan and
Isolde was at bottom carnal, that the music revealed it as such.
Mandell quietly asked him how he could be sure it was; and
Sam, blushing, said he had once felt exactly such things as Wag-

ner's chromatic music implied for a lady of his acquaintance, a
married woman. Mandell gave him a gently reproving look,
and Sam hastily added that it had all happened long ago, before
he knew anything about "the movement." Mandell, looking relieved, smiled indulgently, and the friends looked at each other
knowingly. "The movement," I thought, must be the secret,
and Theosophy must be "the movement."

The striking difference between the personalities of the two
artists, and their intriguing conversation as they worked, made
me long to know them better. I began to drop in on them in the
late afternoon, just before the light from the north window of
the little back room in which they worked began to wane. Soon
they would put down their brushes and we would talk. One
day I walked Mandell to his house on Tenth Street, and on the
way I asked him about "the movement." Very gravely Mandell
told me that "the movement" was the Theosophical Society, of
which he and Sam were members. Sam had joined only recently,
and had not yet had time to absorb the teachings of Theosophy.
That, said Mandell, smiling indulgently, accounted for Sam's
peculiar outbursts and rather worldly opinions. "I don't want
you, Chotzinoff, to think that I have absorbed *all* the teachings
of Theosophy. Only the pure in soul can do that," Mandell
said modestly. Yet as he spoke, Mandell's face seemed to me to
reflect a soul purged of all human failings. I had an impulse to
tell him that, for his expression touched something in me that
vibrated in recognition. He sensed this and held up a depreca-
tory hand. "You are wrong, Chotzinoff," he said. "I am far
from pure. I am human—'all too human,' as Nietzsche says.
There are people in 'the movement' who *are* pure in soul. Not
perhaps so pure as 'she' is. But compared to me, very pure. If
you are interested, you can meet them."

I was eager to know who "she" might be, and I made so

bold as to inquire. Mandell looked into my eyes intently and
said quietly, in a tone of finality, "Mrs. Tingley." I said, "Oh!"
solemnly, but Mandell saw in my face that the name was strange
to me. "But of course you can't know," he said reassuringly.
"There was a time when I myself didn't know." Again he
fixed me with his eyes. "Mrs. Tingley is 'her' reincarnation,"
he said. I murmured, "Oh!" again, and again my face asked for
enlightenment. "There I go again," he said apologetically. "I
keep forgetting you are not in 'the movement.'" Then, after
a pregnant pause, "Mrs. Tingley is the reincarnation of Madame
Blavatsky," he said simply.

I was conscious of the gravity of Mandell's statement, though
Madame Blavatsky was, like Mrs. Tingley, unknown to me.
I felt I must learn then and there who both ladies were, what
reincarnation was, and what relation it had to "the movement."
"Mandell," I said, "as you see, I am very ignorant about these
extraordinary things. But I want very much to know. I *must*
know. I, too, would like to be pure in soul. I've tried very hard,
but it's difficult with so few good people around to help one to
overcome worldly temptations and one's own desires. I can
see that you know something important that sustains you and
makes you calm and happy, even when you are painting potboilers. Can you share your secret with me, Mandell, as you
have shared it with Sam? Help me, Mandell, please. I want to
be good . . . like you . . . . Show me how, Mandell! . . ." Emotion choked me, and I had to turn away.

Mandell put his arm through mine and we walked up and
down his street. He began by telling me that he, too, was once
exactly like me, a young, idealistic artist struggling with selfish
—yes, even carnal—desires, and finding no solution in art, only
temporary solace. Then one day he was introduced to a man,
a doctor, whose face reflected an inner vision and peace. They

became friends, and in time the doctor initiated him into certain mysteries which have the power to transform doubting and tortured minds into an awareness of man's spiritual destiny. The doctor told him about the spiritual essence of the universe, and about the cycles through which the soul of man must pass until it has been sufficiently purified to join and became a part of the universal "allness," like a drop of water sinking into the vast ocean.

"You see, Chotzinoff," Mandell explained, "Theosophy teaches that we come back again and again on earth. We are reincarnated, and with each new incarnation we slough off more and more of our earthly desires and impurities. After a certain number of incarnations some of us become pure enough to become incorporeal. Madame Blavatsky was—indeed, is— one of these rare essences. So is Mrs. Tingley, though she lives in the flesh, and presides over 'the movement' in our Theosophical headquarters at Point Loma, in California. In fact, Mrs. Tingley *is* Madame Blavatsky—that is, Madame Blavatsky's soul has entered Mrs. Tingley's body. . . . You understand?" I thought I did, but I wanted to know whether Madame Blavatsky had any other existence *outside* Mrs. Tingley. "Oh, yes," Mandell said without hesitation. "She is also around us *at this very moment in the air,* as are many pure spirits who have passed through the necessary number of earthly reincarnations. But, of course, in our present incarnation we are unable to see her. I shall give you her works to read—*The Secret Doctrine* and *Isis Unveiled*. In these books she describes exactly such incorporeal existences. Are you sure you understand, Chotzinoff? Theosophy is not an easy doctrine; it takes years to absorb. But if you are really interested, and I think you are, I'll give you those books and take you to one of our meetings. One thing more, Chotzinoff. You may meet people who will tell you that

Annie Besant and not Mrs. Tingley is the reincarnation of 'the founder' and head of 'the movement.' They are in error. Annie Besant is an impostor. She may have met Madame Blavatsky, but that is all. She represents the forces of evil. Everybody in 'the movement' knows that. I thought you should know it too."

We spent half of the night walking up and down Mandell's street. I asked many questions, which Mandell answered at great length with a simple eloquence that destroyed many doubts that presented themselves to me. But it was not to my mind that Mandell appealed. He spoke to my imagination, to those non-reasoning emotional faculties I called the soul. To it Mandell addressed himself, after he had pointed out the incapacity of reason to apprehend spiritual truth. "The soul, Chotzinoff," he said, "unlike the mind, needs no proof. The mind may say, 'You tell me that Madame Blavatsky is here beside us at this very moment, but can you prove it?' But the soul says, 'I *know* it's true, don't ask me how.' The mind may say, 'How do I know that Annie Besant represents the forces of evil?' The soul simply says, 'I know it.' The soul *knows* that love is good and hate is evil. It only *knows* it. It can't prove it. Can one *prove* the exquisite smell of a flower, the exaltation of Wagner's music, the beauty of great paintings and poetry? No. But the soul knows these things of itself. . . ."

The next afternoon, when I came to Mandell's studio, he gave me five large and heavy books—Madame Blavatsky's *Isis Unveiled* and *The Secret Doctrine*. "I told Sam about our conversation last night," he said as he gave me an affectionate smile. Sam put aside his brushes and pressed my hand significantly. "I knew the first time you came here that you would be drawn to 'the movement,' " he said warmly. I sat on a stool and opened the books. In one of them there was a photograph of Madame Blavatsky. She was a large, coarse-looking woman

with thinning, kinky hair parted in the middle. A shawl was
draped around her shoulders. She looked rather untidy. But her
large, mesmeric eyes stared straight into mine and held them.
When I tried to look away or turn the page, I could not. "Don't
resist her," Mandell said softly, without taking his eyes off his
painting of the little shoeblack. "It's useless. *Yield* to her." It
required a great effort to look away from the photograph and
begin the opening chapter. At one point I looked up from the
page. Mandell had stopped working. His head was poised, as
if to catch sounds in the room apprehended only by him. He
seemed to be looking at something not visible to me. I said to
Mandell, "Do you suppose she is in this room with us *now*?"
I had just read that Madame Blavatsky had on several occasions
become sensible of the presence of certain "pure," incorporeal
souls in her room with whom she undertook to converse. Mandell shifted his gaze to me slowly, as if reluctant to abandon his
vision. He gave me one of his wistful smiles. "I wouldn't be
surprised," he answered softly, "would you, Sam?" Sam, after
considering a moment, said he wouldn't. "All the same," he
added, "I wish she would give us a sign or something." Mandell gave me a private, knowing look, as if to remind me that
as a newcomer in "the movement," Sam had not altogether shed
the common mortal's allegiance to reason, and still demanded
proof of manifestations that are by their nature beyond proof.

Some weeks later Mandell took me to a meeting of the New
York branch of the Theosophical Society, in what used to be a
store, on Fourteenth Street. It was presided over by Mandell's
doctor friend, a pale, ascetic-looking man. Even more than Mandell, the doctor had the look of one who cherishes a precious
secret. He said he had heard about me, and was happy that I
took an interest in "the movement." He then mounted a little
platform and addressed the room, which held about twenty-five

members of the Society. He said, "Our 'leader' sends greetings from California, and hopes that some of the New York comrades will come out to Point Loma and join their brothers in the practice of the principles and ideals of Theosophy as formulated by 'the founder,' and passed on intact to 'her.' " The doctor then read some passages from *The Secret Doctrine,* after which he stepped down and was replaced by one of the male members, who led the assembly in some choral singing. The music was rather ordinary, resembling undistinguished hymn tunes, which they probably were. But the words seemed original. They were, in fact, taken from the writings of Mrs. Tingley, and embodied Theosophical doctrine. The refrain of one began with the line "Peace, perfect peace." Another ended with "Repine not, O Soul, thou knowest well."

When the meeting was over, the doctor, Mandell and I adjourned to a little café nearby for a glass of buttermilk (Theosophy frowned on coffee—indeed, on all stimulants). I examined the doctor furtively for evidences of that greater purity of soul which Mandell said he possessed. And I thought I found them in his spare figure, the delicate structure of his head, the brilliant sunken eyes and the ashen color of his face. Mandell deferred to him openly, as I had seen Sam defer to Mandell. He asked him for my benefit to go more deeply into Theosophical doctrine than he, Mandell, had the knowledge and ability to do. And this the doctor proceeded to do. He begged me to be free with questions, and I asked him whether Theosophy accepted marriage. He said that it depended on the number of reincarnations a person had experienced. Marriage, he declared, was a necessity *only* in early reincarnations. The purer the soul became through successive appearances on earth, the less the body required in the way of physical satisfaction. It was possible, however, by the exercise of extraordinary will power, to "overcome" marriage, even by those on a lower spiritual plane than the "elect." Then the doctor and Mandell could "overcome" marriage? I ventured to ask. As to that, the doctor said, desire was a formidable antagonist, there was no doubt about it. But only time would tell whether they could conquer it. I then pointed out, a little hesitantly, that both Madame Blavatsky and Mrs. Tingley had been married several times. At this the doctor smiled benignantly and said the actions of "the leaders" sometimes *resemble* those of ordinary people. "But we in 'the movement' know better. These deeds are actually spiritual manifestations decreed by the 'all-knowing' ones. It was necessary for the scheme of things that our 'founder' and her reincarnation, our 'leader,' should marry. The unions were, of course, in no sense physical. The number of times is no matter." He then said he had several professional calls to make. He shook my hand fervently and left.

I felt irresistibly drawn to Theosophy. The idea of man, purged of human desires by the successive experiences of reincarnation and ready and fit to become a tiny part of that pure essence out of which all life springs, seemed to explain the phenomena of birth and death and suffering, and an answer to my hitherto futile efforts to be at peace with myself. Yet I still had some lingering doubts. More especially I found Mrs. Tingley, as her photographs showed her, less sympathetic than Madame Blavatsky, whose eyes, at least, bore evidence of the supernatural powers attributed to her. Mrs. Tingley was an enormously fat woman, bearing no visible traces of spirituality whatever. Even the hand, on the second finger of which she wore the large ring Madame Blavatsky had bequeathed to her as a symbol and guarantee of the legitimacy of Mrs. Tingley's leadership, looked outsized, pudgy and gross. I could not, of course, confide my reservations about the spirituality of the present "leader" to Mandell. But I confessed to him that I thought I was, as yet, "too human" to feel and understand all the elements of the Theosophical doctrine. Mandell said there was no hurry, that though there was much to *feel,* there was, in fact, nothing to *understand.* Someday soon, he said, I would experience "an illumination." "It" would come to me suddenly, without warning, as "it" had come to him. And then not a doubt would remain, and all would be crystal clear.

And, indeed, Mandell was right. Some time later, as I lay awake in bed at night, I felt the presence of someone near me. I turned on the light and saw that I was alone. Once more in the darkness, I felt an apparition near me. This time I was aware of someone's concentrated gaze upon me, and presently through the gloom I discerned Madame Blavatsky's penetrating, rhapsodic eyes. They came closer and closer to me, growing ever larger and more penetrating as they advanced. At the same time I heard voices, like music, in the air. These voices must, I thought, belong to the disembodied spirits, the "astral" ones, who were Madame Blavatsky's familiars in her last and final reincarnation on earth, of whose ethereal company she was now a part. I lay in a sweat, wide awake in the darkness, and surrendered my senses to the almost palpable sights and sounds around me. The music had the sensuous purity of the Prelude to *Lohengrin;* indeed, the harmonies were very like. Like the Prelude, this music had traveled from a distance and, coming nearer and nearer, burst right in front of me, like giant fireworks. A fortissimo mass of sound filled the room, then gradually subsided and retreated, and finally vanished into the mysterious region whence it came. An ecstatic lassitude permeated my legs and arms. I closed my eyes and felt a luxurious contentment, like one who arrives home after a long foot journey. I now felt the soft influence of that "Peace, perfect peace"

which had sounded so perfunctory in the Theosophical Society's assembly room. I had no longer any doubts. The very
idea of my ever having had any seemed unreal. Mrs. Tingley,
I could not deny, was massive, but so was the wonderful planet
Earth. It must have been my ignorance and obtuseness which
prevented me from seeing in her fleshy countenance that purity
which it undoubtedly possessed, else she could not have been
selected as the repository of "the founder's" spirit. Everything
that once puzzled me now seemed quite clear. I could hardly
bear the illumination. "It" had come to me in great force and
splendor, as Mandell had correctly prophesied. I awoke next
morning in a new world, and I was a new man. I went at once
to Mandell, told him the strange circumstance of my conversion,
and said I wished to join the New York chapter of the Theosophical Society without delay. Mandell looked at me with compassionate tenderness and quietly embraced me. We were now
brothers, he said. He would ask his friend the doctor to pro-
pose me at the next meeting of the Society. The dues were fifty
cents a month, or five dollars a year. He said I could pay by the
year or month, as I chose.

NORMANDIE-
BY-THE-SEA

꙳ My conversion to Theosophy made it necessary for me
to adjust my relationship with certain people to the precepts
of my new belief. Chief among these people was Elena Kovner.
I realized that it would be years before I could qualify for that
category of Theosophists which "overcame," or bypassed, love
and marriage. But notwithstanding my enthusiasm for "the
movement," I could not endure the thought of renouncing my
love for Elena. I could, however, attempt to convert her to
Theosophy. And if I succeeded there would be some pallia-
tion for my frailty in the fact that its object was a fellow Theosophist. So I spent many evenings reading *Isis Unveiled* to
Elena, answering her doubts as Morris Mandell had answered
mine, and assuring her that the moment of revelation was
bound to arrive; "it" would come to her full blown, as "it" had
come to me, and at a stroke give new meaning to her life.

Elena was willing to listen, even eager. I did not bind her
to secrecy. Indeed, I hoped she would, in turn, discuss Theosophy with her parents, though I was pessimistic about her father's
reaction to "the movement." I soon discovered the nature of his

reaction, which was what I thought it would be. Her father asked me banteringly one day whether it was true that every night before getting into bed I stood on one foot for an hour. He understood, he said, that standing on one foot for an hour each night was an endurance test prescribed for new converts to Theosophy. I did not choose to take offense at this, for Mandell had already prepared me for the gibes and insults of unbelievers. I could not hope that so disillusioned (and also inconsistent) a veteran of Russian Nihilism would ever experience the illumination of Theosophy. But I was worried about the effect of his skepticism on his daughter. I felt I needed allies, and I introduced Morris Mandell and Sam Rubinstein to the Kovners. They were warmly welcomed by Mrs. Kovner, and Mr. Kovner seemed pleased to have his daughter on an intimate footing with a pair of artists, who would be contributing to the all-round education he aimed to provide for her.

Then a sudden turn of events interrupted my plans for Elena's conversion. Her cello teacher accepted a very important teaching post in Brussels, and it was decided that Elena should continue her studies with him in Europe. The decision, coming quickly and without warning, threw me into a panic. Notwithstanding my new Theosophical approach to life, I felt suddenly bereft. There were no grounds upon which I could oppose the move. For not only would Elena continue her studies without interruption, but her intellectual and artistic development could not but be benefited by a year or two in Europe. But I feared that so long a separation might weaken, on her side, the secret emotional bond between us. There was now an air of eagerness in Elena's behavior that I found distressing. Her preparations for departure were too detailed and elaborate to suggest pain, or even regret, at leaving me. I could not part from her without a word of assurance. And on the night before she sailed, at a farewell party, I boldly remained after everybody had left and her family had gone to bed. For once Mr. Kovner, hearing no music from the living room, refrained from calling out the lateness of the hour and throwing out hints for me to leave. Elena and I were left alone without disturbance. For the first time I spoke openly about my love. But even as I pleaded I was aware that I and my love for her were now only of secondary importance, that Brussels and Europe and the implications of her new life filled her heart and mind. I had no position in this new life. Nor could I find any promise for the future, for I foresaw the flowering of her art and personality in her new-found freedom from domestic ties, and in the subtle influences of European culture. Certainly she would come back in a few years quite changed, and with standards that I should not be able, I thought, to meet. Desolate and sick at heart, I tried to get from her a word of hope. "I will always think of you," was all she would permit herself to say. And when I begged for a farewell kiss, the tears came to her eyes, but she would only give me her hand.

With Elena gone, I gave myself up more wholeheartedly to what was once my ruling passion—music. Through the kind interest of I. Jacobs, the young East Side pianist and teacher, I made the acquaintance of his teacher, Bernard Reeve. I. Jacobs had only recently begun studying with Bernard Reeve, and in a short time had added a polish to his technique which made his playing sound (and look) deceptively easy. Mr. Reeve lived uptown on the West Side and charged three dollars a lesson. But he made an exception in my case and brought his fee down to two dollars. Mr. Reeve was a small man, soft-spoken and kind. He taught me how to produce a singing tone by loosening my wrists and depressing the keys, instead of striking them. He insisted, in fact, on such close intimacy between fingers and keys that one could not, if one tried, insert a piece of tissue paper between them. He also insisted on the observance of all dynamics noted down by the composer. He permitted a reasonable amount of liberty in interpretation, maintaining that the value of an artist lay precisely in his individuality and, in general, in the difference between his individuality and that of other artists. My lessons were pleasurable, and I always left Mr. Reeve's studio full of buoyant confidence. I would walk across the park to my sister Hannah's three-room apartment on 103rd Street, between Madison and Fifth. Although Hannah knew nothing about the technique of piano playing, I told her the details of my lesson, and I tried to show her how Mr. Reeve had opened musical vistas whose existence I had never suspected.

Hannah always listened with rapt attention. I was sure she understood the implications, if not the details, of what I told her, the while she cooked up something for me to eat. Before I became a vegetarian she would fry me a piece of steak she had saved for me from her children's lunch. Hannah now had three children, two boys and a girl. (I often thought she considered me her fourth.) Davy, her firstborn, was her greatest concern. From the moment of his birth she had concentrated on Davy all the love of her selfless nature. He was a beautiful boy who knew, unfortunately, no restraints; for Hannah looked on him as a miraculous gift from Heaven, which made up for her arid and impoverished childhood and youth, her unrequited love for one man, and her loveless marriage to another. She could not deny Davy anything, and he became a spoiled child. She refused to take his willfulness seriously, and would not permit anyone to say a word against him. His physical well-being was all she cared about. Notwithstanding her poverty, she managed to keep Davy better dressed than the children of the neighborhood. She heard, or read somewhere, that the blood of the best cut of meat was good for growing children. So she bought the most expensive steak for Davy, squeezed out the blood and threw away the meat. Hannah had, unlike me, always been free of superstitions. But now, when she walked in the park with Davy, and some stranger, startled by the child's good looks, asked her how old her beautiful son was, a look of fear would cross her face, and she would spit three times behind Davy's back—the time-honored antidote against the evil eye. Each year she took Davy to be photographed, and ordered half a dozen pictures at thirty-five cents each. And for each new photograph she bought Davy a new suit. The other two children did not want for care. But it was clear to everyone that her concern for Davy was fanatically extreme. My father often said that such love was not only foolish but sinful, and a direct provocation to Fate. Only Jehovah, he said, merited such uncritical devotion.

I went to Hannah's home not only after my lessons with Mr. Reeve, but after the rehearsals of Sam Franko's Bach Society. This was a small choral group which met once a week, usually on Sunday mornings, in the large living room of a Mrs. John Gerster, a wealthy member of the chorus. And in the course of two years the group rehearsed most of the cantatas of J. S. Bach. I was the pianist for the chorus. After the rehearsals, at Hannah's house, I sang for her certain passages from the cantatas that had impressed or moved me. The name of one of the arias or choruses was *Bleib' bei Uns* (*Stay with Us*). And whenever I got up to leave, Hannah would urge me to stay a little longer, fortifying her pleas by singing *Bleib' bei Uns*. The combination of Bach and Hannah was generally too much for me, and I stayed.

H. L. Greene and I heard a great many concerts and operas together. Seldom wanting money, he had been used to paying

the box-office prices for standing room at Carnegie Hall
and the Metropolitan. But I showed him how simple it was to
bribe the ticket-takers at both places. Thus, for the regular price
of one ticket, he could now attend several musical events. H. L.
generously treated me to a series of Kneisel Quartet concerts
at the Brooklyn Academy of Music. He paid three dollars for
two seats to the subscription series of six concerts. This was an
extravagant outlay even for H. L., and we walked to Brooklyn
and back to save carfare. We did not mind the walk, especially
the return journey. Excited and stimulated by a Beethoven or
Schubert quartet, we walked briskly, talking and arguing about
the music and the Kneisels. And sometimes, unable to resist
the temptation of buckwheat cakes we saw being made behind
the plate-glass window of a Childs restaurant on Atlantic
Avenue, we went in for coffee and cakes, and spent more money
than the carfare we had saved.

H. L. was interested in violinists, especially in public performers. He had heard Ysaye and Kreisler, and he never missed
the debut of a violin virtuoso. He invited me one night to a
concert of the Russian Symphony Orchestra to hear the debut of
Mischa Elman, a young Russian violinist who had been acclaimed in Germany and England. For this event H. L. bought
seats in the top balcony. It was a novelty for me not to stand
up at a concert. Furthermore, the acoustics seemed better in the
balcony than downstairs, even though the stage, from where
we sat, looked small indeed. The young Mr. Elman was vociferously greeted when he came out to play the Tschaikovsky concerto. It was clear that the audience was expecting a revelation.
And, indeed, the young virtuoso provided one the moment he
began to play. It was bold, sensuous playing of a kind I had
never before heard. Everything was startlingly vivid: the tone
rich and full-blooded, capable of infinite gradations and hues;

the technique flagrantly secure; the interpretation passionate, and in the andante passionately lyrical. The double stops in the cadenza poured from the violin like an effortless cascade of sound, brilliant and intense. The debut was a sensational triumph even for New York, and the audience screamed and demanded many encores. I was excited like everyone else. But on our walk home H. L. had certain reservations about the new violinist. Conceding the beauty of his tone and his exceptional technique, H. L. contended that for him there was an exaggeration of sentiment and emotion that went beyond good taste. I asked him if the same charge could not be brought against Caruso, and he said that it could, and that the art of the two had much in common. H. L. then contrasted Elman with Ysaye. Ysaye's tone was also sensuous, but the Belgian had an elegance and nobility the Russian lacked. H. L.'s criticism might have influenced me, had his own playing not belied his words. For, whatever theoretical ideas about style and interpretation H. L. professed, he himself played the violin sentimentally. Indeed, there was such a wide discrepancy between his musical opinions and his playing that I wondered even then whether it was at all possible to know one's own faults and merits.

Yet H. L.'s amateurish playing and dogmatic views on music had no effect on our intimacy. Sometimes I succeeded in overcoming his prejudice, as when he finally admitted that Puccini had some merit as an operatic composer. And along with me he promptly succumbed to the lure of Brahms when Mr. Reeve gave me the Rhapsodies in B and G Minor to learn. Somehow, neither of us had ever heard the music of Brahms; or if we had, we thought it of so little consequence that we forgot having heard it. The reviews in the newspapers of performances of the Brahms symphonies were seldom flattering to that composer. Indeed, at Katz's music store the joke went around that in Car-

negie Hall signs had been put up reading "Exit in Case of
Brahms." I bought the two rhapsodies with misgivings. But
even at my first reading I knew I was experiencing new sensations. I felt assaulted by a kind of large, passionate melodious-
ness, and a rhythm that subjected it to constant unrelenting
pressure and held it, so to speak, within bounds. I played the
pieces for H. L. and they at once struck him as forcibly as they
had struck me. "But," H. L. wondered, "a rhapsody should be
free, wild, soaring, and these rhapsodies are rigid, controlled!"
But I saw clearly that it was exactly this rigidity and control that
had so powerfully affected us. It seemed to me that the highest
function of art was to put emotion under control. Beethoven
did it, and so did Wagner, though it is less obvious in Wagner.
But in these pieces Brahms did it consciously. The control is
so sure that it raises rhapsodic emotion to a vividness it could
not have if undisciplined by rhythm and allowed to spill over.
I tried to convey this idea to H. L. And to illustrate it I played
the melody of Grieg's *Åses Tod,* which is note for note the
second theme of Brahms's G Minor Rhapsody. "Over its simple
harmonies Grieg's melody sounds sad and all that," I said.
"But look what Brahms does for the theme! By placing under
it a ceaseless rhythmic counterpoint, by not letting it sag, he
heightens it. Grieg does let it sag; he kind of slobbers over it.
Brahms makes the theme hurry on in spite of itself. The effect
is noble, poignant, as it is urged on by rhythmic countermelody
in the left hand." Since both had used identical material with
such vastly different results, we agreed then and there that
Grieg was a spineless composer and Brahms a strong and great
one.

My interest in Brahms was augmented the summer of that
year to a reverence that placed him beside Beethoven and Wagner in my private musical pantheon. I got a job as a pianist in

a trio in a hotel on the Jersey coast near Sea Bright. It was the best summer job I had had so far, for it paid the large sum of sixteen dollars a week. Another advantage was the elimination of music at meals. Three evenings a week we played serious and semiclassic music in the large lounge after dinner, and three evenings we played dance music in a casino a small distance from the hotel. One morning, as I was practicing my Brahms rhapsodies in the casino, a middle-aged, white-haired woman came in and listened, and, during a pause, spoke to me. Her name was Geraldine Roeder, her husband was the business manager of the Belasco Theater and of all the Belasco theatrical enterprises. I was awed at this revelation. For while I had never been inside the Belasco Theater, I knew about David Belasco's importance in the world of the theater. Mrs. Roeder went on to say that she herself had been a concert violinist, a pupil of the great Joseph Joachim. Her stage name was Geraldine Morgan. She knew the Brahms rhapsodies well. She had even known Brahms himself!

I could hardly speak for emotion. But Mrs. Roeder quickly put me at my ease. Her hair was snow-white and silken, and her face beautiful and kind. She asked me if I knew Brahms's Violin Concerto, and on my saying I didn't, she went back to the hotel and soon returned with her violin case and the piano part of the concerto. She unwrapped the violin from a large piece of silk. I asked her if she had ever played on a Stradivarius, and she smiled and said her violin was one, and put it in my hands. I felt as scared and self-conscious as I did the first time my sister Hannah put her baby in my arms. And after a hasty glance at the instrument I handed it back. Then, while Mrs. Roeder tuned it, I looked at the first tutti of the concerto and tried to grasp the form and anticipate the technical difficulties with which it bristled. Here, as in the rhapsodies, I was delighted with the angularity of the themes and the inexorable rhythm. Warning Mrs. Roeder that I would leave out many notes, I plunged boldly into the tutti. Repeatedly I heard her say "fine" as I scrambled through a passage. Then at last the violin came in, and I felt less exposed. Mrs. Roeder played with great energy and the utmost assurance. The music of Brahms seemed to be her particular musical idiom. Played thus, Brahms was even more granitic than I had thought. A certain passage evoked a visual image as of giants hurling great boulders through the air. I felt under an immense strain keeping up with the violinist's changes of tempo, and trying to imitate her style and phrasing. But I also felt a great exhilaration as I blundered my way through the score without making any serious musical mistakes. I was grateful for the respite of the cadenza, and while I listened to Mrs. Roeder, I looked ahead to the soft entrance of the piano at the end, and figured out how it should sound. All the same, I was hardly prepared for the ravishing interplay of violin and piano following the soloist's final trill. We finished the movement together, to my surprise and joy. And Mrs. Roeder laughed with pleasure, and paid me compliments, and said we must play together often. But not only solo-violin pieces. The chamber music of Brahms was, according to her, even greater than the concerto we had played. Fortunately, she said, there were among the guests in the hotel two string players besides herself—a banker who played the violin, and a young professional viola player who had recently arrived with his wife from Germany.

Very soon after this memorable meeting, Mrs. Roeder rounded up the banker and the young German. In the morning, while most of the guests went down to the ocean to bathe, the members of the quartet rehearsed in the casino, I and the wife of the German viola player their only audience. They played

Brahms's Quartet in A Minor. At the end I was obliged to agree with Mrs. Roeder. It wasn't as heroic a composition as the violin concerto, but it was a more intimate one and, therefore, more satisfying. It seemed like the difference between a proclamation and a confession. After that I participated in a Brahms piano quartet. The quartet was full of thematic angularities, strong rhythms and unexpected accentuations of notes. The Brahmsian characteristics now seemed quite natural to me, and I did very well. Someone asked Mrs. Roeder to play the Beethoven concerto, which I had heard several times at concerts, and knew quite well and admired. She obliged, and I played the piano part. But now the Beethoven seemed pale beside the Brahms, though I lacked the courage to say so. I could think of no music but that of Brahms, and I longed to hear and play everything he wrote. On my day off, on Monday, I went to New York and got the Brahms songs, the symphonies, the piano concertos and the *German Requiem* from the Brooklyn Library. And in a few weeks I knew these works as thoroughly as I knew the music dramas of Wagner.

Still another musical guest was a Mrs. Meltzer, a young married woman who had a beautiful soprano voice. She had studied seriously with a noted voice teacher, with a view to a concert career. But her parents had steered her into marriage with a rich businessman who was much her senior, and she now sang only for "herself." Mrs. Meltzer was small and attractive. She wore her hair in a bang. Her eyes were like the eyes of a Japanese girl. She seemed always aware of her attractiveness, and she was unable to resist flirting with men, even with youths like me. She had an automobile and chauffeur, both a rarity in those days. Each afternoon, if the weather was fine, she would put on a duster, a hat tied with a large silk handkerchief, and goggles, and go for a long drive. Several times she invited me for a ride. In Long Branch we stopped for an ice cream soda in Huyler's, for which she would pay. Mrs. Meltzer would flirt with the soda clerk or any likely-looking man who happened to be around. I thought her behavior unseemly for an attractive young woman who could sing the lieder of Schubert, Schumann, Brahms and Hugo Wolf. Indeed, her voice, too, was provocative. It had a velvety, sensuous quality that was beautiful but somehow disturbing. One Saturday night she was urged by some of the guests to sing. She had on a low-cut evening gown of some dark shimmering material, tightly fitted down to her ankles and ending in a long train which she swished about her as she took her place near the piano. She smelled of some exotic perfume, and she wielded a large fan made of white feathers. She sang "Vissi d'arte" from *La Tosca* with so much passion that the violinist, who formed the hotel trio with Mike Dorf and me, blushed and closed his eyes.

This violinist's name was Borisoff. He was a young player with an unusually refined tone. But his life was a constant torment to him, owing to his extravagant susceptibility to women. He said as much one day when we exchanged confidences, and I told him the story of my love for Elena Kovner. Borisoff confessed that for some years now he had found it almost impossible to be near a pretty woman. This sounded like an exaggeration. But one Monday, on the New York train, as he and I sat talking, he rose abruptly and went into another coach. I followed and asked him if anything was the matter. He looked self-conscious and unhappy, and he finally stammered out that the woman who sat in the seat in front of us in the first coach had a lovely head, that he couldn't bear to look at it and had to leave. All that summer Borisoff was continually faced with such crises. There were several pretty girls and women in the hotel, and even some of the waitresses were fetching. There was an attractive guest, slender and lovely, who sunned herself on the beach all day long, whom we called *Die Schöninke* (The Pretty One). Borisoff took care to avoid her when he went swimming, even to the extent of swimming out of reach of the jurisdiction of the lifeguard. To avoid women, Borisoff, in fact, spent a good part of the time alone, practicing the violin and reading. Some years later, he married. When I next met him, he told me that his vexatious reaction to women had gradually subsided, and that the proximity of pretty women no longer disturbed him. But at Normandie-by-the-Sea that summer, Mrs. Meltzer and a lot of other attractive women unwittingly caused Borisoff many uncomfortable moments.

Although I was completely absorbed in my love for Elena, I was offended by Mrs. Meltzer's flirtations, especially when she paid attention to men whom I considered unworthy of her. Had she been like the other young women guests, who, during the week, found time heavy on their hands without their husbands and engaged in mild, weekday flirtations, I wouldn't have minded it. But I expected a lovely woman who could sing Schubert's "Du bist die Ruh" with melting spirituality to shun the coarser commercial men who spent their weekends at the hotel, let alone encourage them. And since it was plain that she did not love her husband, it would certainly have been more fitting for her to fall in love with a man like me, a musician with whom she would have everything in common. Of course, it would be out of the question for me to reciprocate her love, since I loved Elena deeply. Yet there were times when I was disturbed by the contradictions in my nature—as when I experienced feelings of jealousy the night Mrs. Meltzer went walking on the beach with a graying, elegantly dressed stockbroker from Newark who didn't know a note of music.

When summer was over, Mrs. Meltzer asked me if I would

like to coach her during the fall and winter, and offered to pay me two dollars a session. I accepted gladly. She lived in an entire brownstone house on the West Side, a few blocks from a subway station, and had a telephone and a Japanese butler. I was bewildered by the elegance and ostentation of the house. The walls were covered with rich, embroidered silk, thickly padded, and on them hung many oil paintings, large and small, heavily framed and glass covered. The furniture was most ornate. Elaborate sofas and overstuffed chairs filled the living room, and there were several inlaid glass-enclosed cabinets, on the shelves of which reposed little mysterious objects in ivory and strange delicate woods. The Japanese servant would answer my ring, show me into the living room, and say Madame would soon be down. And in a few minutes Mrs. Meltzer, dressed in a walking suit and wearing a hat, would come in. She would sing for about an hour, and then we would leave the house together. Her motorcar was at the curb, and her chauffeur in uniform would open the door for us. She would drop me at the subway station and continue on her social rounds, or go on to the best shopping district.

One day she told me that she was planning a musicale at her house for a certain evening. She asked me if, besides playing accompaniments for her, I would like to play in a trio with a violinist from the Philharmonic and the well-known cellist Leo Schulz. There would be a fee of five dollars for my participation in the trio. Of course I accepted with alacrity, and I went to rehearse the trio at Mr. Schulz's studio on Broadway. The trio was Mendelssohn's in D Minor, which I had played with Mike Dorf and Hymie Fink, and knew quite well. The musicale (or "private") came off in fine style. The guests, of whom there were about thirty (I was dismayed to see the gray-haired nonmusical stockbroker among them), sat on rented gilded chairs. There were even little printed programs. After the music we went downstairs to the basement for a magnificent supper served at small tables, each seating four. I thought this must be the kind of "private" I had almost played at in the house of Madame Franko's rich friend, for which I had refused to rent a dress suit. I now realized how ill-informed I had been about "society," and how hasty and bad-tempered my behavior must have appeared to Madame Franko. For Mrs. Meltzer's guests, many of whom wore evening dress, were surprisingly modest for rich people, and they listened attentively to the music, and were not in the least patronizing to the performers. I even felt a bit self-conscious in my dark-blue (good) suit, and rather wished I had a tailcoat to wear, like the violinist and Leo Schulz.

It was when he was leaving after supper that Leo Schulz asked me if I would be free the following Saturday to accompany him at a recital he was giving in Scranton, Pennsylvania. I gasped at the rapidity with which Mrs. Meltzer's "private" had borne fruit, and I hastily accepted. Leo Schulz did not even inquire if I had accompanied anyone in public before. He was, indeed, most matter-of-fact in the way he greeted my passionate assent, and said my fee would be ten dollars and all expenses paid. "You have a tailcoat?" he asked confidently, and I lied and said I had. "Well, then," he said, "meet me at the Twenty-third Street Ferry, at nine in the morning. We'll rehearse in Scranton." I flew home to tell the great news to my mother and father. The following day I rented a tailcoat in a shop on Canal Street. The rental fee was a dollar and a quarter for a week, and a five-dollar deposit against the safe, undamaged return of the suit. I bought a starched shirt, collar and black bow tie, all for a dollar, and a set of burnished gold studs and cuff links for a quarter, to com-

plete the outfit. On the morning of the concert I was at the
Twenty-third Street Ferry long before the appointed time.
Punctually at nine, after I had given him up, Leo Schulz,
carrying his cello and a valise, walked into the ferry house.
He appeared to be quite unconcerned that he was to play a
public concert that evening. We crossed the river and got into
a train on the Jersey side. He placed his cello on the seat beside
him, and I sat in the seat behind. I was nervous and excited,
and hardly glanced at the book I had taken along to read.
Around noon, Mr. Schulz turned toward me and asked if I
was hungry. I had had my breakfast at six, and I nodded.
"Let's go to the diner," Mr. Schulz said in the most offhand
manner imaginable. He could not, of course, know that I had
never been in a diner on a train. I followed him into the dining
car. An elegantly attired, polite man led us to a table and
pushed out chairs for us, and a Negro in a white jacket gave
us each a printed card. I read with astonishment the prices on
the right-hand side of each dish. They were indeed steep, and
I began to be concerned about the ultimate size of the expenses
I would incur for Mr. Schulz by the time we got back to New
York. After studying his card for a while, Mr. Schulz said,
"You don't want a *Vorspeise,* do you?" I gathered he meant
the olives, celery and sardines that stood under the word
"appetizers" at the top of the card, and that he didn't think
much of appetizers at a midday meal. I shook my head, and
Mr. Schulz's eyes traveled down the card. "Soup," he said, "you
don't want soup so early in the day, do you?" I had the feeling
that I was being put on my honor not to have soup, and I shook
my head again. "We now," said Mr. Schulz, looking further
down, "come to the meats. You know, of course, that we will
have a bite at the hotel before the concert. Meat is pretty heavy
in the middle of the day. Would you like some meat?" I said

no, not if we were having a bite in the hotel. "I'll tell you what," Mr. Schulz said with a pleasant laugh. "We'll have tea and bread and butter. It's light, it's filling, and it will hold us till dinnertime." So we drank tea and ate a great many slices of white, cottony bread with butter, while Mr. Schulz told me something about the Scranton concert that he was playing under the auspices of the Sing Verein, an old German organization. "They usually give a big supper afterward too," he added reassuringly.

When we arrived in Scranton we drove at once to the concert hall to rehearse. Mr. Schulz was satisfied with me at the rehearsal, which was rather perfunctory, I thought, for we did not play anything right through, but went over what Mr. Schulz said were rough spots. We then drove to the hotel and were assigned rooms. By then it was seven o'clock, and Mr. Schulz said he always took a little nap before a concert, and advised me to do the same. I was too hungry to sleep, so I went for a walk in the town, returning in time to dress. The dress suit was a little too large for me. I didn't expect a rented suit to fit too well, but in the mirror I looked presentable. Mr. Schulz knocked at my door and we went downstairs, where the president of the Sing Verein was waiting to escort us to the hall.

I was fighting off nervousness as I followed Mr. Schulz onto the stage. He seemed to be a favorite in Scranton, for there was prolonged applause, and he bowed many times. I sounded the A. And as Mr. Schulz began tuning up, he turned his head toward me and whispered, "Big supper after the concert! Knackwurst and sauerkraut!" Food was the farthest thing from my mind at that moment, and I wondered that Mr. Schulz could think of anything but the Schumann concerto which he was about to begin. I had taken it for granted that

artists were unfailingly preoccupied with their art at the critical
few moments before a performance. But equally astonishing
was the passion with which Mr. Schulz threw himself into
the concerto the moment he put bow to strings. At the finish
he received an ovation. When he had taken several bows himself, he magnanimously signaled me to bow with him. But
when we gained the green room, he said, as if the performance
had never taken place, "I could eat a horse. Couldn't you?"
Nor did Mr. Schulz greatly exaggerate the extent of his ap-
petite. For at the Sing Verein supper in a big German raths-
keller, he ate a very large quantity of knackwurst and sauerkraut, and drank many schooners of Münchner beer with the
concentration, gusto and passion with which he had played the
Schumann.

That winter I accompanied Leo Schulz in six concerts,
two of them at "privates" in New York. He was always kind to
me, and never failed to have me take a bow with him. I could
not know what his own fee was. Judging by his reluctance to
visit diners on trains, it could not have been very large. But
after the Scranton engagement, my mother always gave me
a couple of egg sandwiches to take along when we made an
extended rail journey. Mr. Schulz never knew about the sandwiches. Out of delicacy, I always ate them in the toilet of our
coach.

GUSTAV MAHLER

~~ In Katz's store one day I learned that the well-known conductor Gustav Mahler had been engaged by the Metropolitan. I had read a good deal about Mahler in the musical reviews, and I knew that he had lifted the musical standards of the Vienna Opera House to great heights. He had also composed a number of symphonies, none of which I had heard. They were said to be epic in character and of unusual length, and they were controversial, for some people held they were very great, while others said they were worthless. All of us at Katz's were excited at the prospect of his coming.

The Wagner repertoire at the Metropolitan had for years been in the hands of Alfred Hertz. Hertz was a German conductor who went to the Bayreuth Festivals religiously and brought back all the great traditions that animated the performances in that shrine. In consequence, we accepted as definitive his interpretations of the Wagner music dramas at the Metropolitan. Though I never dared to say it, I myself was unable to repress a few reservations about Hertz's musical orthodoxy. For example, I could not understand why his or-

chestra generally overpowered the singers. I wondered if
Wagner intended it; and if he had, why had he bothered to
write elaborate librettos, and a great variety of nuances for both
orchestra and singers?

However, we took Hertz on trust. He was a picturesque
figure as he hobbled with the aid of a cane (he was lame) to
the podium and painfully hoisted himself into the conductor's
chair. He was a rotund man, quite bald, and he had a very big
black beard which came down to his chest. From the gallery all
one could see of him was his shining pate and his spreading
beard. His gestures were so extravagant that I often wondered
(again to myself) whether they were really necessary to convey the varying degrees of loudness he exacted from pit and
stage.

On the night of Mahler's American debut, in *Tristan und
Isolde,* a large contingent of Katz's customers lined the railing
of the Metropolitan's top gallery. Mahler came out hurriedly
and climbed swiftly into the conductor's chair. His profile was
sharp and arresting. He looked and behaved quite unlike Hertz.
His gestures were economical and precise. The prelude sounded
different. It was not as lush as with Hertz. There were fewer
retards and accelerations. There was a severity about this interpretation that, strangely enough, heightened both its sensuousness and its suspense. The curtain went up, the invisible
sailor sang his precarious measures, and suddenly the orchestra
and Isolde plunged me into waves of strong, beautiful, rugged
sound. For the first time I could remember, I heard distinctly
the words Isolde was singing. My eyes turned to Mahler to
find a reason. He was "riding" the orchestra with the calculated
sureness of a master trainer, at one moment curbing it to a
crafty balance between it and the voice on the stage, at another giving it its head as it raced alone. Perhaps at certain

climaxes he was too solicitous for the voice. Though I heard the words and the voice, I was sensible of the reins on the orchestra, and I did not feel the thrill and elation of a great fusion of both, which I had expected. Nevertheless, it was an entirely new *Tristan* for me. Now at last I knew how Wagner should sound. Hertz had misled us. Wagner could be as clear, as understandable, as lucid as *Aïda*.

At Mahler's debut performance of *Tristan* that season Olive Fremstad sang Isolde for the first time. Her appearance in this role had been eagerly awaited at Katz's. Fremstad had long been our favorite artist at the Metropolitan. For myself, I thought her the only true singing actress there. She was beautiful and regal, yet warmly feminine. As Sieglinde and Elsa, among others, she was, for me, incomparable. I expected that Fremstad's Isolde would be different from all other Isoldes at the Metropolitan, but I was not prepared for the original impersonation it proved to be. Hers was no tiaraed, heavy, sentimental and shrewish princess, but a beautiful, *aware* woman in the grip of passion so exigent and overpowering as to make her yearn for the release and oblivion of death. The details of her Isolde were so vivid that the passage of nearly half a century has not dimmed my remembrance. She was, in the first act, one with the raging elements evoked by the orchestra. She held me spellbound with her story of Tristan's love and treachery. In no theater had I ever heard passion and contempt so nakedly expressed. The movements of her body and her gestures were so eloquent that they appeared to be the reflex actions of ideas and emotions possessing her at the moment, which would the next instant find expression in words and music.

Indeed, Fremstad's Isolde was so vivid and, because of Mahler's concern for the audibility and diction of singers, so

clear, that every detail of her characterization was instantly apprehended and related to the drama as a whole. Not a false
move, gesture or nuance marred this extraordinary impersonation. The "Liebestod" was its crown. This "Liebestod" was no
dirge, no farewell, no submission to fate. It was a hymn of
gratitude to death for fulfilling the lovers' true destiny. The
poet Shelley had apprehended this true destiny for insatiable
love when he wrote "one life, one death . . . one immortality,
and one *annihilation*." The "Liebestod" as Fremstad sang it
was a paean to Annihilation. No Isolde before Fremstad had
been aware of this joyful implication of the "Liebestod." I
grasped at this implication, for I had myself vaguely sensed it
at my first reading of the music drama. Now Olive Fremstad,
perhaps unconsciously, confirmed it, and made it clear. By her
rapturous, other-worldly smile as she gazed at her dead lover,
she illuminated the hidden idea of the story—that it was not
King Mark who had stood between her and Tristan, but life
itself.

Mahler became my idol. I attended all his performances.
Hertz still conducted many of the Wagner operas, but I stayed
away. Under Mahler I heard for the first time *Fidelio, Don
Giovanni, The Marriage of Figaro, The Bartered Bride* and
Pique Dame. Fidelio overwhelmed me. I had accepted the
widely held opinion that Beethoven's genius was not suited to
opera, and that *Fidelio* was a serious but unsuccessful attempt.
Yet it moved me in a way that no other music drama had.
Berta Morena, a beautiful woman and a sensitive artist, was the
Leonora. In "Mir ist so wunderbar," the hushed, solemn introduction of muted strings gripped my heart; and when the
quartet on the stage sang, each of his or her hope or fear, I
felt a certain indelicacy in sharing their tremulous confessions.
Throughout the opera I was on the verge of tears, and often

I felt helpless under the constant attacks of the music and the story on my emotions. I could hardly bear the moment when the tattered prisoners emerge from their cells like wraiths and greet the sun with hushed wonder and awe, as if for the first time; the digging of the grave in the hopeless dungeon; the colloquy there; Florestan's innocent "Oh dank!" for a crust of bread; the shattering pianissimo trumpet call from afar; the spiritual summing up of the drama in the Third *Leonora* Overture played in the darkened opera house between the scenes of the last act; the final scene in the full blaze of the sun, so reminiscent of the finale of the Ninth Symphony and as liberating—these tore at my heart and made me weep for pity and joy.

The following year Mahler became the conductor of the Philharmonic Society. I attended all of his concerts religiously. In the concert hall Mahler generated the dramatic excitement of opera. As if to make up for the absence of singers and action, he drove his orchestra hard in building up dramatic tension. I remember his harsh but wildly dramatic interpretation of the first and last movements of Beethoven's Fifth. Though I hardly dared admit it to myself, the performance was technically ragged. But its tragic power more than compensated for its want of refinement. And I was much taken with the solitariness of the man; for Mahler appeared isolated and lonely. He was not a favorite with the public, and he conducted to ever-diminishing audiences. I bitterly resented his lack of popular appeal; yet it secretly pleased me, for it proved that I was one of the elect, one of that small number of connoisseurs who was not attracted by virtuosity, but sought out the nobler attributes of interpretative art. I heard stories of the dissatisfaction of the Philharmonic board with Mahler's programs, which they held to be so austere as to repel the general public, and

of their futile endeavors to make him play the popular repertoire, especially the symphonies of the always magnetic Tschaikovsky, and this made me hold the conductor in even greater
esteem. Yet my heart ached for him when he came onto the
stage of Carnegie Hall and faced half a house. One Sunday
matinee I remember particularly. The audience was unusually
small. Mahler played, among other things, two excerpts from
Busoni's opera *Turandot*. The composer was present in a box.
But when the pieces were over there was hardly any applause,
not enough at any rate to give Mahler an excuse for pointing
out Busoni. Mahler stood irresolute for a while in the disconcerting silence, and then walked sadly off the stage.

After concerts I would walk around the block to the stage
door and slip into the green room to gaze at Mahler adoringly,
as he shook hands with admirers and conversed with friends. I
was too timid to approach him. But it was enough for me to
stand around and look at him. Very often his wife was in the
room. I thought she was the most beautiful creature I had ever
seen. It seemed somehow just that Mahler, whose face was
plain, and who wore spectacles, should by his force and genius
attract so lovely a woman. Sometimes she did not appear in the
green room, and Mahler's friends would presently depart,
leaving him quite alone, except for me huddling against the
wall near the door. He would put on his coat and hat, stare
absentmindedly at me and leave for the Plaza Hotel, where he
lived. I would follow, walking right behind him. He seemed
always intensely preoccupied as he walked, his body bent forward, his hands clasped behind his back. He looked like the
picture of Beethoven walking in the suburbs of Vienna. At
street crossings he would advance a few paces before he became
aware of automobiles and carriages rushing past him, danger-
ously close. I longed to take his arm and lead him safely across,

but I never could summon the courage. On these nightly shadowings I discovered, to my delight, that Mahler was superstitious, like me. He would suddenly pause without warning, swing his right foot behind him, and with the toe touch the heel of his left foot. It was not an easy thing to do. But he must have done it for a long time, for he managed the operation swiftly and skillfully. Once, when I was too close behind him, his sudden stop took me unawares, and I bumped against him, and in a scared voice I begged his pardon. He looked at me blankly and walked on. But half a block farther he repeated the maneuver, unaware that I was still behind him, though at a safer distance. When he entered the hotel I ran across the street into Central Park and sat on a bench facing the Plaza, and watched for a light to go on in a window which would certainly indicate his room. I would wonder whether he would go to bed at once, or sit up and work on one of his long symphonies. I had thus far heard only the second. A good part of it baffled me, but I was impressed by the climaxes, which were always splendidly clangorous, and I was charmed by the pastoral moments. At the time I was coaching Mrs. Meltzer in Mahler's songs *Des Knaben Wunderhorn,* which sounded very much like parts of the symphony. The songs were perhaps a little overloaded with counterpoint and faintly sentimental, and an air of heaviness hung about them. They expressed a kind of sophisticated innocence, which Mrs. Meltzer and I found beguiling.

Great changes were taking place in New York's musical life. The presence of Gustav Mahler was having a tremendous effect on music students and the more discriminating music lovers. And Oscar Hammerstein, a man who had made a fortune in vaudeville, had entered the field of opera, built himself the Manhattan Opera House on West Thirty-fourth Street,

and set about challenging the supremacy of the Metropolitan.
Mr. Hammerstein imported a new French repertoire and a
lot of first-rate singers; and a jaded public, surfeited with the
old operatic standbys and the too-familiar casts at the Metropolitan, flocked to the Manhattan, leaving many seats vacant
at the older house. I learned that the ticket-taker in the gallery
of the Manhattan Opera House was as favorably disposed toward bribery as was his colleague at the Metropolitan, a circumstance which enabled me to witness *Pelléas et Mélisande,
Louise,* and two or three other French operas of lesser mag-
nitude. To hear the piano version of *Pelléas* translated into
orchestral sound was, for me, a never-to-be-forgotten experience. Though I had tried to "visualize" Debussy's orchestration, the actuality exceeded anything I had imagined, while the
stage performance realized perfectly all the poetic implications
of the play and the music. Mary Garden, the Mélisande, seemed
to have been especially born to sing and act the role. I was
deeply affected by her artistry. I was, from the very first, quite
aware that her Mélisande was a new kind of operatic impersonation, one entirely created from within the character. It
never failed to meet all the demands of the words and music,
as in the utter innocence of Mélisande's question to Pelléas,
"Why must you leave?"; and at times Mary Garden went far
beyond these demands—when, as if impelled by pure terror,
she ran headlong before Golaud's vengeful sword, uttering
short, despairing, little cries as she fled. On the surface Mary
Garden's terror, coming a moment after her display of reckless courage, might be thought inconsistent. But it was con-
sistent with the imaginative composition of her character, for
Mélisande was at heart a child whose instincts were elemental.
This I did not fully know until I saw Mary Garden abandon
the slain Pelléas and run for her life, as if pursued by a thousand devils.

TOSCANINI

The year after Gustav Mahler came to New York, the Metropolitan engaged Giulio Gatti-Casazza, the impresario of La Scala in Milan, as director. Mr. Gatti-Casazza, in turn, was bringing along his conductor in chief, one Arturo Toscanini. This move, someone told us at Katz's, was the Metropolitan's answer to the threat posed by the Manhattan Opera House. We were all mystified by the news. Few, if any of us, had heard of Gatti-Casazza, or of his compatriot Toscanini. It seemed to us naïve on the part of the Metropolitan to expect a pair of Italians to draw away the patrons of the Manhattan Opera House, who were now enjoying fresh, new voices and an entire new repertoire. Even so great and renowned a musical figure as Gustav Mahler had not been able to do it. What could these Italians do to counteract the appeal of Mary Garden, Nellie Melba, Giovanni Zenatello, Luisa Tetrazzini, Alessandro Bonci and other fresh luminaries? And there was Cleofonte Campanini, chief conductor at the Manhattan, who was by now an idol with the public. True, the Metropolitan still had Caruso, Farrar, Scotti and one or two other favorites; and of course it had the Wagnerian operas, most of which were not given at the Manhattan. But viewed realistically, Mr. Hammerstein's position seemed impregnable.

Mr. Gatti-Casazza and Mr. Toscanini duly arrived, and the papers announced the first week's repertoire. At Katz's we were not surprised that Mr. Toscanini should begin the season with *Aïda*. The ignorant public loved melody for its own sake, and *Aïda* was a good "vehicle" for popular singers like Caruso, Scotti, Louise Homer and the new Bohemian soprano, Emmy Destinn. But a month later Toscanini was also to conduct *Götterdämmerung*. We could hardly believe it. An Italian conducting *Götterdämmerung!* It was unthinkable. Even Mr. Katz, who did not care much about the later Wagner operas, expressed astonishment at such presumption, and said that the new impresario was crazy, and his conductor overambitious. I was puzzled. I wondered how anyone used to the tinkly music of Verdi could comprehend an intricate score like *Götterdämmerung*. Even if he succeeded in learning the music, how was it possible for an Italian to grasp the epic dimensions of that music drama! Nevertheless I felt an obligation to go and hear *Götterdämmerung* and see for myself, if only to be a witness of the fiasco it would deservedly be. Mr. Katz was more interested in the *Aïda*. And to get some measure of the capabilities of the new Italian conductor, I decided to accompany him on the opening night. Because of my intimacy with the ticket-taker at the top gallery, we did not have to join the queue at dawn and wait for the doors to open in the evening. We arrived at seven-thirty, like any ticket-holder. By then people were standing three deep behind the gallery railing, and we had some difficulty in maneuvering our bodies into a position where we could catch an occasional glimpse of the orchestra pit and the stage.

The houselights dimmed and, through a chink between

two standees in front of me, I looked down on the orchestra pit. I saw a small figure make its way quickly to the podium and spring onto it. The conductor's chair had been removed! Toscanini bowed once to the audience, turned his back to it and cut off the applause by rapping a violin stand sharply with his baton. The Italian conducted standing up, as if he were facing a symphony orchestra. There was no score on a stand in front of him! He placed his left hand on his hip; his right hovered in the air for a second. His silhouette was neat, precise and elegant. He began the prelude. From the opening bar I felt a tension in myself and in the air. The late-comers, as usual, poured into the orchestra and boxes. My eyes caught them, but they made hardly any stir, and I heard only the music. I knew the prelude—indeed, I knew all of *Aïda*—well, but now it sounded strange. The little phrase on which it is built floated up to me like a thought, delicate and pure. It did not appear to come from the instruments in the pit. It was shaped and wafted by the little stick in Toscanini's right hand, a stick that behaved like a sensitive wand. The prelude gradually became corporeal (something like the prelude to *Lohengrin,* I thought irreverently), accumulated weight, filled the big auditorium with magnificent, balanced sound, receded and died out in a whisper. I had listened to a poetic, even noble introduction. When it died out, serious implications, like over-tones, still hovered in the air. For a moment I forgot that I knew the story of *Aïda,* and I wondered what the nature of the ensuing drama could be to meet the promise of these intimations. Mr. Katz broke the spell by nudging me and whispering, "Not bad, this Toscanini!" It brought me back to earth. I was now ashamed that I had succumbed so com-pletely to an Italian opera and an Italian conductor, and I whispered back, "No, not bad. But wait till *Götterdäm-*

merung." Yet throughout that evening I frequently forgot my
surroundings and lost myself in the performance. In the intermissions I gave way to dejection, for Mr. Katz was loud, even
maliciously so, in his praise of *Aïda,* the artists on the stage
and, most of all, Toscanini, and I could honestly muster no
counterarguments, and only reiterate, "Just wait for *Götterdämmerung!*"

A month later we spoke to Jake Belkin, one of the Metropolitan second-violin players, who occasionally came down to
Katz's to buy music at a discount. We bombarded Belkin with
questions about the new conductor. But what Belkin had to tell
us only added to my mystification and discomfort. He said
that there had been a rehearsal of *Götterdämmerung* that very
morning. The orchestra had been impressed with Toscanini's
abilities at the *Aïda* rehearsal. But they were hardly prepared
for what had happened that morning. The librarian had placed
the huge score of the first act of *Götterdämmerung* on the
music stand in front of the podium. When Toscanini saw the
score, he lifted it up and threw it on the floor. He then conducted *Götterdämmerung* entirely from memory. But that was
not all. He actually knew every note, every nuance; he heard
mistakes even in fortissimo passages and corrected them; he
sang the German words, every one of them. In short, Belkin
swore that Toscanini was a prodigy whose like had not been
seen at the Metropolitan. Furthermore, his power over singers
and orchestra was from the first absolute, and everybody on
the stage and in the pit already stood in awe of him. Mr. Katz
greeted this news triumphantly. I was crushed, but I managed
to say, "But what about the *spirit* of *Götterdämmerung?* The
German soul of the opera? How can any Italian understand it,
let alone bring it out?" Belkin laughed. "He's got that too,

believe me," he said. "He's a devil, that's all I can say, a real devil."

The next evening H. L., Mr. Katz and I lined the gallery railing at the Metropolitan. Mr. Katz disliked *Götterdäm-merung*. But he accompanied me to verify Belkin's extravagant praise of Toscanini and, I presume, to gloat over my discom-fiture should the praise prove deserved. Very quickly I saw that Belkin's report was accurate. Toscanini stood in front of his orchestra without the benefit of a note of music before his eyes. He restored the Norn scene, which Hertz had always cut. Though I knew it from the piano score, this was the first time I heard it in performance. But the whole opera was in a sense a restoration for me. The "sunrise" episode in the orchestra blazed with a new effulgence; the Rhine in Siegfried's Journey was a new, imperious, jubilant river; the chorus of Hagen's men rent the air with a new, exigent, lusty rhythm; the death and funeral of Siegfried were grandiose and emotional beyond tears; the Immolation scene and the final pages excited in me a feeling of exaltation that I had never before experienced.

I left the opera house in a daze. Mr. Katz took the streetcar home. H. L. and I walked. For a long time we did not talk. When we reached Union Square I could no longer contain myself. I sat down on a bench and cried, as if something dreadful had happened. Then I felt better, and we continued on our way, talking, discussing and dissecting the performance, and the incredible new conductor. I still could not understand how a *mere* Italian could transform *Götterdämmerung* as Toscanini had done that night. H. L. said the only way he could account for it was that Toscanini was a throwback to the Italian Renaissance. In the Italy of the fourteenth and fifteenth centuries there were giants in literature, painting and sculpture.

Toscanini was an artist of the same epic proportions. Yes, I
said, but it doesn't explain the man's identification with the
German soul. H. L. wondered whether there was such a thing
as a German soul, or, for that matter, an Italian or any other
kind. "What," H. L. asked me, "was the soul of Hamlet: English? Faust: German? Peer Gynt: Scandinavian? Nonsense.
The soul cannot be localized. Each soul is a part of the universal soul. The *Götterdämmerung* we heard tonight was not
a German *Götterdämmerung,* but the world's *Götterdämmerung.*" H. L. was very eloquent and persuasive on the subject. What he found difficult to reconcile with Toscanini's
genius was the Italian's willingness to conduct trivial operas
like *Aïda* and *Madama Butterfly* ("Oh, *Butterfly* is all right
in its way, but not good enough for a Toscanini"). "But perhaps he really hates these Italian operas, and he conducts them
only because he is required to in his contract," I put in. But
H. L. thought that in view of what Belkin had said about
Toscanini's intransigence, *that* was hardly likely.

At Katz's the question of Toscanini versus Mahler could not
be long avoided. The Mahler adherents claimed that Toscanini
was beautifying Wagner—"gilding" they called it. He was
sandpapering the rough, strong German texture of the music;
in a word, he was Italianizing Wagner. Toscanini's Wagner
was admittedly lucid and beautiful, but it was *not* Wagner.
Mahler, on the other hand, while achieving orchestral clarity,
still remained *echt Deutsch* in his concern not to rub down
the gritty texture of the music. "Wait till Toscanini attempts
Die Meistersinger," one diehard Mahlerite cried. "That'll tell
the story. That's one opera you can't prettify. It's as German as
sauerkraut." I kept out of these discussions, mainly from a
feeling of guilt. Toscanini had overpowered my senses and my
judgment. He had made me *forget* Mahler, a conductor whom

only a few months earlier I had looked upon as the greatest in the world. I was feeling disloyal to Mahler, and I was ashamed of having to be. Fortunately Mahler was also a symphonic conductor, and as far as I knew, Toscanini was only a conductor of opera. To ease my conscience I decided to believe, and openly acknowledge, that Toscanini was supreme in opera —that is, in Wagner; and Mahler, while a great opera conductor, was supreme in symphonic music. In that way I could be loyal to both and enjoy without misgivings the specialty of each. And a year later the situation was entirely cleared up for me; Mahler left the Metropolitan and gave all his time to the New York Philharmonic, and Toscanini reigned supreme at the Metropolitan.

KIAMESHA REVISITED

꩜ My life at home was busy yet serene. My earnings in the aggregate were sufficient to see us through each year, and my mother was now only seldom obliged to borrow small sums to tide us over periods when my pupils took sick or left me for some other teacher. Summer, which used to be the leanest season financially, now held no terrors for me, for I was in demand for jobs at hotels in the Catskills and on the Jersey coast. In July and August I sent my mother, father and little sister to the country. I engaged a room for them in the cottage of a Jewish farmer near Flemington, New Jersey, for three dollars a week. This sum included the use of the kitchen and cooking utensils. I gave my mother four dollars a week for food and incidentals. Since I earned sixteen dollars a week in my first summer at Normandie-by-the-Sea, I had nine dollars left. This quite covered the rent in Henry Street, my laundry and occasional trips to New York on Mondays.

The next summer I was again offered Normandie-by-the-Sea. But just as I was about to accept, I received a counteroffer from Mary Sklar's father to go to Kiamesha Lake. Mr. Sklar had formed a company with four of his friends and had rented the Grand View House, a large hotel at Kiamesha Lake, which they expected to open for business on the fifteenth of June. Mr. Sklar seemed eager to have me, and offered to match my salary at Normandie-by-the-Sea. I accepted. Although my former stay at Kiamesha Lake had not been a happy one, I had not forgotten the beauty of the mountains and the lake. Mary Sklar was to spend the summer at her father's hotel, and the idea of working for friends instead of strangers made the prospect a pleasant one. Still another inducement was the promise of seeing a good deal of I. Jacobs, who was a permanent summer fixture at *his* old friend's hotel in Kiamesha. Now that we were both studying with the same teacher, I. Jacobs and I had much in common, and I could look forward to very profitable exchanges of ideas on piano problems and music in general.

To meet the musical requirements of the Grand View House, I engaged Hymie Fink, Mike Dorf and a cornet player. Hymie, Mike and I played together for lunch and supper, and in the evening the cornetist, John Kapolski, a Pole, joined us in the ballroom in dance music. The four of us shared an elongated room with one window on the top floor of the hotel. Each of us had a cot to himself. As leader of the quartet, I took the cot closest to the window, a choice I very soon regretted. For Kapolski, before going to bed, hung his socks on the windowsill to air every night. Out of delicacy, I bore with Kapolski's distressing bedtime routine, but I spent many sleepless hours, especially on warm nights. Otherwise, Kapolski was a well-meaning fellow and a good cornetist.

We arrived at the Grand View on the day of the scheduled official opening. But much to our surprise, we found the hotel completely empty of guests. The only residents were an army of servants and the four partners and their families. The latter included grandparents, in-laws, nieces, nephews and even quite distant relations. These were all, of course, nonpaying. Yet they were so many that the large dining room at mealtime looked half filled. I wondered, when I first saw this large array at supper, how the partners expected to make any profit. However, I could see how their presence might not altogether be a loss. The paying guests (when they arrived) might, in their ignorance, take the relations for paying guests like themselves, and conclude that the Grand View was an unusually popular and desirable hotel.

The Grand View, unlike the majority of the hotels in the vicinity, was nonkosher. At least, in its prospectus it avoided the word "kosher," and spoke of its food only as "tasty." It seemed obvious to me by the general breezy tone of the brochure that the partners hoped to attract quite a different clientele from those of their orthodox competition, the Pine View, the Mountain View and several other large hotels. The partners were liberals in politics and agnostics in religion, and they hoped to appeal to the more solvent of the Jewish intelligentsia. They also hoped to attract Christians, since there was no mention of race or creed in the prospectus. However, until the first week in July they attracted nobody. Three times a day for two weeks the hotel's surrey left for the railroad station and returned without a single guest. Our quartet, however, performed its duties regularly, quite as if the hotel were full. We played in the dining room for lunch and dinner, and in the evening we played dance music in the casino. The families and relatives of the partners applauded us, and some of them danced a waltz or a two-step in the evening. But as the days passed without the arrival of a single guest, the anxiety of the partners became quite evident, and even communicated itself

to their families. The partners spoke sharply to each other,
when they spoke at all. Dissension broke out at table, tempers
flared up, and at last there were open insinuations about the
unfairness of a policy whereby a partner with a small number
of relatives—like Mr. Sklar—was obliged to be on the same
financial footing as one who had brought along twice as many
relations—as in the case of Mr. Freund, the senior partner.

One afternoon, at the height of this unpleasant situation,
the hotel surrey returned from the station bearing two guests.
This event was so unexpected that there was no one at the desk
to greet the strangers. It was some time before the partners were
rounded up; and when they were, the newcomers were received
with elaborate subservience. They were a middle-aged couple,
and they signed the register as Mr. and Mrs. Albert Anderson,
Troy, New York. They were without a doubt Christians, and
their advent as the very first guests of the season was considered
most auspicious, indicating, perhaps, a trend toward the kind
of clientele the partners had hoped to attract.

Mr. and Mrs. Anderson were given a table close to the
piano, and at supper they applauded every number. The next
morning they were sitting in two rockers on the veranda, the
only persons there, for the relatives were, as if by magic, no
longer to be seen anywhere, except in the dining room during
meals. The Andersons greeted me in a most friendly manner
and invited me to take a rocker next to them. They told me
how they had enjoyed the music and how glad they were to
be at the Grand View. Their choice of the Grand View had
been accidental, they said, for they got out of the train at
Kiamesha Lake having no hotel in mind, and climbed into
the first buggy they saw, which happened luckily to be the
Grand View surrey. We chatted for a long time. As I sat there
rocking and conversing, one or another of the partners passed

in front of us and looked pointedly at me. Then Mary Sklar's little brother Charlie appeared and told me his father wanted to see me in the office. I excused myself and went inside. Mr. Sklar, in his office, looked disturbed. He said, with much stammering, that he hoped I wouldn't misunderstand what he was about to say. In short, his partners (and he, too, for that matter) felt that it was improper for those who worked in the hotel to mingle with the guests. He hastened to add that Jewish guests did not, as a rule, mind, but that Christians might. I felt bitterly affronted, and pointed out that the Andersons had invited me to take a chair. I also told him, with a good deal of heat, that I did not consider myself a servant, that at Normandie-by-the-Sea I was treated by management and guests as an equal. I said I was quite ready to leave the Grand View. Whereupon Mr. Sklar looked unhappy and asked me to do nothing rash. He would explain to his partners that I had not forced myself on the Andersons. He begged me to forget the whole interview, and I said that if I stayed on, it could only be on terms of equality. To this he agreed, much to my relief. For thus far the musicians had received no pay, and if the Andersons were really the advance guard of a great influx of guests, the management would soon be in a position to pay us in full. In any event, the summer was too far advanced for me to look for another job, and I had to think not only of myself, but of my family in the New Jersey farmhouse.

Around the middle of August, the hotel really began to fill up. But the expected Christian trend did not materialize. The Andersons departed after a fortnight's stay. As the surrey waited to take them to the station, Mrs. Anderson, in my presence, congratulated Mr. Sklar on the music, and presented each of the quartet with a fountain pen as a keepsake, and as a mark of their appreciation and our affability (Mr. Anderson was a dealer in fountain pens). Mr. Sklar was very pleased at this, for it justified the stand he had taken against his partners on the controversial subject of my mingling with the guests. I was sorry to see the Andersons go, they were so agreeable and sympathetic. But I soon forgot them, for the Grand View was now a lively hotel indeed. The Jewish intellectuals with their wives and children were as noisy and expansive as the kosher patrons of the Cedar View had been on my first visit to Kiamesha Lake. Whatever these lusty and vigorous people did, they did enthusiastically. They ate heartily, went mountain-climbing with gusto, danced extravagantly and flirted openly. At meals they quieted down and shushed each other when Hymie and I played. Their taste in music favored Italian opera, though their requests also ran to the symphonies of Mozart and Beethoven. Once, as an experiment, Hymie, Mike and I played the "Prelude and Liebestod" from *Tristan* in a violin, cello and piano arrangement, for which we were, greatly to our delight, applauded. These arrangements of symphonies and overtures often taxed our capabilities, but we tried to make up for technical inadequacies by our sincerity and the genuineness of feeling we put into what we played. We were always tumultuously acclaimed. I recall only one instance of criticism or disapproval, and even that was implied rather than avowed. We had finished an enthusiastic but rather technically faulty rendition of the overture to *William Tell,* and were bowing to great applause, when a man at the table nearest to us raised his knife in the air and began to wipe it deliberately and ostentatiously, suspiciously in the manner of an assassin wiping bloodstains from his weapon. The man's knife, for all we knew, may have needed wiping. But he looked meaningfully at us during the operation. At least so we thought. And thenceforth we were careful to choose easier numbers for our programs.

Around the middle of July, Mr. Sklar, owing us for a month, paid us two weeks' wages. This was a godsend, for I had hardly enough money to buy postage stamps, and my mother was keeping her summer landlord, the Jersey farmer, at bay with the kind of fabrications she used in the old days to enchant dunning grocers and butchers. Hymie and I celebrated the event by hiring for a dollar apiece a horse and buggy for an afternoon, an adventure we had long desired. We drove at breakneck speed, putting the horse into a lather from the first. Once we arrived at a railroad crossing whose presence was hidden by woods, and we reined in the horse just as a train flew past our faces. The horse backed up and hit a tree, ripping off the back side of the buggy. To repair this the owner of the livery stable collected four dollars from us. Nor was this our only mishap. I had taken off my coat, the better to enjoy the breeze our fast-trotting horse raised. The next morning I rose with a sore throat and a high temperature. Mary Sklar insisted on fetching the town doctor, who said I had pneumonia and put me to bed. There I remained helplessly for ten days, nursed by Mary and her cousin Florence. Mary played the piano a little. Our concerts at meals were temporarily discontinued, but Mary took my place in the evening for dancing. When I got better she and her cousin brought me delicacies from the kitchen, and three times a day regaled me with "guggle-muggles," a kind of milk shake with brandy. Soon I was well again, and I resumed my full routine. In the afternoon, Mary, Florence, the daughter of another partner and I repaired to a certain beautiful glade near the hotel, where I read *Tess of the D'Urbervilles* aloud. The novel made a deep impression on them and on me, though I had read it before. So much so that when I came to the execution of Tess I could not continue for emotion. At the same time, I knew that in the girls' minds I was associated with the pathos, romance and tragedy of the book. Indeed, I used to feel at times, when reading aloud, as if I had written it myself. At the very least, I had the satisfaction of introducing the young ladies to the glamorous, pathetic literary world of Thomas Hardy.

With all I had to do and all I wanted to do, the days flew by. In the morning I practiced in the empty dining room. Often I visted I. Jacobs in his luxurious hotel. I found him on the veranda, usually surrounded by admiring young ladies, but he always excused himself and took me into the ballroom, where he played the piano for me, and we compared notes on the compositions we were both studying. In the afternoons I climbed mountains and read aloud to Mary and her relations and friends, and wrote love letters to Elena Kovner in Belgium, and corresponded with Morris Mandell on the fine points of Theosophy. Somehow, I could find no time to write home or to my sisters Hannah and Molly, both of whom I loved dearly. The hotel itself provided excitement in the shape of celebrities, who arrived in August and remained till Labor Day—Mr. and Mrs. Alexander Carr and Mr. and Mrs. Tomashefsky. Mr. Tomashefsky was not *the* Tomashefsky, but a distant relation. Nevertheless, the name was magical, and people from other hotels came to have a look at him. Alexander Carr was a celebrity on his own. He was a headliner in vaudeville, and was presently to play one of the partners in the Broadway success *Potash and Perlmutter*. Mrs. Carr, a former actress, was a platinum blonde, the first I had ever encountered. Nearby she looked painted and rather faded. Yet, like her husband, she represented for us the stage, and both husband and wife com-

ported themselves with the dignity and aloofness we thought
natural to luminaries.

One day, who should appear at the Grand View but H. L.,
wearing a fedora and carrying a pilgrim's staff, on his back a
knapsack. H. L. had embarked all alone on a walking tour
from Albany to the Adirondacks, and had detoured to Kiamesha Lake to surprise me. I was overjoyed to see him, and I
took him along on a picnic Mary Sklar and some other girls
had arranged for that afternoon. H. L. was, as always, lofty
and condescending; and when he left us that evening to continue on his tour, I felt the necessity of excusing and explaining
him to the girls, citing his great scholarship, especially in the
field of drama, his devotion to his family and his generosity
to friends. Neither Mary nor her friends seemed impressed
with my estimate of him. A few days later I received a postcard
from H. L. from Au Sable Forks, in which he thanked me for
a pleasant visit and asked to be remembered to the girl "with
the coal-black eyes." I was astonished at his remembering Mary
Sklar, for he had been more condescending to her than to the
other girls. I hastened to give Mary his message, adding that
it was unusual for H. L. to notice anyone. But Mary was again
unimpressed, and called H. L. a pompous oaf.

On Labor Day the Grand View began to empty, and the
day after, not a guest was left. As if by magic, we were suddenly back to the bleakness of opening week. Again the dining
room at meals contained only the partners, their families and
relations. Some days later, having finally been paid in full,
Hymie, Mike, Kapolski and I departed, leaving the nonpaying
contingent to wind up the affairs of the Grand View. Later I
learned that the venture had been unprofitable and that the
partners, with the exception of one who had shrewdly made no
monetary contribution on the grounds that he had thought

up the scheme, had lost whatever money they had put into it. They consoled themselves, rather naïvely, with the thought that they and their dependents had been enabled to spend a luxurious summer in a fine hotel in the Catskills.

Back on Henry Street, I resumed my teaching and attended classes at Columbia. Late one afternoon as I sat at the dining-room table doing my homework, there was a timid knock at the door. I called out, "Come in," but no one entered. I got up and opened the door. There was no one in the hall. I resumed my studies. A few minutes later there was another knock. As I opened the door quickly, I heard someone rushing down the stairs. I followed. When I came out on the stoop, I saw, to my astonishment, Mary Sklar running down the street. I ran after her and caught up with her at the corner of East Broadway. I hadn't seen Mary in weeks, not since I left her at the Grand View in Kiamesha Lake. I was astonished at her conduct, and so, it appeared, was she. She had tears in her eyes, and at first was unable to speak. At last she said that she had found herself near my house and thought of paying me a visit. But her courage had failed her. I asked her to go back with me, but she refused. I walked with her to Delancey Street, where she took a streetcar for home.

Some days later, on returning from a concert, my mother told me that a very pretty girl who said her name was Mary had called that afternoon, and had waited for me several hours. I had been confused about Mary's first attempt to see me. Her second, bolder visit seemed to point to a strong desire on her part to renew our old friendship at Kiamesha Lake. At the same time I felt vaguely uneasy about where this might lead. I thought of H. L. and my loyalty to him. H. L. had not forgotten Mary, and in a burst of confidence unusual for him (it was on our walk home after a performance of *Tristan*) he told me that he had been unable to banish her from his mind, and was now forced to admit to himself that he was in love with her. He said this in such a way as to make me think that Mary was a lucky girl indeed, and that there were no reservations in his mind about Mary's affections, once he had declared himself. In view of all this, I decided that it was my duty to bring the two together before I saw Mary again alone. I wrote to her and invited her to go with H. L. and me to a Kneisel Quartet concert in Brooklyn the following Tuesday. H. L. bought an extra ticket, and the three of us met at my house, walked to the Brooklyn Bridge and boarded a streetcar to the Academy of Music. After the concert, at H. L.'s invitation we stopped off at Child's on Atlantic Avenue for buckwheats and coffee. The concert had been magnificent and the buckwheats were delicious. Yet the meeting between H. L. and Mary had missed fire. H. L. had not been his usual confident self, and his pontifications about music and the drama for once lacked conviction. For her part, Mary was thoughtful and mostly silent. H. L. suggested walking to New York, but Mary, who lived in Yonkers, said that would get her home too late. We took her home, and returning to Henry Street, we walked and talked through half of the night. For the first time since I had met him, H. L. seemed unsure and nervous. When I finally left him, I promised him that the next time I saw Mary I would try to ascertain the exact state of her feelings about him. I was able to keep my promise sooner than I expected. For the very next day Mary came to my house directly after school. We went for a walk in Jackson Street Park, and I soon broached the subject, though with much hesitation and self-consciousness. And as I spoke to her about H. L.'s talents and suitability and his love for her, I was surprised to find myself hoping that what I was saying would not make the impression

I thought I wanted to make. I kept thinking of John Alden and Priscilla, and apparently that was in Mary's mind too, for when I finished she said with a smile, but with tears in her eyes, "Why don't you speak for yourself?" This threw me into a turmoil of conflicting emotions—vanity, pleasure and disgust with myself. Mary was beautiful and attractive, and she had chosen me over H. L., who had an importance as a man and scholar that I did not have! I gloried in the fact. Then I thought of H. L. and the allegiance I owed him; and lastly I thought of Elena Kovner, to whom I had written a love letter that very day. But Mary was walking beside me, and I felt a vague pleasure in being close to her. After a few minutes every other consideration seemed unimportant. I took her hand and we walked on in silence. When we came behind the porticoed bandstand at the end of the park and saw that we were for the moment alone, we kissed. I felt heroic and triumphant, yet a little uneasy. Life had suddenly, in a moment, grown complicated. My relations with H. L. and Elena, which only yesterday were honest and simple, were now disturbingly complex.

I began to see Mary almost daily. To do so I neglected my friends, my college homework, my piano practice and sometimes my pupils. Mary was not yet sixteen, but she was already in her junior year at Yonkers High School. She kept her visits to my house a secret from her family, but she had confided in her cousin Florence, who was a few years older than she. Florence, in turn, had confessed to an attachment for my friend Hymie. The two had been much together in Kiamesha Lake. We made a romantic foursome. I saw myself and Mary as Tristan and Isolde, and Florence and Hymie as Kurvenal and Brangäne. Florence lived in White Plains with her old, widowed mother in a little house on the outskirts of the town. I came often to their home to meet Mary, who was able to visit her

cousin openly. The four of us spent many happy evenings
there. Hymie and I would bear the expense of suppers consist-
ing of cold cuts and potato salad and pickles. There was an upright piano in the parlor. After the girls washed the dishes, I
played from the Wagner operas, especially *Tristan,* singing all
the parts with finesse and emotion. Though I never designated
them as such, Florence and Hymie assumed on their own the
subordinate roles of Kurvenal and Brangäne I had in mind for
them, and were indefatigable in arranging meetings between
Mary and me, and shielding us from suspicion. It was Florence
who suggested the plan whereby Mary and I succeeded in
spending one whole weekday together without the senior
Sklars' knowledge. I thought it a most ingenious plan at the
time, and only much later realized the enormity of the deception. One winter morning, around ten o'clock, I presented
myself to the principal of Mary's high school and introduced
myself as Mary's brother. I told her that my mother had been
taken ill, and I asked if Mary might be excused for the day
and sent home. The sympathetic lady principal expressed concern for my "mother," at once sent for Mary (who, as prearranged, showed surprise at seeing me), and excused her for
the day. It was a bitter-cold morning, and we walked the
streets for some hours, happy at the success of our ruse. When
we no longer could bear the cold, we went into a café, where
we stayed as long as seemed proper over a cup of coffee and a
piece of spongecake. Again we braved the cold for a while,
and then Mary had the bright idea of spending a few hours at
the public library. To allay suspicion we entered the library
separately and sat down as if by accident next to each other
at a long table. The book-lined room was delightfully warm.
We were the only "students" at the table. We consulted the
card catalogue, took down several books from the shelves and

pretended to be deep in study. At the same time we conversed
in low tones. We talked of many things, laying plans for future
meetings. Mary said the time had come for me to visit her at
her house and to make myself agreeable to her family. She was
sure her mother would take to me. But her father looked on
Mary as still a little girl and he had an uncontrollable temper;
however, she thought my visit would dissipate any suspicion
on his part. From time to time Mary or I would get up, return
a book to the shelves, consult the catalogue again, bring another
book to the table and resume our pretended studies. But around
half-past two, a librarian came up to Mary and said she was
sorry, but her orders were that the reading room was closed
during school hours to children and young people of grammar-
school and high-school age. Mary blushed, put on her coat
and left. I lingered on for a quarter of an hour, for appearance'
sake, simulating an absorbed interest in the book that lay open
before me. When I came out on the street, Mary was nowhere
in sight, but I soon found her walking up and down a side
street. We walked two or three miles, and then spent another
twenty cents on coffee and cake in a Thompson cafeteria. By
then it began to grow dark and flurries of snow suddenly
whirled all around us. We went into a doorway of a tenement
and kissed and embraced a long time, then came out separately,
like strangers, and went our ways in opposite directions.

But we had been observed by a friend of Mr. Sklar's who
knew me by name! For I received a letter from Mary the next
morning telling me that our walk in the cold had been reported to her father, who had railed against me as an unprin-
cipled musician and seducer. Mary had scornfully repudiated
the accusation, and finally succeeded in mollifying him by
swearing that we were only resuming an intellectual friendship
we had formed in Kiamesha. She urged me to come to supper

the following evening. She had prepared her mother, and her
mother had undertaken to soften her father toward me. Mary
was certain that nothing untoward would occur during my visit,
and cautioned me to behave with indifference.

I went to Yonkers the following evening. A place had been
set for me at table. Mary greeted me with simulated heartiness,
and I tried to be breezy and impersonal. Mrs. Sklar, whose eyes
were, like her daughter's, black and sparkling, received me
in motherly fashion. I had a feeling that she had guessed our
secret and was not displeased. Her husband was reserved and
formal. With Mary's older and younger brothers, David and
Charlie, we made six at table. I played the part of a man of
the world, hardly ever looking at Mary, and addressing myself
mainly to Mr. and Mrs. Sklar. David was a fellow student at
Columbia; I talked to him about the college and the various
professors. As Mary had foreseen, nothing untoward occurred,
except for an unsolicited observation by little Charlie. In a
pause in the conversation, the boy exclaimed, apropos of nothing, "I don't care—*I* will not ignore Chotzinoff!" His brother
David said, "Oh, shut up, Charlie," thereby making matters
worse. But Mary at once set things to rights by saying merrily,
"Well, I like Chotzinoff too. I think we all do, don't we?" This
sounded so impersonal that Mr. Sklar laughed and said
rhetorically, "Why shouldn't we like him?" The rest of the
dinner went off pleasantly.

As the evening wore on it began to snow and then to sleet.
When I rose to go, around midnight, Mrs. Sklar looked at the
icy windowpanes, shook her head and invited me to spend the
night. I laughed off the invitation, saying I did not mind the
weather and wouldn't think of putting them to any trouble.
But Mrs. Sklar said it would be no trouble, she would make
me up a bed on chairs right there in the parlor. David and

Charlie added their pleas, and finally Mr. Sklar, in a tone of voice and with the look of a man whose suspicions of his visitor had finally been proved baseless, said, "Yes, Chotzinoff, stay. In the morning you and David can go to Columbia together." Mary had not said a word, and managed to look coolly disinterested. With a great appearance of reluctance, I let myself be persuaded. Dining-room chairs were brought in, quilts, sheets and a pillow, and in a moment my bed was ready. Good-nights were exchanged, and I was left alone. I undressed to my long woolen underwear, put out the light and climbed into my chairs.

I lay awake a long time. After a while the house was silent. The blobs of sleet that dashed against the windows sounded like toy pistol shots. Suddenly I heard a whisper from the doorway. It was Mary's voice telling me to make no sound, and a second later she stood by me, a dim figure in a long nightdress, her loose hair reaching down to her shoulders. I made room for her on the chairs, and she crept in and lay down beside me. Her boldness and recklessness in coming to me took my breath away. We embraced and kissed and clung to each other. "Supposing *he* heard you? Supposing he comes here?" I said. She whispered back, "Let him, let him. . . . I don't care," exactly like Mélisande when she saw Golaud approaching, sword in hand. I, too, strangely enough, felt no fear. Yet *he* might appear before us at any moment! I must be prepared to tell him how wrong he would be in thinking the worst of us. Of course, he might not wait for an explanation and kill us outright. But if he should hesitate, I must quickly tell him not to judge us by his own worldly, immoral code. I must be eloquent, and convince him of the purity of our love. "Mr. Sklar," I must perhaps be prepared to say, "you've heard of Dante and Beatrice. . . . Dante didn't even know Beatrice; he only saw her once from a distance. Yet he loved her all his life. Love is not

what you think it is, Mr. Sklar. . . . True lovers can even lie
in bed together and not succumb to . . . what you imagine.
Believe me, Mr. Sklar, you are wrong. . . . I am not ashamed
of my love. . . . But it is not what *you* think."

We spent the dark of the night in whispered corroborations
of our emotions and our courage, both of us aware of our danger and glorying in it. The storm outside subsided, and there
was no longer the noise of sleet against the windowpanes. At
last the faint light of an uneasy dawn stole into the room. We
were safe so far. I realized this with a kind of regret. I had
been prepared for *his* coming. I almost wished he had come.
Mary, seeing the encroaching light, sighed, embraced me for
the last time and crept out of bed. I felt triumphant and light-
hearted. "It is the nightingale and not the lark," I whispered as
I clung to her, reluctant to let her go. "Oh, it's the lark," she
said gravely, and disappeared down the hall. I lay back in
luxurious ease, waiting for the house to awake.

At breakfast Mr. Sklar read aloud items of interest from the
morning paper. One of these related to a notorious suit for
divorce of the moment. A "society" man was suing his wife
for a divorce on the grounds of infidelity. The defense contended that the visit of the wife to the hotel bedroom of the
correspondent had been in the nature of a social call. Mr. Sklar
read out the details of this case with great relish. "And listen,"
he went on, "to what Judge Gaynor said in his charge to the
jury. 'Gentlemen,' he said, 'when a woman goes to a man's
bedroom in the middle of the night she doesn't come to pray.'
Ha, ha," Mr. Sklar chuckled. "A smart judge, this Gaynor;
he knows human nature, all right." "Mr. Sklar," I interposed
with heat, "it seems to me that that is a cynical attitude. There
are men and women in the world who would meet in a bedroom at midnight to pray, or for some purpose equally inno-

cent." Mary and I looked at each other boldly across the table, and Mrs. Sklar covered us with a benignant smile. Mr. Sklar, his eyes glued to his paper, frowned. "I wonder at you, Chotzinoff," he said. "You talk like a child." "Oh, leave Chotzinoff alone," murmured the irrepressible Charlie. His sister gave him a tender look and an affectionate pat on the head.

I cannot recall just how or why our virginal, springlike romance came to an end. Perhaps our love was "of imagination all compact." Perhaps we were consciously re-enacting the famous romances of literature and music. Certainly music and poetry did much to inspire it. And Mr. Sklar's cynicism and opposition, and my triumph over H. L., helped to sustain it for a time. Then one day there was a letter from Mary complaining of my growing indifference. I replied with a painfully vague, stilted and insincere note, to which I stupidly subscribed myself "Sincerely, Samuel Chotzinoff." Mary's reply to this began "My sincere Samuel Chotzinoff," and ended with a proud farewell. I was much upset by this exchange, and despised myself for a while. But other things and other people pressed upon me, and I was soon deep again in music, piano practice and teaching; and I resumed my old friendships with the Kovners, the Lessers and Morris Mandell. My correspondence with Elena, which had been for some time sporadic, took a spurt, and I reverted to the passionate tone of my earlier letters.

It was soon after my parting with Mary that Mandell himself behaved so out of character that I began to feel skeptical about him as a Theosophical leader and, finally, about Theosophy itself. Though Mandell always modestly disclaimed any superiority, I had taken it for granted that he was one of the elect. Because he had reached the advanced age of twenty-five without getting married or indulging in love, I assumed that he was one of those fortunate Theosophists who had "over-come" love and marriage, and was tending toward that absolute purity of body and soul essential to those who were destined, like Madame Blavatsky and Mrs. Tingley, to evolve into disembodied spirits. Thus it was that I was bewildered and shocked when Mandell announced suddenly, and without warning, that he was about to be married. Furthermore, the prospective bride wasn't even a Theosophist; but *that*, Mandell explained, would come later. She was a teacher in a primary grade in a public school. When I told all this to Hymie he couldn't believe his ears. But after giving it some thought, he said it was disloyal for us to question Mandell's actions. He thought it could be that marriage was necessary to Mandell's evolution as a spirit. He reminded me that both Madame Blavatsky and Mrs. Tingley had been married. In other words, he attempted to console me, and himself, with the notion that the spirits themselves had ordained that Mandell must undergo the experience of love and marriage, like any Theosophical novice. It was all too clear that Hymie was arguing against his own feelings.

Hymie and I were permitted to meet Miss Bella Korn, Mandell's affianced. We tried hard to like her and to imagine her in the important role of wife to so pure a nature and so devout a Theosophist as Morris Mandell. But comparing notes later, we found that we had both been disappointed in her. Miss Korn was a short, stout, fleshy young woman with a mass of blond hair that was sufficiently luxuriant and glossy to excite the most ordinary, uncultured, nonspiritual male. To my extreme distaste, she seemed to flaunt her sex. And when Mandell looked at her, a curious change came over his benign face, and I saw plainly that he was still a long way from overcoming desire.

Their wedding took place in the bride's home in the Bronx. Hymie, Mike Dorf and I provided the music. We decided not to let our feelings about the marriage stand in the way of our arranging a lofty and beautiful program. We played, in an arrangement for piano, violin and cello, the Prelude to *Lohengrin,* Wolfram's "Oh Evening Star" from *Tannhäuser,* the third-act Prelude from *Die Meistersinger* and the "Liebestod" from *Tristan.* All through the festivities I felt sad and bereft. There was that in the bride's aggressive demeanor that foreshadowed the severance of our intimacy with Mandell. The music we played brought tears to my eyes, for it related to a different Mandell from the one who sat close to his frowsy bride, paying little attention to what we played, thinking of God knows what! As we placed the music of the "Liebestod" on our stands I saw Hymie mournfully and imperceptibly shake his head. He seemed to be asking himself what possible resemblance there could be between Isolde and Bella Korn.

HANNAH BEHAVES
LIKE A CHRISTIAN

My sister Molly, her husband, Sergei, and their little son, Walt Whitman (hopefully so named at my suggestion), were now back in New York, after two years in Waterbury, Connecticut. Sergei had moved his family to Waterbury with the hope of improving his financial position by taking up house painting. He soon discovered that house painting was a seasonal profession, and that it was impossible to take on enough jobs in spring, summer and early fall to tide him over the idle winter months. In any case, Molly pined for New York. Though she attended conscientiously to her household, she was not a dedicated housewife like her sister Hannah. Her energy, high spirits and curiosity were wasted in Waterbury, where the married women of the small Jewish colony spent what little leisure they had in gossiping and playing pinochle or "pish-a-paysha" (Pit Your Patience), a card game of childish simplicity. Molly missed *me* most of all. She had been my companion and confidant, and always shared my ever-changing intellectual interests.

Molly moved into a three-room tenement on 102nd Street,

between Madison and Park Avenues, rather closer to Park Avenue, for the noise of the New York Central trains could be heard all day long. Underneath her apartment was a bakery, the yeasty odors of which were so pervasive that they seemed the chief component of the air in Molly's rooms. Yet, not withstanding the noise and the smells, it was pleasant to spend an evening at Molly's. Formerly an active participant in the Russian Social Revolutionary Movement, Sergei, in three years of marriage, had turned into a quiet, thoughtful family man. He had gone back to his old job at the Beylinson ice cream factory on Houston Street, where he worked long hours. He cheerfully minded Walt Whitman on nights when I took Molly to the opera, to my friends' houses or to a Theosophist meeting. I had very quickly converted Molly to Theosophy, and I frequently brought Mandell and Rubinstein to her house for a Sunday supper of salami and pickles, and to talk about "the movement." Rubinstein, especially, was charmed with Molly, thought she had an interesting head, and set about painting her portrait.

Sometimes I wondered at Sergei's patience with Molly, for she was ready to drop everything and accompany me at a moment's notice wherever I went. If I dropped by at her house, as sometimes happened, around noon of a Saturday after a morning class at Columbia, and said I was on my way to a matinee performance of a Wagner opera at the Metropolitan and she could come along if she liked, Molly, though she might be in the middle of giving Sergei his lunch, or feeding Walt Whitman, would instantly discard her apron, grab her hat and coat, shout a few instructions to her husband and leave with me. Sergei never seemed to mind these sudden abandonments. Indeed, he loved Molly so unselfishly that he was always happy to see her go. Sergei loved me too, "with all his

heart," so Molly assured me. He was about ten years older
than I, but he had a high regard for my judgment, and he
consulted me about his problems, such as they were, at home
and at the ice cream factory. He was remarkably, even inhumanly, reasonable about everything, and his obvious purity
of heart and selflessness made me ashamed of my own willfulness and vanity, which I tried so often and in vain to overcome
with the various social philosophies and spiritual "movements"
I took up.

I invited Molly to go with me to the first *Fidelio* performance
conducted by Mahler. We were to meet at the gallery entrance
of the Metropolitan. But Molly distrusted this arrangement,
fearing she might miss me, and said she would rather come
down to Henry Street and we would go to the opera together.
On the day of the performance it rained very hard. Molly was
to be at my house not later than seven o'clock, for *Fidelio* began
promptly at eight and I wanted to be there in good time for
the overture. Unaccountably, Molly failed to show up at seven.
By then the rain was coming down in torrents, and my mother
begged me to wait a few minutes more before starting out alone.
It was a distance of a mile between my house and the subway,
and I was eager to set out. I waited, tense and nervous, till
ten past seven. Then I left the house, ran at top speed down
East Broadway, turned into Canal Street and made for the subway. I had almost reached the subway kiosk when I stumbled
and fell full length into a puddle. I picked myself up and
scampered down the subway steps. I was embarrassed and quite
conscious of the grimy, watery spectacle I presented, but I could
not afford to lose time in attempting to tidy myself up (clearly
an impossibility). When I reached the Metropolitan I saw by
the clock on Broadway that it was two minutes to eight. I flew
up the interminable flights of stairs to the gallery as if on wings.

And as I gained the railing in the already darkened house, I heard, to my joy, the opening bar of the *Fidelio* overture.

When I got home after the performance, my mother was waiting up to tell me that Molly had arrived not more than five minutes after I left, and that, finding me gone, she had abandoned herself to hysterics so extravagant as to alarm the household. In the hope of calming her down, my mother forced her to munch a lump of sugar saturated with Hoffman Drops (my mother's own remedy for palpitations of the heart). When I next saw Molly she did not upbraid me for not having waited for her. She knew, of course, how unreasonable it was to expect me to miss a note of *Fidelio*. She had "given way" at my house, she said, only out of anger at herself for not allowing sufficient time to get to my house.

As I told Molly everything, or nearly everything, about myself, she knew about my romance with Mary Sklar. One Saturday I invited her to go with me to Florence's house in White Plains, where Mary was spending the night with her cousin. But early that morning I was summoned to the corner drugstore, where there was a telephone call for me. It was Sergei, who said that Molly had been taken ill, and I must come right up. When I arrived at Sergei's I found the doctor there. He said that Molly had suffered a "breakdown," an ailment I had never before heard of. He prescribed no medicine, but only a sedative to calm her "nerves." He ordered that Molly must never be left alone. She required, he said, rest and fresh air, and the patience and understanding of those around her. For fresh air we moved her bed from the single-windowed, dark, stuffy bedroom to the parlor, which had two windows facing 102nd Street. Molly behaved strangely, weeping and laughing alternately, apparently without cause. Sergei, Hannah, my mother and I took turns staying with her. Molly told me she felt safer with me than with the others, even safer than with Sergei, with whom she was now unaccountably capricious and high-handed. She slept mostly in the daytime, and was wide awake at night. Sergei (or I, when it was my turn to spend the night) slept, or tried to sleep, on an improvised bed on the floor near her. At times each night Molly would scream that "things" were pursuing her, that she was going to die, and implore us to fetch the doctor at once. Sergei was helpless with her, and once actually ran out in the dead of night and came back with the doctor, who gave her a sedative, and warned Sergei never again to rout him out of bed at night. Molly did feel, as she maintained, "safer" with me. When she awoke me and called for the doctor, I gave her the sedative and took her mind off "things" with anecdotes and stories of people we both knew, or I lit the gas and read Walt Whitman or Shelley to her. After a month or two she got better, and had fewer hallucinations. But her dependence on me did not grow less, and I spent at her house every moment I could spare from college and my teaching. The one alternative to this was to have Molly and her husband and child move in with us on Henry Street. Our front bedroom was rented to a middle-aged bachelor, a cross-eyed man whose face, when he came to the kitchen in the morning to wash himself at the sink, looked as if it had been smeared with castor oil. I explained to him the nature of Molly's illness and our need for his room. He was very understanding and found himself other quarters nearby. And soon after, Molly and her family moved in. All three slept in the front bedroom.

Now Molly improved rapidly. She was never alone for a moment. On Sunday, if the weather was fine, she and I and little Walt Whitman went to Jackson Street Park, I wheeling the baby carriage. Sergei in the meantime cleaned their bedroom and smeared the coils and joints of the bedspring with bedbug powder. My father was not too happy with our new tenants, because little Walt made a great deal of noise and often cried at night. My father and mother slept in a window-less bedroom between the dining room and parlor, and one had to go through this room to get to the front bedroom, whose only door opened on the parlor. Sometimes in the night Molly or Sergei was obliged to pass through my father's room to get to the kitchen or the toilet, which was in the hall; and though they walked on tiptoe, my father, who slept lightly, would wake up and give vent to his displeasure. But on the whole we enjoyed having Molly, Sergei and Walt with us. For one thing, I got to know Sergei better, and to admire and love him more than ever. He was the purest in heart of any person I knew. This baffled me. For Sergei had not, like me, the spiritual guidance of Theosophy. Nothing remained of his early revolutionary ardor, and he was a professed atheist be-sides. Yet he was a good man in the absolute meaning of the word. I was quite aware of his uniqueness, and so was Molly. Yet she did not cherish him as such a man deserved. I was reading at the time Arnold Bennett's *The Old Wives' Tale,* and I found the greatest resemblance between Mr. Povey, the good, kind, innocent, self-sacrificing linen-draper's apprentice, and my brother-in-law. I began to be hesitant about inviting Molly to go with me to the opera, because it meant that after a hard day's work at the ice cream factory, Sergei would have to sit up with Walt Whitman, feed him, put him to bed, etc. It was Sergei himself who, with some diffidence, asked me one day why I had stopped taking Molly to the opera. And when I next invited Molly to accompany me, he looked so pleased that I was convinced my compassion for him was misplaced.

Hannah's boy Davy was going on six, and I thought it was high time for him to begin his musical education. Once, when Hannah brought him to Henry Street, I tested his ear and found it good. Hannah had no piano and couldn't afford to get one, even on the installment plan. At one point she seriously considered selling her diamond ring and buying a second-hand piano. The ring, for which she had paid ninety dollars, had appreciated somewhat in the six years she had owned it. But always, just as she made ready to take it downtown to see what it would fetch, some friend or relation in temporary distress would borrow it and take it down to the Provident Loan Association, on the corner of Grand and Clinton Streets, in exchange for a loan which represented not more than half its value.

The absence of a piano in the homes of the poor was not, however, considered a serious handicap. Most piano students owned no piano, and practiced an hour a day at their teachers' houses. I started Davy on my piano and gave him a lesson whenever he visited us. He was intelligent and quick, but unruly, and he cannily took advantage of my affection and his mother's passionate love for him. Hannah usually sat in the dining room, listening tensely and eagerly while he had his lesson. Wishing to spare her, I would hesitate to reprimand him for willful inattention. Once, when I lost my temper and rushed into the dining room to cool off, the sight of Hannah sitting dejectedly, with tear-stained eyes, upset me more than her son's behavior. I pretended I had come in search of a pencil, and I quickly returned to the parlor and Davy.

When the Easter holidays came around I suggested that Davy should spend a week with us, so that he could have several piano lessons, and I would be around to superintend his practicing. Hannah brought him downtown, stayed a few hours and, after a tearful farewell, left for home. Davy at first looked upon his visit as a lark. But on the second day he grew restive, pretended not to hear me at the lesson and flatly refused to practice. With Hannah away, I could be stern with Davy. I got him to sit down at the piano at first by threats and, those failing, by the promise of an ice cream soda after his lesson. But notwithstanding the bribe, he became more inattentive than usual. Then, when I grew angry, he began to cry. My mother, hearing him, came into the room. She looked into his face, which I now saw was covered with small red spots, and felt his head. "He's sick," she said. "He has fever." And indeed, Davy's eyes shone brightly, and the little red spots multiplied even as I looked at them.

Our doctor lived a few houses down the street, and I lost no time in bringing Davy to his office. Before he took his temperature and examined him, the doctor said it was unmistakably scarlet fever. I asked him whether we should take the child to his own home or put him to bed at our house, but he said that was for us to decide. On the way back I thought the matter over and decided to send Davy home. He would be better off with his mother. I was not unmindful of the risk involved in subjecting a feverish child to an hour's ride on a streetcar. But if we put Davy to bed in our front room, the house would be disrupted for at least a fortnight, my mother would have to be his nurse, little Walt Whitman might catch the disease and my father would make matters worse by being disagreeable. I considered all these things. But I was also conscious of the inconvenience it would cause *me*. For an unspecified length of time I would not be free to play the piano, and I would have to forgo seeing my friends. Yet it was with secret misgivings that I asked my father to take Davy home. And even as Davy was being bundled up (though it was May and warm) and made ready for his journey, I was several times on the point of changing my mind and putting him to bed on the lounge in the front room.

After a few days Davy was better. My mother went each morning to Hannah's to help her with the children, and brought home reports of his improvement. He no longer had "temperature," and had so far recovered that he refused to lie quietly in bed, but kept jumping up and down. A week passed since my father had taken him home. One morning when I got up, I discovered that my mother had not come home the night before. I was alarmed, and on my way up to Columbia I stopped off at Hannah's. I found my mother making breakfast for the children. Davy had had a relapse the preceding day, his temperature had suddenly risen, the doctor had been summoned. He had pronounced the case serious and had telephoned for a district nurse (who showed up an hour later and took command of the sickroom). Finally he suggested calling in a child specialist, the renowned pediatrician Dr. Koplick. Hannah was distraught. For the first time since I could remember, she seemed indifferent to my presence.

Dr. Koplick's fee was twenty-five dollars, a sum quite out of the question for Hannah or me to raise. Hannah's ring was out on loan, and there was nothing in either of our houses that would fetch more than a few dollars in a pawnshop. Instead of going on to Columbia, I took a streetcar downtown and went straight to Dr. Lesser, told him about the desperate situation at Hannah's, and asked for a further advance of thirty dollars against his children's piano lessons. Without a word the doctor took out his well-filled wallet from his back pocket and peeled off three ten-dollar bills. I went back to Hannah's. The doctor was there again and I told him to go ahead and call in Dr. Koplick. The doctor went down to the corner drugstore and telephoned the specialist's office. It appeared that Dr. Koplick was in such great demand that the earliest he could come was the following afternoon at three. I spent the rest of the day at Hannah's, and in the evening I went down to visit H. L. Though I pretended to be cheerful at Hannah's, and spoke about scarlet fever as a commonplace of childhood (I reminded Hannah of the time she and Molly had had the disease 'way back in Russia and they had to have their hair cut off, and how funny they looked to me; I was hoping to make Hannah laugh, and indeed she permitted herself the ghost of a smile), I was full of forebodings, and I listened only halfheartedly to H. L.'s comments on life and art. The next afternoon I cut a class at Columbia and was at 103rd Street a little before three. I did not go into the house, but took up a position across the street. Soon a motorcar drew up at Hannah's house and a man with a small satchel got out and entered the vestibule. Half an hour later he came out. I ran across the street and intercepted him as he was about to enter his car. I said I was Davy's uncle and asked him if there was any hope. "Oh, yes," he replied, "there is always hope," and got into his car and drove away. I ran up to Hannah's apartment. My mother was in the sickroom. Hannah was sitting alone in the kitchen. I took her in my arms and poured out words of hope and assurance, and quoted Dr. Koplick as their source. My mother came into the room and cried with joy at my news. The nurse now appeared and said she had orders from the specialist to put the child into a very hot bath. Something had gone wrong with Davy's bladder, and a great deal now depended on his voiding of urine, even the smallest quantity, and she hoped the hot bath would have that effect. The nurse and I carried Davy, his features looking strangely awry, like a caricature, into the bathroom. He moaned feebly as we carefully

lowered him into the scalding water. My mother stood by
with an empty bottle, and when we lifted him out of the bath
she held it close to him, and to our inexpressible joy Davy
voided a little water. My mother called them precious and holy
drops, and said that all would now be well, and ran into the
kitchen to show the bottle to Hannah. Back in his bed, Davy
fell into a deep sleep. The nurse and I conversed in a whisper,
and when he awoke suddenly I asked him how he felt and
he murmured, "Good," but without opening his eyes. Before I
left for the night I went out to an ice cream parlor on Madison
Avenue and bought, for seventy-five cents, a large box of candy
with a blue ribbon around it, which I presented to the nurse
in appreciation of her kindness. She insisted on opening the
box then and there and offering the candy around, and we
each took a piece (even Hannah) for fear of displeasing her
and in recognition of the optimistic significance of her gesture. It seemed obvious that Davy was no longer in danger,
and that the change in his condition called for the passing of
refreshments.

I went to the Lessers' that night with a lighter heart and a
better conscience; for I could not banish the thought that if I
had put Davy to bed in my house he would be up and about
by now. After dinner there was a pinochle game and Mrs. Lesser, as usual, made me her silent partner in the game, and, as
usual, she came out a winner and handed me two dollars as
my share. It was one in the morning when I got home. I found
no one in the house but an old woman, a next-door neighbor,
who was sitting in the rocker in the dining room. She told me
that a message had come through the telephone at the drugstore that Davy had died at ten o'clock that night, and that
my father, Molly and Sergei had all gone to Hannah's, and
had asked her to sit up with Walt Whitman until I came home.

I sent the old woman back to her house, and I stretched out on the lounge to wait for morning. I was determined to postpone all thought and feeling until morning. And I deliberately fixed my mind on extraneous matters, and tried to exhaust each subject thoroughly before going to the next. Then in the middle of something I fell asleep, and a moment later I awoke with a start, remembering clearly what I wanted to forget. Then I saw to my horror that it was eight o'clock, and the room was full of sunlight. I called in the woman neighbor and asked her to mind little Walt. An hour later I was in 103rd Street. As I walked reluctantly up the stairs (I even thought of running away somewhere and not coming back for weeks) I heard the sound of weeping and hysteria, which I expected and dreaded. Inside there were many strange people, all crying. In the kitchen on an empty grocery box sat Hannah, and standing over her was my father. No one else was in the room, though a few people peered through the doorway. Hannah, tearless and strangely composed, had her eyes fixed on the floor, modestly. When I came in she raised them and gave me the faintest smile, as if we were conspirators in something, and no one but us knew about it. She then clenched her hands, and I heard her knuckles crack, but she looked calm, as before. She lowered her eyes and again regarded the floor intently. My father, whose exhortations I had evidently interrupted, now appeared to lose all patience with Hannah. "In God's name," he shouted at her in Yiddish, "let yourself go! Cry! Lament! Rend your garments! Be a woman! . . . She hasn't shed a tear," he said to me, accusingly, "not a single tear! . . . Why do you resist nature and God? You are committing a sin! Unburden yourself! Open your heart!" And suddenly my father murmured incoherently to himself in Hebrew and burst into tears. Hannah did not appear to hear him, remaining unmoved. I led my father out of the room. Hannah's husband, Jake, was in the bedroom giving his year-old son, Shelley, his bottle. His eyes were tear-stained, but he was giving all his attention to the baby, as if in doing so he might erase all thoughts of what had happened. I asked him if any arrangements had been made and he said, without taking his eyes off the baby, that his lodge had been notified and had made arrangements for the funeral that afternoon, but that it was necessary to get a burial permit from the Board of Health. I left the house, hailed a taxicab and told the driver to take me to the Board of Health. I had ridden in a cab but never paid for one. I sat on the edge of the seat and watched with fascination as the meter jumped five cents every four blocks. Why had I not taken Davy home in a taxicab that fatal morning? And what was my haste now? At one moment I felt myself engulfed by a feeling of terrible guilt, and I sank back in my seat and wept bitterly and silently into my handkerchief. We drew up at the Board of Health. There I reported Davy's death, filled out a form and received a burial permit. I returned to Hannah's house. At the curb stood a hearse and two carriages. Now I could not summon courage to go upstairs. I remained outside until Hannah, dressed in a hat and coat, was led out by my mother. Hannah's demeanor and expression had not changed. She seemed impersonal, even unconcerned, just like a Christian mourner. I remembered the mother of Howard Haskins, my schoolmate in Waterbury, at her son's funeral. Hannah behaved like Mrs. Haskins. I got into the carriage with Hannah, Jake, my mother and Molly. It was a horse-drawn cortege and it took quite two hours to get to Cypress Hills Cemetery. At the grave Molly became hysterical and had to be led away. A perfect stranger, an old Jew with a long beard, suddenly stood in front of us and began a eulogy of Davy, addressing Hannah directly, in a passionate, heart-wringing manner, as if he were talking about someone he knew and loved. But Hannah stood immobile, silent, her eyes demurely on the ground, even when the gravedigger began rapidly to heap earth on the coffin, and Hannah's friend, Mrs. Berger, who had pawned Hannah's diamond ring only a fortnight before, fainted dead away and was given ammonia to smell. Five hours after we left 103rd Street, we were back. Hannah took off her hat and coat and resumed her seat on the empty grocery crate. She said nothing, and turned away all offers of food and drink. I stayed until evening. Then I went downtown to H. L.'s house. He greeted the news without emotion. "Well," he said, shrugging his shoulders awkwardly, *"c'est la vie,* you know." Later he took me for a walk in Jackson Street Park. He tried several times to engage me in some literary or musical argument, and once I asked him if he knew of any passage in music or literature that might relate the outrageously senseless tragedy that had overtaken a pure and spotless creature like Hannah to any possible scheme of nature or God. H. L. considered awhile and said, "The Book of Job. But then Job, though he doubted Him, believed in God. Hannah believed in Davy."

We came back to H. L.'s house. A piano arrangement of the Ninth Symphony was on the music rack. H. L. opened it to the Adagio. "This doesn't explain," he said, "but I guess it reconciles." I began to play it. Its unearthly serenity washed me like a wave. Tears trickled down my cheeks and I felt their salty taste on my lips and in my mouth. For the first time that day I did not think of Davy or even of Hannah. I thought only of playing the Adagio with the utmost care, so that no human sentiment might blemish its mystical joy.

THE ENCHANTED
WORLD OF
DAVID BELASCO

〜〜〜 When the prescribed seven days of mourning were over, I brought Hannah to stay with us in Henry Street. Her two children had been sent to their aunt, Jake's sister, in Kingston, New York. Hannah seemed equally indifferent to the departure of the children and to her visiting us. She suffered herself to be combed and dressed for her journey on the Second Avenue El to our house. It was the middle of June. In a fortnight the children would return from Kingston and they and Hannah would go for the summer to a farm close to the one in New Jersey where my mother, father and little sister were going to stay.

Hannah shared Molly's bed in the front bedroom. Jake and Sergei slept on the living-room floor. My mother busied herself all day cooking and cleaning, and Hannah, who had always been eager to do more than her share of work when she visited us, did not now lift a finger to help her, but sat in a rocker, without rocking, and stared impersonally into space. At night, on going to bed, she undid her skirt, stepped out of it and let it lie on the floor where it had dropped. I felt at a loss what to do about Hannah. Her affection for me, once so strong, seemed to have disappeared. My father, however, continued to lecture her. "Do your two children mean nothing to you?" he would say, raising his eyes from his Hebrew book. "They are living creatures. They have done no wrong to deserve such treatment. Your behavior is sinful. You are neither dead nor alive. Be one or the other, so your children will know if they are motherless or no." My sister never replied. She looked, indeed, as unconcerned as if she thought he was talking to someone else in the room about something that didn't apply to her. These diatribes became annoying to the rest of us, and when I could stand it no longer I told my father in Hannah's presence to leave her alone. His only comment was a tart *"a mishoogine heus"* (a madhouse). But he did as he was bid.

In the first week of July our household dispersed: Hannah and her children, my mother, father and little sister went to Flemington; and I, for the second time, went to Normandie-by-the-Sea. I was happy at the change from the constrained atmosphere of Henry Street to the sunshine and crisp breezes from the ocean and the Shrewsbury River. Many of the guests of two seasons before were again spending the summer in the large, wooden hotel. *"Die Schöninke,"* now married to the successful theater-ticket broker who had courted her, was there again and, as formerly, a delight to the eye. Also Mrs. Meltzer, Mrs. Roeder, the banker violinist and the German viola player. We resumed our chamber-music sessions in the casino in the afternoons, and I played violin concertos and sonatas for violin and piano with Mrs. Roeder and coached Mrs. Meltzer in classic lieder, operatic arias and modern songs by Strauss, Mahler, and Pfitzner.

One Saturday night in the casino, Mrs. Roeder, sitting at a

table with a large party, called me over and introduced me to
her friends the Belascos, and their two married daughters,
Mrs. Morris Gest and Mrs. William Eliot, who had arrived
at Normandie-by-the-Sea that afternoon. My excitement was
great at meeting this noted theatrical family. David Belasco
looked exactly like his pictures in the papers. He was dressed
in black and wore a clerical collar. His large, swarthy, fleshy
face, liquid black eyes and benign look (a little lock of hair
was always falling over his right eye) made me think, irreverently, of a female Anglican bishop. Mrs. Roeder placed a
chair next to hers and offered me a glass of champagne, the
first I ever tasted. One of the gentlemen at the table took
from his pocket a little gold stick that separated at its end into
a cluster of what looked like curled needles, stuck it into his
glass of champagne and turned it quickly around and then
in reverse. This had the effect of bringing powerful bubbles
to the surface of the glass and made the wine brim over. At that
point the man raised the glass to his lips. I made a mental
note of the odd instrument, vowing to get one someday for
myself, when I should be in a position to drink champagne
frequently.

The talk turned to a new play Mr. Belasco—or "The Governor," as he was called by everyone at the table—was going to
produce in the fall, a comedy from the German called *The
Concert*. The play was about a famous concert pianist. Mr.
Leo Dietrichstein, the actor who was to play the part of the
concert pianist, was, I was told, no pianist himself. Indeed,
he could not play the piano at all. But in the play he was required to play, or, at any rate, to appear to play, in full view
of the audience. The difficulty would be solved by having Mr.
Dietrichstein pretend to play on a dummy piano, while a real
pianist played backstage. As Mr. Belasco went into the details

of this arrangement, my heart started to beat fast, for I felt
that he must be leading up to engaging *me* to be the pianist
behind the scenes. And, indeed, he did ask me, the next moment, if I would be interested in the job, adding that Mrs.
Roeder had suggested me and had vouched for my ability to
play like a concert pianist. I was speechless from gratitude
and joy, and it was with difficulty that I stammered my acceptance. I was then taken aside by Mr. Roeder for a discussion of
the terms, etc. These were highly gratifying. My salary would
be thirty-five dollars a week, starting from the tryout performance in Pittsburgh in the middle of September. Rehearsals,
however, would begin in the middle of August. Mr. Roeder
said that he had already obtained from Mr. Bellak, the manager
of the hotel, permission for me to come daily to New York
for rehearsals, provided I was back in time to play each evening. Furthermore, the Belasco office would pay for my transportation to and from New York. Nor would I have any
expense in the matter of lunches in town. The Belasco office
supplied sandwiches and coffee on rehearsal days. When Mr.
Roeder had settled these practical matters, we went back to
the table and I was offered another glass of champagne. This
time I politely asked the gentleman with the golden wine
stirrer if I might borrow the instrument for a moment. With
it I created innumerable bubbles, and when they were at their
height I quickly drained the glass, as I had seen the man do.
In my haste I gulped. This brought on a fit of hiccups. Everybody at the table laughed, and Mr. Roeder gave me several
thumps on my back, after which I regained my breath and
composure. Someone filled my glass again. This time I was
careful not to gulp, but sipped the wine slowly. I felt warm
and pleasant, and I conversed easily, even volubly. Mrs. Roeder
begged me to repeat some stories I had told her of my child-

hood in London and on the East Side. I did so without hesitation, and Mr. Belasco and the other people were amused,
and they kept me talking about myself and my family until
it was time for the dancing to begin. I excused myself and
went to the piano. But my legs suddenly felt light, and it
seemed to me that some outside force was hurrying me along,
so that I flew, rather than walked, across the room. When I
gained the piano chair I felt all right again, though the notes
on the music sheet danced before my eyes, and I was obliged
to look down and play by heart. Once, while I was playing
away, exaggerating the rhythm of a waltz, Mr. Roeder brought
over a full glass of champagne and placed it on top of the
piano for me. His thoughtfulness filled me with gratitude, and
without ceasing to play, I rose from my seat, turned toward his
table and made a low bow. This was greeted with laughter
and applause, and made me very happy indeed. My glass on
top of the piano thereafter seemed always full, though I sipped
from it continually. After we played "Home, Sweet Home,"
the usual signal that the dance was over, I started toward my
friends' table to say good night. This time my legs were not
light but heavy, and the distance seemed long. Though my
feet dragged and tried to hold me back, I had never felt so
happy. Mrs. Roeder, looking radiant in a spangled evening
gown, regarded me with such loving-kindness that I asked
her, in front of her husband, if I might kiss her. Mr. Roeder
appeared not to resent my boldness and gave me a friendly
smile. His wife did not even wait for his consent, but leaned
over and gave me her cheek. I kissed her tenderly, and again
there was laughter and applause. I staggered up to my room
feeling that I had been vouchsafed everything that life had
to give. I sat down on the bed, the better to review my good
fortune. And as I began to unbutton my shirt, oblivion over-

came me, and I knew nothing more until I was awakened late the next morning by excruciating pains in the back of my head.

Mr. Belasco had gone back to New York, but his daughters and their husbands remained for a vacation. On Monday I went into the barbershop to get a haircut and I found Mr. Morris Gest, the husband of Renee, the older Belasco daughter, in the chair. He was getting a complete, expensive shave and haircut. His face was being massaged with a kind of putty, and then laved with a stinging liquid. Ed Pinaud tonic was applied to his hair. In fact, his face and head were rubbed with an assortment of liquids from bottles that lined the shelf under the large mirror. At the same time a manicurist attended to his nails, and a boy shined his shoes. I could only guess at the cost of such a complete beautification of his person. Mr. Gest saw me in the mirror, and spoke to me in the most friendly fashion, saying how amused he had been at some of the hard-luck stories of my youth I had told the night of the dance at the casino. "But they were nothing compared to the troubles I had with The Governor," he assured me through the mirror; and disregarding the presence of strangers in the room, he related, with a certain relish, the tribulations attendant on his wooing and gaining the hand of Belasco's daughter. "Y'see, Sammy," Mr. Gest said (I was flattered by this intimate address), "I was an immigrant boy out of Russia, a ticket broker *noch zu*"—in the bargain—"and The Governor thought I showed *chutzpeh*—you know, gall—to want to marry his daughter. When I came to his theater he threw me out. When he found me in his house he threw me out. Every time he threw me out I came back. He threw me out at the front door, I came in by the back door. That's the American spirit, Sammy!" Mr. Gest, shining from top to toe, got up from the chair. He looked, I thought, artistic, though he had a walleye.

His face was broad, he had full, sensual lips, his hair kept falling over his right eye, like his father-in-law's, and he wore a black, flowing tie. "Come for a walk on the beach with me, Sammy," he said familiarly. "You can get a haircut another time." We strolled along the beach, and he talked more about himself and his stamina in his unrelenting pursuit of Miss Belasco. "She herself didn't care too much for me at first," he said, "but I never let up. Not me. No, sir! This is a wonderful country, Sammy. Don't ever forget it. You can get anywhere you want if you want it bad enough. You know what, Sammy? Mrs. Gest sings a little. For pleasure, I mean. But she needs to be coached. Why don't you give her an hour a week? You know, she don't want to be a professional. Just for pleasure." I said I would be delighted. He asked what I charged and I said boldly, "Two dollars an hour," and without blinking an eye he said that would be all right. I told him we might start the lessons early the next morning, whereupon he stopped in his tracks and smiled at me. "Look, Sammy," he said, "have a heart! We're on our honeymoon!" I understood the implication and blushed, and asked him to set a date. After considering a moment, he said, "How about a week from today, say eleven A.M.?" So it was agreed. But on the appointed morning I waited in the casino from eleven till noon for Mrs. Gest, but she did not appear. After lunch I encountered Mr. Gest in the lobby. He said Mrs. Gest was sorry she couldn't keep her appointment with me, and I said I hoped there was nothing wrong. "Oh, no," he said broadly, "everything's fine. Only eleven o'clock is a little too early, you know, Sammy, you understand!" and he gave me a knowing thump on the shoulder. I advanced the hour, and the next day at noon Mrs. Gest appeared for her first lesson. She was languid and slim, and had a wonderful milky complexion, dark eyes and hair, though her nose was quite long and sharp, and almost met her pointed chin. Her voice was small, hollow and rather shaky. She wanted me to teach her the aria "Un bel di" from *Madama Butterfly*. I told her she was not equipped technically for such a difficult aria. She said she understood that she was no Farrar, but she wanted to sing it for her "pleasure." Mr. Gest wandered in, listened for a moment and left. We spent a month (the duration of her stay at Normandie-by-the-Sea) on "Un bel di," for Mrs. Gest did not care to learn anything else for her "pleasure." I found the lessons quite a trial, and I felt I was robbing Mr. Gest. But I salved my conscience by remembering the expensive operations Mr. Gest indulged in once a week in the barbershop.

All this time I awaited with the greatest impatience the day of my first rehearsal at the Belasco Theater. A week before that event, I used my day off to journey to Flemington to visit my family and Hannah, and tell them the great news. At the Flemington station I hired a carriage to take me to Hannah's place. Hannah was not in the farmhouse, and there was no one about. I set out to find her in the woods, and presently, in a clearing, I saw Hannah, sitting on a boulder, looking from a distance like the picture I had often seen in the Metropolitan Museum of Joan of Arc in the forest of Domremy. She showed no surprise on seeing me, suffered herself to be kissed, and listlessly answered my inquiries about the children. She had not changed since I last saw her, except that she looked more unkempt. It was two months since Davy died, and it was obvious that Hannah was still perversely suppressing her grief. I felt I should make an effort to unfreeze her heart, and it came to me all at once to do what everyone had thus far refrained from doing—talk unreservedly about Davy. I told Hannah how I was being constantly haunted by Davy's beautiful face, especially when I was in bed at night. This was an exaggeration. But I often thought of him, and sometimes saw him before me when I put out the light at night. I recalled his virtues, his aptitude for music, even his mischievousness. And as I talked, Hannah looked at me wonderingly, tears sprang to her eyes—perhaps the first she had shed since Davy's death—and suddenly she threw herself in my arms and opened her heart to grief in the extravagant Jewish way that my father had in vain commanded her to do. We talked about Davy for a long time, between us recalling what he said and did. Then we walked back to the house. Hannah led me into her room and from under the mattress of her bed she took out Davy's last photograph, wept over it, covered it with kisses, gave it to me to admire and then returned it to its secret place. When she could cry no more, I told her about the visit of the Belascos and my engagement for *The Concert*. Hannah showed an interest in the news and said I must hurry to tell it to my mother. So I left her and walked the half mile to where my mother lived.

On an unforgettable Monday morning, a week later, I presented myself to Mr. Roeder at his office in the Belasco Theater for the first rehearsal of *The Concert*. To my surprise Mr. Roeder was not as affable as he had been on weekends at Normandie-by-the-Sea. He was rather curt, and turned me over to a man at a desk, who gave me a contract to sign and then took me down to the rehearsal room in the basement of the theater. This was a very large room decorated in Oriental fashion. Enormous china vases stood about, and the walls were hung with painted silks. A grand piano struck the only modern note. The chairs and tables were of various French, Italian and Oriental periods. It was a truly exotic place, and I felt as if I had touched Aladdin's lamp and found myself suddenly in a mandarin's palace. Several men (two of them quite bald and middle-aged) and many women, most of them young and pretty, stood about. Mr. Roeder's secretary introduced me to each one in turn. One of the bald-headed men turned out to be Leo Dietrichstein, the adapter and the star of the play. I was disappointed in Mr. Dietrichstein's looks and figure. I had pictured the great concert pianist of the play as a romantic-looking musician, not the short, hairless man with bags under the eyes who stood before me. On the other hand, Miss Janet Beecher, the leading lady, was very beautiful and soft-spoken, the ideal stage wife for a romantic concert pianist. Presently a large man without a jacket, his shirt sleeves rolled up, came into the room and began rehearsing the first scene of the play. I had expected Mr. Belasco to do the rehearsing and I asked Mr. Stuart Walker, the stage manager, in a whisper whether Mr. Belasco was indisposed. Mr. Walker, a tall, thin young man with pince-nez, smiled at me indulgently and whispered back that "The Governor" appeared only after the preliminary staging had been set by his assistant, the man with the rolled-up sleeves. Mr. Walker also gave me copies of the music I was to play—Liszt's Tenth Rhapsody and Schumann's *Warum*. Somewhere in the play I would also be required to improvise scales, arpeggios, etc., showing the great pianist at practice.

That morning I was not required to play, and I sat and watched and listened, fascinated, to the unfolding of *The Concert*. I thought the play witty, amusing and true to life, though the character of the great concert pianist did not square with my own lofty idea of what a great concert pianist should be. For in the play, Mr. Dietrichstein, with the loveliest of women for a wife, could not resist the appeal of his young, beautiful and adoring lady pupils, and at the end of the first act actually ran away with one of them to his hideout in the

Adirondacks. I was relieved to find, in the course of the play, that the great pianist engaged in these amorous adventures more out of vanity and fear of growing old and losing his hold on his feminine public than from indifference to his wife. Mr. Dietrichstein played the musician as a fatuous, vain, imperious but susceptible artist, who really loves his wife, but yet expects her to look upon his amorous adventures as legitimate extensions of an artist's temperament. I wondered whether this cynical evaluation of an artist's romantic inclination could be a true one, and remembering my own susceptibility to several women at the same time, I had to admit that the greater provocations and opportunities in the life of an established concert artist might easily prove irresistible. At any rate, I found myself blushingly identifying many of the foibles and inconsistencies of the artist in the play as my own.

About a week later, the rehearsals were transferred to the stage of the theater and Mr. Belasco arrived to confer the finishing touches. The stage of the Belasco seemed even more exciting to me than the Oriental cellar. I gazed in wonder at the many ropes which hoisted walls and ceilings and gardens up to the flies, at the complicated electrical panel, at the multifarious props in rooms on each side of the stage. A cage had been built to house me and a grand piano directly in back of the large fireplace in the Adirondack lodge of the second-act set of *The Concert*. Through a large fire screen I was able to see all of the stage, but neither the piano nor I was visible from out front. I watched Mr. Dietrichstein carefully as he pretended to play scales and exercises and, later, *Warum* on his dummy keyboard. We had by this time practiced these musical movements together many times, and the synchronization of the actor's hands, head, body movements and facial expressions with the music I played was now perfect. When I was not playing I went out front to watch Mr. Belasco rehearse. Though it was very warm, he wore his clerical collar and priestly jacket. He gave instructions and made comments in a low, gentle tone of voice. I had heard stories of his terrible outbursts at rehearsals, and I felt disappointed at his modest behavior. Curiously enough, he never addressed a word to Mr. Dietrichstein. I wondered whether Mr. Dietrichstein was so fine an actor that he required no instruction, or so hopelessly incompetent as to be beyond guidance. To me he seemed a fine actor indeed. And when lunchtime arrived, I complimented him on his performance. "I suppose," I added encouragingly, "you hope to become a David Warfield someday." I said this not only to encourage him, but also to let him know that I was not without a knowledge of the American theater and its greatest actor. Mr. Dietrichstein, however, did not acknowledge my compliment, but moved away from me without saying a word. A few minutes later, the secretary appeared and told me I was wanted upstairs in Mr. Roeder's office. I found Mr. Roeder alone. "Well!" he said, regarding me with a hostile air. "You almost did yourself out of a job. Dietrichstein just left here in a fury, calling for your blood. He screamed that you had deliberately insulted him, and swore that if you were not dismissed he would throw up his part." I was aghast, and so bewildered and upset by this unfounded accusation that it was some time before I was able to refute it. "Insult him!" I gasped. "I complimented him. Why, I even asked him if he hoped someday to become a David Warfield." Mr. Roeder searched my face as if to discover whether I was joking. Then he burst into shockingly loud laughter. "You nitwit!" he roared. "No wonder he was fit to be tied. Don't you know that you never ask an actor whether he'd like to be like another actor? Don't you know that Dietrichstein believes he is a better

actor than Warfield? Wait till The Governor hears about it!"
And Mr. Roeder went off again in a fit of laughter. "Now go
back and apologize to him. And don't ever say such a thing
again—to any actor." I returned to the stage in the greatest
dejection. Mr. Dietrichstein was in his dressing room. The door
stood open and I went in and told him I was sorry and hoped
he'd forgive me. He nodded. But his face expressed sullen
displeasure. I don't think he ever really forgave me.

We opened in the Nixon Theater in Pittsburgh. At the
end of the play, Mr. Belasco assembled the entire cast on the
stage and pointed out what he thought had gone wrong. Then
he turned to Stuart Walker, who stood near him with a pencil
and pad, and asked him how many "laughs" he had counted.
Mr. Walker consulted his pad and said eighty-nine. Mr.
Belasco looked very disappointed at this, and stood in thought
for a while, sampling with the thumb and forefinger of his
right hand the lock of hair that had fallen over his eye. "We
estimated a hundred and fifty, didn't we?" he mused. "Rehearsal tomorrow at ten," he then murmured softly, and walked
away. I went back to my hotel, wondering why "laughs" had to
be counted, and, if they did have to be counted, how Mr.
Belasco had estimated the surprising number he mentioned.

After a week in Pittsburgh, we went to Baltimore. One afternoon the seven young ladies who played the parts of Mr.
Dietrichstein's pupils gave a tea party for themselves and invited me and Mr. Walker. We were the only men present. Mr.
Walker was a very cultured man (he later produced "literary"
playlets like *Six Who Pass While the Lentils Boil,* and toured
the country with a "portmanteau" theater, a small collapsible
stage which could be set up in hotels or even outdoors). He
had a sweet nature, and seemed naïve even to me. As stage
manager, he was treated with respect and even affection by the
ladies of the company. I, too, was made much of, the ladies

vying with each other in filling my cup and offering me little pastries in corrugated-paper containers. When the party was over, I started out for a walk, and Miss Edith Fallon, one of the ladies, asked if I would mind if she accompanied me, as she too craved fresh air before the evening performance. I said of course I wouldn't mind, and we walked in the direction of the Peabody Conservatory, the famous Baltimore music school, which I wanted very much to see. On the way we talked about music and literature, both of which interested my companion greatly. We gazed at the façade of the Conservatory. I had not the courage to go inside, for I knew no one there. However, it was pleasant to be with Miss Fallon, who listened to everything I said with ostentatious attention, and I prolonged our walk until dinnertime. Miss Fallon wanted to know about my family and upbringing, and I recounted with relish what I considered the salient facts of my life. I then asked her, out of politeness, about herself. She told me that Fallon was her stage name, that she was married to a Mr. John Mitchell, a New York representative of the American Tube Company of Chicago, and that *The Concert* was her second part in a Belasco production. She asked me if I had ever seen Shaw's *Candida*. I hadn't, and I said I would get it and read it. "You remind me of a character in the play called Marchbanks," she said as she entered the revolving door of her hotel.

Back in New York, we had three or four days of rehearsals before the opening night. On that momentous evening we were all drawn up at the front of the stage behind the closed curtain, a few minutes before curtain time. Nervousness was written on all faces, from Mr. Dietrichstein's down to mine. Mr. Belasco, in clerical garb, emerged from the wings and stood in front of us. Fondling his errant lock of hair and looking at the floor, his face benign, as always, but with more color, he softly exhorted the company to give of their best. He himself, he

assured us, was confident of a hit. "Now God bless you!" he
finished, waving his hand at the long line of actors before him.
His tone of voice recalled to my mind *A Christmas Carol* and
Bob Cratchit and Tiny Tim's "God bless us every one!" Mr.
Walker now warned that the curtain was about to go up and
I ran to my cage backstage to be ready with the fortissimo
opening chords of Liszt's Tenth Rhapsody. I had no sooner
taken my seat at the piano when the canvas door of the cage
was pushed open and Mr. Belasco stood before me. "I expect
you to play," he said sweetly but firmly, "as if you were getting
a thousand dollars a night." It was a startling suggestion at
such a moment. Fortunately, the little red light in my cage
signaled me to begin, so I had no time to reflect on the obvious
disparity between a thousand-dollar-a-night and a thirty-five-
dollar-a-week performance. Curiously enough, my nervousness had vanished, and I knew I was playing well. Not even
suspecting my existence, the audience applauded Mr. Dietrichstein wildly at the end of the Rhapsody for a performance
that was not his. Mr. Belasco's private belief was speedily justified. The house constantly shook with laughter (Mr. Walker
later reported that the "laughs" greatly exceeded the desired
150). The play was an instantaneous hit. And as I waited at
the front of the theater for Dr. and Mrs. Lesser, who had purchased seats in the balcony, I saw several speculators selling
seats for future dates to people leaving the theater. The Lessers
were delighted with the play, and Dr. Lesser invited me to
Childs on Broadway to have a supper of buckwheat cakes and
coffee, after which we walked downtown and I left them at
Avenue B and 9th Street.

§ II

The success of *The Concert* was a guarantee of financial
security for me for at least a season. What with the lessons I
gave, I now earned between fifty and fifty-five dollars a week!

Almost at once I began to consider ways of spending it. My father suggested saving a certain sum each week, but added that in money matters I was my mother's son, not his, and he was sure that his advice would not be taken. I told him I had every intention of saving money, and that I would begin doing so after I had bought some things for the house which I always wanted and now felt I could afford. For some time I had admired and coveted a large sepia-toned copy of Whistler's "Mother" in a dark three-tiered frame, that hung tantalizingly in a shop window on Madison Avenue. The price, twenty dollars, was dismaying, but it was now unthinkable that I should not buy it. One payday I brought it home and hung it where I had always imagined it would hang—on the wall directly over the lounge on which I slept. It looked magnificent there, and was greatly admired by everyone, even by my father. But I saw immediately that the dirty, drab and torn leather of the lounge was entirely out of harmony with the lovely, severe tones of the picture and the frame. In my mind's eye I saw a green velvet cover over the couch. Mrs. Lesser helped me find one with just the right color. When at last it was draped over the lounge, it was a delight for the eye. In turn the lounge now *demanded* several pillows of the same hue to adorn it and give it the air of a rich divan. Mrs. Lesser bought them for me as a gift. But at night the double gas jet that hung from the ceiling cast a forbidding cold light over the entire room which was quite unflattering to Whistler's mother and made the green velvet cover and the pillows look bilious. It came to me then that the only proper light for the room would be one from a shaded lamp, and I purchased, at some expense, in Siegel Cooper's a table gas lamp with a green glass shade and a rubber gas tube of sufficient length to reach across the room to the gas outlet on the baseboard of the opposite wall.

One night as I sat on the draped lounge under Whistler's

"Mother," my eyes rested with dissatisfaction on the rented upright piano against the opposite wall. It was clearly out of harmony with the lounge, the subdued light and the sepia work of art on the wall behind me. What the room needed as a final crowning touch was a grand piano. Aside from any aesthetic consideration, my new importance as a pianist clearly indicated the presence of a grand piano. I was almost twenty years old, I was playing what amounted to a small recital each night and Saturday matinees at the Belasco (though I remained anonymous to my audience) and my earnings were substantial. I couldn't think of a more propitious moment to acquire a grand piano. Then and there I decided to negotiate for one the very next morning, and I spent a sleepless night imagining a big ebony grand in the room. At nine in the morning I was at Mason & Hamlin's Fifth Avenue shop, trying out a number of pianos. I chose one next in size to a concert grand, and signed a contract to pay fifteen dollars down and fifteen dollars a month until the purchase price of $1,300 with interest should be paid off. In a matter of only eight years the piano would be mine.

My rented upright piano was removed to Spector's store on Grand Street, and on the Saturday, as prearranged, my new piano arrived. The hoisting of it through a living-room window attracted a crowd, for a grand piano was a rarity on the East Side. Both elated and concerned, I watched it being maneuvered through the window, and when the padded covers were removed, I was relieved not to find the slightest scratch on the wonderfully glazed ebony. When the movers screwed the legs and the pedals onto the piano and stood it up properly, I was so overcome with emotion that I recklessly gave them a dollar as a tip. With my mother's and father's assistance, I then moved the great instrument about until I found its predestined position in the room. Then I raised the piano lid concert-fashion, sat down on the ample ebony bench that came with the piano, and played the loud opening chords of Liszt's Tenth Rhapsody. Never had I heard an instrument give forth such ravishing, brilliant sound. To test the piano's tone quality, I switched to Schumann's *Warum*. The soft velvety sounds fell caressingly on the ear. I asked my mother to walk about and tell me how the piano sounded in different parts of the room. She listened attentively and said it sounded beautifully alike everywhere. My father, for his part, gave his entire attention to the polished case, and rubbed with his sleeve a spot whose sheen seemed to him somewhat subdued.

My room (my studio, I called it) was now beautiful to behold, and my happiness was complete. My mother thought that a man of my position also required a new suit of clothes. But I had already spent so much money that I was obliged to cut down temporarily my mother's allowance for running the house. Besides, I had no interest in clothes and in how I looked.

Pleasant rumors began to reach me about my performances at the Belasco. Many people who saw *The Concert* believed that Mr. Dietrichstein himself played the Tenth Rhapsody and all the other things I played, so realistic was the actor's behavior at his dummy piano. Musicians were, however, skeptical, and I heard of several bets that had been made that someone backstage was providing the music. On the other hand, the great pianist Josef Hofmann had bet that Mr. Dietrichstein actually played, and what was more, that he sounded like a first-rate pianist and musician. This rumor filled me with pride. But my joy was tempered by an editorial in *The Musical Courier*. The anonymous writer said that he couldn't tell whether Mr. Dietrichstein was playing, but that whoever did play the Liszt

Rhapsody didn't seem to be quite sure of his octaves. This dismayed me, for I considered my octaves quite good. But from that moment on I became self-conscious about them. My wrists tended to stiffen, and frequently an octave passage emerged ragged. If I was sure of my octaves before I read the reflection on them in *The Musical Courier,* I was never quite sure of them afterward.

Never had I been so occupied as now. Between my last class at Columbia and the evening performance at the Belasco, I had barely time to attend to my pupils at home. My homework I did at the theater between the Tenth Rhapsody, which opened the play, and *Warum,* which came in the middle of the second act. Between *Warum* and the very end of the last act, when I played some scales and arpeggios, I had another three-quarters of an hour for study. When there was little or no homework, I went for walks around Times Square, always returning in plenty of time for my cues; or I hung around backstage, which I found continually fascinating. I was soon on the most friendly terms with the cast, the stagehands, the electricians and with Gus, the stage-doorman. Gus was a charming, voluble old man who was only too eager to satisfy my curiosity about the theater in general, and about the many actors and actresses he had known. I sat often in his little room at the stage entrance and listened to him with the greatest interest. His stories were interwoven with his own estimates of people, and with his own observations on humanity. "Now take women," he said once, "and I don't mean actresses." He had been telling me about the long run at the Belasco of *The Easiest Way,* and how "The Governor" had taken an unknown young lady, Francis Starr, and made her the star of the show. "I ain't talkin' of Miss Starr right now, but of the women who came to see the play. Now, there was two men in the cast of *The Easiest Way*—the hero, a

nice good-lookin' feller, and a big fat, husky man who played
the rich man who with money and that kind of thing made
Miss Starr go wrong. Well, d'ye know who got the most
letters?" and Gus pointed to the mail cabinet on the wall.
"The bad feller, not the clean, good one. Y'see that third
pigeonhole there? It was too small to hold all his letters. And
he showed me many of them. They were from rich, fashionable
ladies who wrote, 'Y'know you can have me if you want me!'
Well, now, you would think they'd of went for the good-
lookin' hero. Not them! Ladies in fur coats and jewelry would
barge in here after the performance trying to see the old fox.
He coulda had the pick of the town. But he was a married
man and had no use for them gals." About "The Governor"
Gus was reticent, but whenever I mentioned him he made
knowing faces at me. "The Governor" occupied what was
rumored to be a fabulous apartment on the top floor of the
theater. It was fitted out with all sorts of Oriental objects and
contained an extraordinary library of printed and manuscript
plays. A tiny elevator connected the apartment with the stage.
Sometimes, though not frequently, I would become aware of
Mr. Belasco during intermissions talking to one or another of
the ladies in the cast. One of the ladies had to make a quick
change of costume in a certain scene. Her dressing room was
on the second floor and Mr. Walker was always afraid that
she would be late for her entrance. When *The Concert* had
run a month or so, Mr. Belasco generously ordered a little booth
erected backstage. This arrangement gave the actress more
time to change and removed Mr. Walker's anxiety about a
late entrance. The Governor sometimes went into the lady's
booth for a whispered chat. One night, as I was conversing
with Gus, Mr. Walker stuck his head into the room and asked
if he could see me for a moment backstage. I went backstage

with him and he pointed to the little booth. "Would you mind knocking on the door and telling her her cue is coming up? I think The Governor is in there. You don't mind doing it for me, do you?" Wondering why Mr. Walker was delegating one of his duties to me, I rapped softly on the booth. It was some time before the door opened and the actress came out. She made her entrance on the stage not a moment too soon. Mr. Walker had discreetly vanished, and I went back to resume my talk with Gus.

Miss Beecher, the leading lady, liked my company and often invited me to her dressing room. She was so beautiful that I would sit and gaze at her lovely face and light hair, and quite forget to listen to what she was saying. She was a Christian Scientist and a philosopher in general, and had only nice things to say about everybody. "One must think beautiful thoughts about people," she would say, "and everyone will *seem* beautiful." I had noticed that after the first-act curtain (Mr. Dietrichstein had just kissed her good-bye on the stage), Miss Beecher, upon gaining her room, always seized an atomizer and sprayed first her throat and then the room. I asked her one night why she did that. She astonished me by saying it was because she couldn't *bear* Mr. Dietrichstein. She said this with ill-concealed hatred. While I admired Mr. Dietrichstein as an artist, I couldn't take to him as a man. He did appear cold and cynical. Yet I found no reason to hate him. But I had watched Miss Beecher in the play, and her behavior toward Mr. Dietrichstein was always so radiantly affectionate that I had supposed she might easily be in love with him in real life. Quite unprepared for such a revelation as I had just heard, I excused myself and beat a retreat from the dressing room so that I might think over the discrepancy between Miss Beecher's usual overgenerous estimate of humanity and her aversion to her leading man. I appealed to Mr. Walker to explain this curious lapse in Miss Beecher's otherwise noble nature. Mr. Walker, whom I considered an authority on the drama and the stage, smiled indulgently and said, "She's a darling. But she's an actress too, and stage people are often jealous of one another. Not that she hasn't cause to be. Just watch Dietrichstein when he takes a curtain call with Janet. He's a fox. A real fox." I watched. I saw nothing foxy in Mr. Dietrichstein's behavior. But Mr. Walker, who watched with me, nudged me and said, "See what I mean? The way he grabs her hand and leads her forward patronizingly like— What a fox!"

However, while I never saw Mr. Dietrichstein behave like a fox, I did see him once behave like a boor. On his way to his dressing room one night after the play, he caught up with one of the girls who played the part of an amorous, hysterical pupil. "I'll thank you," he called out in a voice that everyone could hear, "not to be so realistic when you embrace me. I don't like to be mauled." The poor girl flushed with embarrassment. "I'm playing it as Mr. Belasco told me to," she replied heatedly. "I assure you it's nothing personal. I don't like it any more than you do." "Well, then, don't do it!" he retorted icily, and hurried to his room. Mr. Walker, passing me on his way out, touched me on the shoulder. "See what I mean?" he called out genially.

EUPHORIA ON EAST
BROADWAY

That renowned actor David Warfield, who unwittingly almost cost me my job at the Belasco, was rehearsing in a play called *The Return of Peter Grimm,* and the cast of *The Concert* was invited to the dress rehearsal. Mr. Warfield played the part of a crusty, well-to-do old bachelor who dies at the end of the first act and returns—in spirit—in the second and third acts in order to foil the machinations of his evil relations to do his little, sensitive orphaned nephew out of the lad's inheritance. Hoping that the subject of life after death would appeal to Hannah, I persuaded her to go with me to the dress rehearsal of *Peter Grimm.*

Hannah watched *The Return of Peter Grimm* with deep interest. Peter Grimm's little nephew looked a little like Davy, but thinner, as Davy had looked during his illness. It was evident from the start that the child was too ethereal for this world, and would die at the end of the play. His frailty and the doom that seemed to hover over him touched both Hannah and me deeply. And when at last the boy's incorporeal uncle took him by the hand and led him offstage to eternal life after death,

Hannah sobbed quietly into her handkerchief, and I knew her heart was eased. Some time later I stopped off at Hannah's on my way to Columbia early in the morning. I had had no breakfast, and Hannah went into the kitchen to make me something to eat. I heard her singing in a low voice as she put the kettle to boil. "What shall our wedding breakfast be? Hard-boiled eggs and a cup of tea." It was a refrain that the child in the play had sung in his delirium. And now Hannah had so far forgotten her pain that she could sing. I felt sure that she was returning to the realities of life from which she had for so long withdrawn herself. I bought two balcony seats for *The Concert* for her and Molly. This time I told Hannah I wanted her to hear for herself how my playing sounded in a theater. The ruse worked. Molly reported that Hannah had laughed in spite of herself at some of the more amusing episodes of the play, and that she looked pleased when the house broke into applause after I played *Warum.*

My association with the theater brought with it many benefits. I found a notice posted on the board naming several theaters on Broadway that would welcome the cast of *The Concert* on Wednesday matinees. Our own midweek matinee came on Thursday. One Wednesday, at Miss Fallon's suggestion, she and I went over to the Empire Theater. Miss Fallon, who had printed cards with her name and *The Concert* on them, showed one to the man at the box office, who thereupon gave her two complimentary tickets for the matinee. The play was *Smith,* a comedy by Somerset Maugham. The star was John Drew, and his leading lady was Mary Boland. Smith was the name of a ladies' maid played by Miss Boland. In the play, Mr. Drew, a wealthy English colonial bachelor visiting his sister in London, becomes so fed up with the heartlessness of the upper classes that he marries his sister's maid, Smith, and re-

turns to India. The climax of the play is a bridge game during
which one of the elegant society ladies receives a message that
her child has just died—obviously through maternal neglect. I
was shocked at this state of affairs in English society, and I
heartily approved Mr. Drew's choice of the pretty, simple-
hearted Cockney maid for a wife over the more socially eligible
ladies who were trying to marry him. But the play was generally
delightful. In spite of the grave shortcomings of English society
which Mr. Maugham revealed, I rather liked the witty, snob-
bish, attractive people on the stage, and I wondered if I should
ever get to England and circulate among them. I should like
that very much, I thought. In the meantime it was pleasant to
sit (without cost) in a red upholstered plush seat in the orchestra of the lovely Empire Theater and feel myself a part of New
York's acting fraternity.

Mr. Belasco's successful play *The Girl of the Golden West*
had been made into an opera by Puccini. The composer was
in town for its world premiere at the Metropolitan, and rehearsals were in progress. Mr. Belasco generously invited the
cast of *The Concert* to the dress rehearsal. For the very first
time in my years of attendance at the opera house I sat in the
orchestra. The physical grandeur of the great theater, which I
had always looked down on from above, now pressed on me
from every side. I found a seat close to the stage, so close that
I could distinguish the features of Arturo Toscanini when,
with raised stick in hand, he turned toward us to ensure absolute quiet in the auditorium. I thought he had the face of a
fiery, handsome Italian brigand. Soon after the curtain fell
on the first act, it was raised again, and there on the stage stood
Mr. Toscanini, Mr. Gatti-Casazza, Mr. Puccini and Mr. Belasco! They were talking to each other, Mr. Toscanini vehemently, the others placidly. Then Caruso and Madame Destinn

and Mr. Amato, the three principals in the cast, were summoned to the stage, and Mr. Belasco talked to them, making what appeared to be suggestions to improve their acting. They all comported themselves as naturally as if there were no one out front to look at them. I felt as if I myself were a participant in their deliberations.

The curtain was at length lowered, and ten minutes later it went up on the second act. The three principals sang magnificently, and Mr. Amato, dressed like a dandy, gave me the illusion of a cruel, handsome, sophisticated sheriff. But my proximity to the stage proved otherwise disillusioning. Miss Destinn looked fat and unromantic, and Mr. Caruso was physically less alluring than Mr. Amato, the villain, thus setting me to wonder about Miss Destinn's feelings in the matter. When Miss Destinn awkwardly maneuvered her wounded lover into the attic by way of a ladder, I suppressed an impulse to laugh. It seemed to me I would have been better off in my usual place behind the railing of the topmost gallery. For now I realized that distance was flattering to oversize or bulky singers. Indeed, it was with a certain relief that a week later I paid my twenty-five-cent bribe to the gallery ticket-taker, and took up my old position where I could look down on the diminutive figures performing *Tristan* on the stage below me.

Miss Fallon, as one of the seven lady pupils of the "master" —Mr. Dietrichstein—had nothing to do after the first act of *The Concert*. One night she remained backstage and came to my cage to hear me play *Warum*. I placed a chair near me and I played *Warum* with unusual ardor, I thought. Miss Fallon thought so too. We whiled away the time when I was not playing by watching the actors on the stage. When the play was over Miss Fallon invited me to eat Chinese food in a restaurant on Forty-fourth Street, close to the Belasco. Miss

Fallon spoke English beautifully, and referred familiarly to certain authors and their works, as she daintily stuck a tooth-pick in a chunk of pickled watermelon rind. She quoted Ben-nett, Galsworthy, Shaw, even Stevenson, whom she called familiarly "R. L. S." She talked about music. "My own piano playing," she said, "is confined to teasing the keyboard with what R. L. S. called 'a melodious forefinger.'" She would like, though, to learn to play better, she said, and wondered whether I could endure giving her a few lessons. When we were about to leave, she took two dollars from her purse and handed them to me. "Remember, I invited you," she said. For appearance' sake she wanted me to pretend to pay. We walked all the way down to West Fourth Street, where she lived. She asked me to have "dinner" at her house on Sunday and meet her husband.

On Sunday, when I rang Miss Fallon's bell, the door was opened by a Negro woman in a white apron and cap. She showed me into a parlor, where Miss Fallon was sitting on an overstuffed sofa reading a book. Beside her sat a large gray cat, and on a table nearby I saw a light-blue china cat almost as large as the real one. Miss Fallon greeted me warmly, as if she hadn't seen me for a long time, though she had stopped to talk to me after the first-act curtain the night before. "John!" she called out in the direction of the kitchen, and Mr. Mitchell came through a swinging door. He too, like the Negro maid, had on an apron, on which he wiped his hand before offering it to me. "John is a good cook," his wife explained. "What is more, he likes to cook." Mr. Mitchell was a youngish man with a pleasant face and kind eyes. He spoke with a Southern drawl, exactly like the black-faced comedians in vaudeville. He was extraor-dinarily courteous, especially to his wife; so much so that it surprised me to hear him call her Edith instead of Mrs. Mitchell. Presently he returned to the kitchen. I went to the upright piano and tried it. On the music rack stood a vocal score of *Tristan*. "Oh, I just peck away at it with my forefinger," Miss Fallon said. "Please play it." I played the Prelude and skipped over to the "Liebestod." Miss Fallon took a chair close to me. I was aware that she was looking at me intently as I played. I felt myself blushing at first, but I was soon immersed in the music. The final chord of the "Liebestod" was still reverberating softly when Mr. Mitchell came through the swinging door and announced cheerfully that dinner was ready. We went into the dining room. The table was elaborately set for three. Miss Fallon sat between her husband and me. On either side of my plate—a large one with a raised, painted flower border—were ranged a series of knives, forks and spoons, all of heavy, shining silver. Mr. Mitchell had discarded his apron and put on a jacket. The table, with its white damask cloth and a china bowl full of flowers in the center, the silver, the general elegance of the room and the fine appearance of Mr. and Mrs. Mitchell made me conscious of extreme gentility, and reminded me of my first tea party at the Masons' on Fifty-sixth Street. But this time I was not embarrassed. I watched Mrs. Mitchell carefully, and followed her example in the use of knives, forks and spoons. Mr. Mitchell's amiable politeness and Mrs. Mitchell's unconcealed pleasure in everything I said gave me a certain assurance and boldness, and I soon enjoyed that feeling of superiority toward my hosts which I felt at home toward my family. Spurred on by Mrs. Mitchell, I talked about the East Side, Jewish life and Jewish characteristics in general. Mr. Mitchell was interested and amused, and in turn told us that in the small Alabama town where he was born and brought up, there was only a single Jew, an itinerant peddler with a beard, whose kindness to the little boys (he gave them candied apples for nothing) could not quite overcome their fear of his strangeness.

Mr. Mitchell's Southern speech fell musically on the air, and to
keep him talking, I asked him about the customs, manners and
folk songs of the South. He sang a few "darky" songs he had
learned from Negroes in his childhood. One of them went, I
believe, like this:

> Sixteen yea-ahs o' courtin', sixteen yea-ahs an' mo',
> Ain't no nearah married than I was befo'.
> Sunrise! Sunset! White folks got me gwine,
> Every time the sun goes down,
> Yallah gal in mah mine.

After dinner we sat in the parlor. I noticed that every time
Miss Fallon left or came into the room, her husband jumped to
his feet, quite as if she were a stranger. Later we went for a
walk. Returning, I left the Mitchells at their house. I saw Mr.
Mitchell holding the front door open to let his wife go in first,
and as she passed him he raised his hat to her with his other
hand. It wasn't as if he wished to impress anyone, for I was by
then out of his sight, and there was no one else about. I did not
know what to make of such excessive courtesy. I could only
account for it as an importation from the South.

I came often to Fourth Street. Mr. Mitchell, though unfailingly polite, was always friendly. I wondered at that, for I had
none of the outward graces that made him appear exceptional.
I had no elegant manners—indeed, few of any kind—and I was
outspoken and passionate, and intolerant in my opinions. I
sometimes caught a look between husband and wife that made
me feel ill at ease, a look of amused tolerance following something I said or did, as, for example, when Miss Fallon poured
me out a cup of tea and said, "How many lumps?" I was
talking to Mr. Mitchell, and I replied absently, "Oh, the usual."

Looking up, I caught a smile on both their faces, and I wondered if I had said anything amiss.

Mr. Mitchell's job took him to Chicago frequently. During his absence Miss Fallon would wait for me at the theater, and I would accompany her to her house, where we stayed up late drinking tea and smoking cigarettes. Miss Fallon introduced me to cigarettes. On the East Side, women did not smoke. I thought it rather daring of Miss Fallon to smoke in restaurants, and I admired the boldness with which she would tap the back of her hand with a cigarette to pack down the tobacco. She always expected me, I suppose for the looks of it, to offer her a light, even when she was within reach of a box of matches. I soon understood that it was part of my training in manners, and I did not mind humoring her in such small politenesses. When we went walking, she managed to have me walk on the outside. I knew, of course, that she was not expecting me to protect her from a runaway horse or a reckless driver of an automobile. She merely wanted me to do the things that gentlemen did. I read Shaw's *Candida* to find out why I had reminded her of Marchbanks. Marchbanks, I discovered, was rude and outspoken and terribly vain, though a poet. If I resembled him—and Miss Fallon liked Marchbanks—why should she want to turn me into an excessively well-mannered gentleman like her husband? I realized I could do with some manners. But I would never humor her to the extent of lifting my hat to her with no one around to see.

The Mitchells lived comfortably, and even had a private telephone. But I figured they were not really wealthy, else Mr. Mitchell wouldn't always be doing the cooking and the dishes at home. The colored maid I had seen the first time I dined in Fourth Street was only a cleaning woman who appeared sporadically. Yet Miss Fallon bought herself beautiful clothes and hats, which she never paid for in cash, but charged to her "account" at the best shops on Fifth Avenue. Sometimes she did not even bother to ask the price of what she "charged," saying simply, "Send it, please." She frequently hailed cabs, and when I dined at her house, we would ride to the Belasco in an I.T.O.A. taxi, for which she would telephone. She had a charge account with the I.T.O.A. One Sunday she called an I.T.O.A. car and we drove up Riverside Drive and stopped at the Claremont Restaurant for lunch. The Claremont was a most expensive eating place overlooking the Hudson. It had a large fish tank, and customers pointed to the fish that took their fancy, which a waiter then hauled out with a net and sent to the kitchen to be cooked and served up. Miss Fallon had long since assuaged my pride in the matter of accepting her invitations to lunches and dinners by assuring me that it didn't really matter which one of us happened to have what she lightly called "the where-withal." Yet, what with her taxis, her constant shopping and the many meals we had together in restaurants, she spent more money than she could afford. One day Mr. Mitchell said to her with a pleasant smile, "Would you mind, dear, going easy in Wanamaker's for a month or two, and give me a chance to catch up?" Miss Fallon flushed and looked embarrassed and said, "Yes, of course." I could not help feeling guilty about my share in her extravagances.

The Concert ran steadily along as a solid hit all winter and into the spring. Except for Mr. Dietrichstein, who deliberately stayed aloof from his colleagues, the actors and actresses and Mr. Stuart Walker were most friendly to me. I invited some of them to dinner at my house. They made much of my mother and her cooking and admired the parlor, which, with its green-shaded lamp, green burlap window draperies, ebony grand piano and Whistler's "Mother" on the wall, seemed to me, at night especially, a vision of subdued elegance. Miss Proctor, who played the part of a spinster secretary to Mr. Dietrichstein, and her sister, who was my understudy, spent a Sunday evening with us, and expressed themselves as enchanted with my parents and our way of life, and in turn invited me to dinner at their apartment. All through the winter my understudy had nothing to do at the Belasco except sit around in my cage and watch Mr. Dietrichstein and me when we had our musical intervals. But in the early spring, just when it seemed that she was never to have the chance of playing, the opportunity suddenly presented itself for her to replace me. I had, as usual, gone for a walk on Broadway, and had stopped for a while in the lobby of the Metropolitan to look at the photographs of the singers and conductors on the wall, and to listen, at the same time, to the faint sound of the performance that in forte moments reached me. On my way back to the theater, I found fire engines drawn up at the corner of Forty-fourth Street. A cordon of policemen held the crowds back and permitted no one to enter the street. I pleaded with one of the policemen to let me through, but he was adamant. The clock on the Cadillac Hotel on the corner pointed to twenty of eleven. In five more minutes my last cue would come up. Although I had left Miss Proctor sitting in my cage, I was worried that something would go amiss. I ran back to Forty-second Street, then to Sixth Avenue, and flew through the stage door of the Belasco just in time to hear the scale in tenths that Mr. Dietrichstein pretends to play. Relieved that my understudy had picked up the cue, I glanced at the stage. The stage business required Mr. Dietrichstein to start in the lowest part of the keyboard, continue nimbly toward the treble, stop abruptly on catching sight of Miss Beecher, then leave the piano and go up to her. At the moment when he

reached the treble and, looking up, saw Miss Beecher, the most
dreadful thing happened. As Mr. Dietrichstein rose from the
piano stool and walked to the center of the stage, the scale in
tenths did not cease, but continued mounting in the treble. Miss
Proctor, out of nervousness, had taken her eyes off Mr. Dietrichstein for a moment and was not aware that he had left the
piano! There was a roar of laughter from out front. Only
then did the sound of music cease. The final curtain descended.
Terrified at what had happened, I fled. But not before I heard
Mr. Dietrichstein's howl of rage, and his agonized, "Where is
that son of a bitch? I'll . . ." The next evening I arrived earlier
at the theater, knocked timidly at Mr. Dietrichstein's dressing-
room door and went in. The star was adjusting his wig, and he
gave me a terrible look through the mirror. I told him about the
fire on Broadway, and apologized for Miss Proctor's unfortunate
failure to cease playing at the right moment. I promised not to
leave the vicinity of the Belasco during performances for the rest
of the run of the play. This mollified Mr. Dietrichstein. And
Miss Proctor never had another opportunity to substitute for
me.

At Christmas I received cards from the entire cast, including
Mr. Dietrichstein, and presents from Miss Beecher, Edith Fallon
and Miss Proctor. Miss Proctor's gift was a plaster figure of an
angel, Miss Beecher's a little book bound in leather. *Is Happiness Attainable?* was its provocative title. Impatient to know the
author's conclusion, I began the book at once. I had not read
three pages before I found that the answer was affirmative. Love
was the simple and only key to happiness—love for every
human creature. (I wondered if Miss Beecher had read the book,
and if she had, what she was going to do about her animosity
toward Mr. Dietrichstein.) Edith Fallon, however, gave me
what I most wanted—a tall ebony cabinet to hold music. It

harmonized with my ebony piano, and it had no less than sixteen separate drawers, graduated from extreme shallowness for sheet music, to a depth that would hold six fat volumes of the size of a volume of Beethoven sonatas. I spent many happy hours cataloguing and arranging my music so that I could put my hand on anything I desired. The cabinet, when I saw it displayed in Schirmer's window, was marked twenty-seven dollars, and Miss Fallon bought it during one of the periods during which she had been asked to "go easy" on her purchases. Mr. Mitchell was in Chicago at the time.

Another happy surprise awaited me on New Year's Eve. From the time they had become prosperous, the Lessers had spent New Year's Eve at a supper and dance at some Broadway hotel. This New Year's, Dr. Lesser invited me to join a party, which consisted of six dentists and their wives, at the Cadillac Hotel on Broadway, the magnificent façade of which I passed every night on my way to the Belasco. Tickets, including supper and champagne, cost seven dollars apiece, and Dr. Lesser had laid out twenty-one dollars at a stroke! Five minutes after the fall of the curtain on *The Concert,* I was fighting my way into the Cadillac Hotel, for the New Year's Eve celebrants were already massed solidly in Times Square, blowing horns, linking arms to avoid separation, screaming, laughing and shouting. There was a crush in the lobby of the Cadillac, and it was with much difficulty that I gained the restaurant door, presented my ticket and found my party. The dentists and their wives, wearing paper hats at a rakish angle, were in the middle of supper, eating turkey and cranberry sauce. Mrs. Lesser had kept a place for me next to her. I was given a paper hat, a whistle that unrolled itself like a caterpillar when I blew it, and a ratchet. A glass of champagne soon raised my spirits to the prevailing high level. I felt happy being part of the big, gay celebration. Between courses, ladies and gentlemen left their seats and sat down for a moment in the vacated chairs, greeting strangers as if they were old friends. All of a sudden a man jumped on a chair and held up his hands. The room gradually quieted down, and soon there was utter silence. Men took out their watches and waited breathlessly. Then the man standing on the chair shouted, "Happy New Year, ladies and gentlemen," a siren outside set up a wailing, everybody jumped up, screaming, "Happy New Year," men and women fell to kissing one another, and men and men warmly shook hands. Having kissed and embraced their friends and relations, people flew around the room kissing and embracing utter strangers. I shook hands with Dr. Lesser and the dentists, and kissed Mrs. Lesser and the dentists' wives. Mrs. Lesser's little face glowed feverishly, and her eyes burned, so that I thought she might be running a temperature. Her husband, too, was worried about her heightened color and offered to take her home. But she said she was feeling fine and enjoying herself, and wouldn't hear of leaving. All this time waiters were removing the tables and chairs. At the same time an orchestra appeared out of nowhere and struck up a two-step. In an instant everybody was dancing. Indeed, so many couples were crowded in the room, wheeling around with difficulty, that they looked almost stationary. Against the advice of her husband, who warned that a two-step was too strenuous for her, Mrs. Lesser insisted on dancing with me. We started off and were quickly engulfed in the maelstrom of bodies around us. The faces of all the lady dancers looked flushed, like Mrs. Lesser's. Many of the women had exotic-looking flowers pinned on their shoulders. Once I caught a whiff of a gardenia, a flower with a disturbing smell, which a flower woman sold nightly in front of the Belasco. Mrs. Lesser, too, smelled of a perfume equally disturbing. The noise, the shouting, the music, the jostling, my close-

ness to Mrs. Lesser, were all extraordinarily exciting. At one
point Mrs. Lesser raised her eyes to mine, and I saw they were
tear-stained. I asked her if she was tired, and ought we to stop?
"No, no," she whispered. But I knew by the spasmodic rise and
fall of her chest that she was crying. "I can't . . . I can't . . ." she
murmured between sobs, the words she used when she lay on
her couch in great pain. I held her very close, and I tightened my
grasp on her thin, wet fingers. I felt intoxicated and triumphant.

The next day, Mrs. Lesser had one of her severe attacks,
running a temperature and spitting blood. Dr. Lesser blamed
the New Year's Eve celebration, especially the two-step. When
I left his house late that night, he offered to walk me home. He
was full of fears about his wife, which I tried to dispel. And
he soon felt easier, and talked about his early days in America,
his meeting with his wife and his strenuous courtship. He told
me that the first thing about her that had impressed him had
been her neatness. She always looked immaculate. She was
then very poor, working twelve hours a day in a garment factory. "In those days she had only one blouse," he said with a
reflective smile that lit up his homely features. "And every night,
before going to bed, she washed it and hung it up to dry, and
in the morning she'd iron it. I never saw her when she didn't
look fresh and clean. Now I don't know what to do," he added
irrelevantly. I comforted him as best I could, reminding him,
as I always did at such moments, of the many setbacks she had
suffered, and her inevitable recovery. A few days later she was
on her feet again. And on Wednesday she expressed a desire to
go to the theater, and the doctor himself begged me to take
her to a matinee. We took a streetcar for Times Square, and
bought balcony seats for a musical play, the star of which was
the celebrated Lotta Faust. I had never seen a musical play. It
was well known that musical plays were concocted for the

amusement of the thoughtless and the rich, and I felt apologetic
to myself as we entered the theater. But the enlarged photograph
of Miss Faust in the lobby, showing her in an arresting pose,
smoking a cigarette, looked compelling. Inside, after a few
moments of doubt, I found myself succumbing to the cheerful,
blatant music, to the amusing situations on the stage and, above
all, to Miss Faust's charms and artistry. Miss Faust combined
feminine allure and sophistication. When she came out to sing
her big number, she wore a low-cut, tight-fitting short dress; a
Spanish shawl covered her left shoulder only, the right being
quite exposed, and a large sailor hat sat jauntily on one side
of her head. Simulating haughty boredom, she advanced slowly
and sinuously to the footlights and in a subdued, beautifully
husky voice began, "I'm weary of taxicabs, balls and cafés. . . ."
I forget what sentiment this prelude led up to. But as Miss Faust
wearily enumerated the particulars of high life which no longer
pleased her, she somehow created a longing in me for the very
things she was renouncing. I liked Miss Faust very much, and
so did Mrs. Lesser, and the show was exciting in a way that recalled the New Year's Eve party at the Cadillac. On the way
out I bought a copy of Miss Faust's hit number, which I played
and sang later for Dr. Lesser. From then on, and for a considerable period, I took unashamed pleasure in musical plays, and I
saw many of them with Mrs. Lesser and sometimes with Molly.
Molly enjoyed them even more than I did. Her unrestrained,
hysterical laughter was often embarrassing. One time she was
unable to stop laughing long after the comedian had left the
stage and another number was in progress. All my efforts to
quiet her down proved unsuccessful. To avoid the further anger
of the audience, I hustled Molly out of the theater in the middle
of the play, and took her home. She was very contrite and cried
in the streetcar. I thought it prudent not to take her to musical
comedies again.

In early spring, I finally realized my childhood ambition to live in a brownstone house on East Broadway. My mother had long been on the lookout for a suitable apartment on that most desirable of East Side streets. We moved into a five-room flat on the first floor of a fine-looking house on the corner of East Broadway and Montgomery Street. Each story had a single tenant. Thus we had the toilet in the hall all to ourselves. There was a bathtub in the kitchen and a grate in the parlor. The rent was thirty-five dollars per month. My father called it sheer lunacy, as in a way it was, for the new apartment was no larger than the old. However, Molly paid us ten dollars for the front bedroom, so our rent was actually only twenty-five dollars. My father, unlike my mother, had no feeling for "locale," else he would have considered our rent not excessive for the pleasure of looking out the window at the beautiful wide avenue (East Broadway was more an avenue than a street) stretching before one's pleased vision from the East River to the Bowery. Nor could he appreciate the social implications of the street. Right underneath us lived a doctor! Indeed, there was hardly a brownstone between Montgomery and Jefferson Streets that did not house a doctor and his family. At night people from all over the East Side sauntered past our house for pleasure, as the rich paraded on Fifth Avenue. Standing in front of our stoop (sitting on stoops in ordinary streets was permissible; on East Broadway it was frowned upon), I watched the passersby of an evening, and overheard scraps of arguments or conversation. Overheard is perhaps incorrect. For talk was uninhibited and loud, and one could sometimes make out the sense of a colloquy taking place half a block away. The range of topics was vast, the languages many—Russian, Rumanian, Hungarian, German, Polish, Hebrew, Yiddish and sometimes English. I heard snatches of conversation about *The Origin of Species,* Theodor Herzel, *Daniel Deronda,* the ban on the use of parallel fifths in

music, the Emperor Franz Josef, anarchism, Walt Whitman
and the Talmud. Once, on leaning out the window, I was able
to distinguish above the general din a disputation on a Biblical
matter. And scanning the block, I made out at a distance of
perhaps three hundred feet two bearded figures gesticulating
wildly. They were conclusively the disputants. Soon one of
them, apparently outraged by the absurdity or the enormity of
the other's argument, suddenly ran across the street in protest,
and finding his companion hot after him, as suddenly recrossed.
In this zigzag fashion the two came into view and proceeded
in the direction of the river. I followed them with my eyes till
they dwindled quite away.

Established now on fashionable East Broadway, I regarded
myself among the Jewish elite. For a dollar and a quarter, I had
a new plaque made advertising my father's religious calling,
which I nailed to the brick wall on the right of the entrance
over the stoop. This was balanced on the left side by the doctor's
severe plaque. My mother thought I should have my own plaque
as pianist and teacher, and also have visiting cards printed with
that information under my name. These ideas I vetoed for no
reason that I could formulate, except perhaps through modesty.
Constantly aware of my new surroundings, I experienced waves
of undefined elation, and was generally in a state of expectancy.
The apartment was a never-ending delight. I bought six teacups
and saucers at Woolworth's five-and-ten-cent store on Fourteenth Street. They had a dense blue design on the outside and
were white inside. The people I had in for tea were no longer
obliged to drink out of a glass, Russian fashion, though my
parents and their friends continued to drink their tea out of
glasses. Miss Fallon, too, when visiting us, favored a glass.
Indeed, she professed to like everything Russian. One day when
we were expecting Miss Fallon and her husband to dinner, I

could not find a clean shirt to wear. I borrowed a Russian blouse with a high collar and belt that my brother-in-law Sergei had brought with him from the old country, and so garbed, received the Mitchells. Miss Fallon was delighted with my costume, thought it extremely becoming and begged me to wear it to the theater. She hoped I would set a fashion, and American men would then discard their starched collars and begin to look romantic. Mr. Mitchell was amused, but less optimistic than his wife about its general adoption in America. Mr. Mitchell appeared always amused by what I said and did, and by his wife's romantic attitude toward me and my surroundings. Often I had the feeling that he did not take me seriously, and that his geniality and politeness toward me were merely the expression of his indulgence toward what he believed were his wife's harmless and transitory passions for alien people and strange customs. For my part, though I felt a little uneasy with a man who never for a moment let down his guard, I admired and envied his elegant, inhuman aloofness and restraint, and his general air as of a bystander in his own home, and in a situation that must have concerned him. Except for music, husband and wife had, it seemed to me, everything in common for a happy marriage. I could only account for her deepening interest in me by my music and my lack of that Anglo-Saxon polish which her husband had in such abundance. The attraction of music was, of course, the more powerful of the two, for I knew from my earliest youth that the beauty and perfection of music, great and near-great, clung to the performer like a strange perfume, and invested him with a borrowed allure. In that respect I had an unfair advantage over Mr. Mitchell—indeed, over all non-performers. For when I played the piano, I was at that moment, and for as long as the impact of the music continued after I stopped playing, an idealized being. *The Concert* at the Belasco

proved conclusively this transference of the aura of music from
itself to the performer. I proved it when I played for the
Mitchells, and I felt Mrs. Mitchell vibrating in sympathy (as
when a glass or metal object in the room responds clearly when
the piano strikes its "note") and saw Mr. Mitchell's quizzical
smile, as if he understood what was taking place, yet was un-
equipped to cope with it.

The Concert ended its run in May. Mr. Mitchell had been
transferred to Chicago a month earlier. He had taken a house
in Evanston, and expected his wife to give up their apartment
on Fourth Street and come out to him following the close of
The Concert. As the time approached for her departure, Miss
Fallon grew nervous and depressed. I, too, felt sad at the
prospect of her leaving, but I affected a melancholy when with
her or with Molly out of proportion to my true state of mind,
which was a combination of regret and relief. For Miss Fallon
had become possessive, and I saw my freedom curtailed. She
had not been able to reconcile her aim to turn me into a gentleman with her desire to have me retain or adopt the dress and
characteristics of a Russian peasant. Her efforts in both directions had become, I thought, ludicrous. In any case, when I
made sure beyond any doubt that she loved me, I became capricious, forgot to keep appointments with her and gave way to
"moods" when with her. I began to miss all the friends I had
neglected for her. Molly, who knew everything, was glad that
Miss Fallon was leaving New York for good. She was appre-
hensive that Miss Fallon's husband might otherwise, as she
picturesquely put it, "bust out of Chicago," with intent to do
me harm. I had no such fears. I could not imagine Mr. Mitchell
in any other role but that of civilized, sophisticated and rather
helpless onlooker. But Molly, who had met Mr. Mitchell on
several occasions, insisted that natures like his were like sleeping
volcanoes whose potential for eruption was incalculable.

I made no effort to keep Miss Fallon in New York. When she dismantled her apartment, she gave me as a parting gift the "Mona Lisa" which hung over the piano, whose under-standing eyes and skeptical smile I had often found disconcert-ing when Mr. Mitchell was around. I hung it opposite Whistler's "Mother." As I looked from one picture to the other, I felt there was nothing more to be learned about women. I saw Miss Fallon off at Grand Central Station. She cried a good deal, and so did I a little. When I left the station I did indeed feel bereft. I walked aimlessly on Broadway. I went into the lobbies of several theaters and looked at the enlarged pictures of "stars." It was with a shock and a sense of shame that I realized an hour later that I had not thought about Miss Fallon since her train left. That night I had dinner with the Lessers, the first time in weeks, and later I met H. L. and we walked, as we used to so fre-quently, in Jackson Street Park, and talked literature and music. A month after her departure, Miss Fallon had receded almost totally from my memory. She had written me every day at first, and I had put off writing, until too much time had elapsed. Then her letters ceased. One day, while I was out, a strange man knocked on our door and asked for me by name. My mother managed to convey to him that I was out, but was expected home for supper. I was mystified when told about this visit. The man never came back. Molly conjectured that the stranger might be a friend of Miss Fallon's, who had been asked by her to find out whether I still lived in the same place, or was, indeed, alive. For, failing to hear from me, Miss Fallon might have thought I had moved, or else something had happened to me, and her letters had never reached me. It turned out later that Molly was right.

No other year had been so prosperous for me. Yet at the beginning of summer I had not managed to save any substantial sum. I considered taking a summer job, but unfortunately

Normandie-by-the-Sea had been all but washed away during a
November hurricane. I could have found a job somewhere else.
But my mother thought that after my success in *The Concert,*
any hotel job would hurt the reputation I had gained on Broadway and among musicians. She held that *"ess passt nit."* And to
keep my reputation spotless, she was willing to forgo her by-
now accustomed vacation in New Jersey. This I wouldn't hear
of. By the first of July I would still have fifty dollars left. I
therefore made her write to the Flemington farmer and reserve her old room. For myself, I was prepared to spend the
summer on East Broadway, practicing the piano and reading
great books. My mood was optimistic, and I frequently felt a
nameless elation as I walked the streets reading the latest copy
of *Musical America* or *The Musical Courier.* These absorbing
trade journals told me all I wished to know about the lives and
activities of the famous and the nonfamous musicians of that
period. I read about debuts in Paris, Vienna, London and Berlin.
The pictures of persons I had never heard of appeared on the
front and back covers of both magazines. On the inside pages
there were innumerable advertisements of artists unknown to
me, but apparently of great importance in the musical world.
Accompanying their names in bold type were snatches of critical
approval from newspapers: "Marvelous!" (*Boston Globe*),
"Magnificent!" (*Glens Falls Courier*), "Unequaled!" (*Rome,
Georgia, Express*). Dates for these artists were always booking,
but their number was designated as limited, and local managers
were advised to lose no time in writing before it was too late.
I was particularly fascinated by articles from the magazines'
foreign correspondents, for Europe was still the continent of
music and musicians. Thus it was that I read about the debut
of a young Russian violinist, Efrem Zimbalist, who was said by
critics to be the equal of Mischa Elman. Both Elman and

Zimbalist were products of the St. Petersburg Conservatory, and pupils of Professor Leopold Auer. For the last two years I had followed young Mr. Zimbalist's career in the musical journals. And in a recent issue of *The Musical Courier* there was an announcement that the Russian violinist would in the fall and winter tour the United States under the management of the Wolfsohn Bureau. Mr. Zimbalist would, I assumed, bring his accompanist with him, as Mischa Elman had done. To be a solo performer was any pianist's ultimate ambition. Yet accompanying a great violinist on the piano offered a satisfaction of its own. I had envied Mr. Percy Kahn, who played the piano for Mischa Elman with an artistry worthy of the great violinist, especially in sonatas of Mozart, Beethoven and Brahms, the difficulties of which were equally taxing for both players. I could appreciate the happiness Mr. Kahn felt when he shared the applause with Mr. Elman, like an equal; and I already envied the pianist Mr. Zimbalist would bring along with him from Europe.

I lived in a state of euphoria that was almost tangible. I walked happily along the streets reading the musical papers or, on Saturdays, the literary section of the *New York Evening Post*. The latter was my favorite newspaper because I admired the intimate, urbane essays and literary criticisms of Simeon Strunsky. I also liked its music critic, Henry T. Finck. It is true that Mr. Finck was overenthusiastic about certain non-Wagnerian prima donnas and many non-Wagnerian operas, and he wrote much and irrelevantly about gardening and cooking (silly preoccupations for a music critic, I thought). But I dismissed these aberrations as inconsequential in the face of his admiration for, and championship of, the music of Wagner. "If," he wrote in a memorable review of a performance of *Tristan,* which I cut out of the paper and treasured for years, "if everything ever composed disappeared, and only a score of *Tristan* remained, the whole history of music could be easily reconstructed from that stupendous music drama," or words to that effect, for I no longer possess the clipping. If I had nothing with me to read, I composed entire music dramas of my own as I walked, to German texts and for an orchestra resembling Wagner's. The stories of these operas were epic but vague. The only detail I can recall now is the unvarying fate of my heroines, which was a sacrificial death, for the eventual spiritual benefit of the hero. Sometimes, as I improvised, I was so carried away by the pathos or grandeur of my declamation that passersby stopped and gazed at me in astonishment. But by the time I got to a piano, my inspiration was gone, and the leitmotifs and recitatives that had seemed original and beautiful in the open air now sounded derivative and commonplace. Yet the next time I went walking, I felt again surging within me *true* inspiration, and before I knew it I was composing still another music drama.

It seemed to me that I was on the brink of a world of new sensations, of physical and spiritual discoveries that would further enrich my already full existence. And, indeed, hardly a day went by that did not present me with some adventure. On the streets I encountered strange and beautiful faces that gave me a sudden start, and impelled me to walk after them for a while, so eager was I to grasp at accidental embodiments of feelings and ideas that I might perhaps be allowed to share. Past me went—I knew by their looks—musicians, painters, sculptors, poets, who would, I was certain, be as grateful for my understanding and appreciation of their art as I would be grateful to be near them. I was too timid to approach them, and I had to content myself with staring at their faces and figures and imagining their inner life.

One Sunday, in the cool of the early morning, I took my

volume of Shelley and walked to Jackson Street Park. I sat down
on a bench to read *Prometheus Unbound,* a poem which baffled
my understanding. Except for some isolated stanzas whose
beauty was clear and immediate, I could not, though I bent my
mind and sympathies to it, grasp the "meaning" of the greater
part of the poem. Perplexed and disturbed at my obtuseness, I
tried to find the meaning of some obdurate lines by declaiming
them, when I became aware of a man sitting near me. The man,
pointing to the book in my hand, said, "That is Shelley's greatest
poem." I looked at him in wonder. He was a large, handsome
youth with black hair and classic features. I was overjoyed
at this delightful, unexpected adventure, and I was also sharply
aware that instant of the unlimited possibilities residing in mere
existence. Here I was sitting on a park bench quite unaware
that a kindred spirit had sat down by me. The man knew many
lines of *Prometheus Unbound* and recited them in a theatrical
manner, and with a foreign accent I could not immediately
identify. He soon enlightened me by telling me that he was a
Greek, born in Athens. My astonishment and delight were now
indeed great. I was actually close to a Greek who looked like the
Greeks of the marble statues in the Metropolitan Museum and
the plaster casts in the art classes of the Educational Alliance.
Perhaps his ancestors had fought at Thermopylae and had sat,
enchanted, at Socrates' feet! I asked him if he had read Homer
in the original, and he said, "Yes, of course, how else?" and I
blushed for my obtuseness. He was pleased to hear that I was
a musician and a student of world literature. An hour passed
like a moment, and we had barely touched on the books we both
had read and admired. He was himself, it transpired, a playwright and a poet. For the time being he earned his living washing dishes in a Greek restaurant on Madison Street, close to the
Bowery. He was at the moment in the middle of a drama on

the subject of the trial and conviction of Socrates. He lived nearby on Montgomery Street, and would be happy to show me the first act of his play.

We repaired to his hall room on the top floor of a tenement. It was a shabby, dark, small room. I made out a rusted folding bed, unmade, a table with some books and papers, a single chair and a one-burner gas stove resting on an overturned grocery box. A fitting place for a poet, I thought. He warmed up some coffee. As I sipped mine, he read me passages from his play. It was in Greek and I understood nothing. But it fell nobly on the ear, like Hebrew. I told him it sounded like music. It was getting late and I rose to go. Suddenly all color left his face, he stared fixedly at me, then without warning he flung his arms around me and held me as in a vise. Frightened and dismayed, I shook him off. Then, avoiding my gaze as I avoided his, without a word he opened the door for me and I ran down the stairs. I had reached the first floor when I heard someone behind me. It was my Greek. Still avoiding looking at me, he handed me my volume of Shelley, which I had forgotten to take. "Your *Prometheus*," he murmured, and ran up the stairs. The accent on the penultimate syllable brought back the circumstance of my strange encounter on the park bench only an hour ago, and restored a perspective that had all but been obliterated. After all, he *was* an authentic Greek, and he read Homer in the original! I felt sorry for him. But I felt even more sorry for myself for having to forgo the friendship of a man whose ancestor could have been the poet Agathon in Plato's *Symposium*.

WHILE WAITING FOR
A LETTER

One of my pupils, Dora Feller, worked as a stenographer in the office of a musical agency on Thirty-fourth Street. Among the artists managed by her firm was Horatio Connell, a concert baritone. One day Dora showed up for a lesson bearing extraordinary news. That morning Mr. Connell had called at his agent's on matters of business, and had, as usual, stopped to chat with Dora. "You wouldn't happen to know a fine pianist who could act as accompanist to Efrem Zimbalist on his American tour?" Mr. Connell asked Dora, as he took an opened letter from his pocket. Dora said her own piano teacher would be the very man. Mr. Connell, turning over the pages of his letter, paused. "Mary writes," he said, "Mary Fels, you know, of Fels-Naphtha Soap; she lives in London and seems to be a great friend of Zimbalist—Mary says here the man for Zimbalist must not only be a fine pianist, he must also have the best moral character." Mr. Connell smiled. "Has your piano teacher the best moral character, Dora?" Dora assured Mr. Connell that I was both a fine pianist and a virtuous man. Mr. Connell then read more of the letter, for

Dora's further information and his own amusement. Mrs.
Fels wrote that her friend and protégé, Zimbalist, was an in-
experienced and impressionable artist, and that she thought it
of the utmost importance that his pianist in America should
have moral and ethical qualifications. If her friend, Horatio
Connell, could put her in touch with such a person, she would
feel easier about the American tour, etc. Mr. Connell gave
Dora Mrs. Fels's letter to show me. If I was interested, I might
communicate with Mrs. Fels directly, stating both my musical
and my moral qualifications.

I was too agitated by this turn of events to give Dora her
lesson. Instead, we composed a letter to Mrs. Fels together. I
realized that this letter was likely to be a turning point in my
life. Its composition called for the most painstaking care, if
it was to impress Mrs. Fels and Mr. Zimbalist. So eminent a
virtuoso (Mr. Zimbalist's continuing triumphs in Berlin and
London were features of the latest issues of the musical magazines) required, and no doubt expected, his accompanist to
be a pianist of experience, something which I certainly was not.
Yet I felt that my musicality, my knowledge of the repertory
of the violin—I knew several violin concertos and a few of the
violin-and-piano sonatas of Beethoven and Mozart—and my
flair for reading at sight might be, in a way, the equivalent of
actual experience. At any rate, it was imperative to assume a
boldness I did not possess. Without actually prevaricating, I
succeeded, with Dora's astute help, in giving the impression
that I was a most capable pianist, with considerable experience
in accompanying. After all, I reflected aloud to Dora, if this
statement were ever challenged, I could point to my experience
in Kiamesha Lake with Sol Rashkin, and in Normandie-by-the-
Sea with Geraldine Morgan, and to my concerts with Leo
Schulz. While a trip to Scranton did not constitute a tour, any

move out of New York might, in a sense, be called touring. As for my moral character, since no man could be an unbiased judge of his own, I referred Mrs. Fels to my old friend Mr. Connell. "My old friend" was Dora's suggestion. When I pointed out that I had never met him, she assured me that Mr. Connell would not mind in the least my claiming friendship. She would see to that. We both agreed that I must not mention my age. I was not yet twenty-one, and Mrs. Fels might consider me too young to exercise that moral influence on her protégé which she expected of Mr. Zimbalist's American companion.

As for Mrs. Fels, her name was even more celebrated than that of Zimbalist. I recalled that only a few years previously, Fels-Naphtha soap had been launched on the world with large advertisements in the papers and magazines, and samples had been lavishly distributed without cost to residents of the East Side, and, presumably, of the West Side as well. At this very moment there was a cake of Fels-Naphtha in our own kitchen. It seemed incredible that I was writing to the owner of this universally popular and famous product. Fels-Naphtha was, indeed, a household word. And when I showed my mother Mrs. Fels's letter to Mr. Connell and read out the signature, my mother involuntarily added, "Nepteh!"

Mrs. Fels lived in Regent's Park, London. As I addressed the envelope, the misty London I had known for a brief time as a child of six rose up before me. I saw again the Tilbury Docks where a ship had deposited our family, twelve strong, and I remembered the desperation of my father and mother when they learned that we had been set down not in New York, our proper destination, for which we had paid, but in London. A year later we succeeded in reaching New York. But London had left a lasting impression on me. I had only to shut my

eyes to see before me Black Lion Yard in Whitechapel, where
we had lived, London Bridge, the Tower and the boats sail-
ing up and down the Thames. Since that time I had come to
know another London, a London of my imagination and the
novels of Dickens and Thackeray, Henry James and George
Gissing. It seemed to me that I knew the London streets even
better than those of New York. If I should ever get there, I
should easily know my way about. How often had I dreamed
of my being set down again—but now as a man steeped in the
literature and history of England—on Tilbury Docks, and
starting out on foot to "verify" the places I had known, read
about or only imagined. My first stop would be, of course,
Black Lion Yard. There I would stand on the curb and look
up at the windows from which as a child I had looked down
on the teeming street. Perhaps, as in Heine's (and Schubert's)
"Doppelgänger," I would see the image of myself at the window, wringing its hands in despair. Then I would leave Whitechapel and make for the Strand. In the Inner Temple I would
easily spot the house in which Charles and Mary Lamb once
lived and gave those supper parties (which Crabb Robinson
in his diaries so glowingly describes), where the fare was so
frugal and the talk so rich. The benches in the court must
surely still be there, and I would perhaps see the ghost of Mr.
Salt, described by Lamb in one of the essays, sitting on one.
And now I was most incredibly writing to a Fels who resided
in Regent's Park, London. For all I knew, Mr. Zimbalist would,
on the completion of his American tour, engage me to play
for him permanently, and take me back to London with him.

The letter to Mrs. Fels in Regent's Park was posted and I
awaited a reply. For the next two weeks I steeled myself to
glance once a day only, perfunctorily, at the three little holes
in our mailbox in the vestibule downstairs. I figured out that

it could not possibly take less than a fortnight for my letter to arrive and a reply to reach New York. When the two weeks were over I began to worry. I slept badly, rose early and watched for the mailman from our parlor window. A month passed slowly, and no reply came. I acquired several new superstitions and practiced them rigidly, hoping that they would somehow facilitate the arrival of the letter. They were of no avail. I then decided to take an altogether different tack. I would pretend that nothing had happened, that Mrs. Fels had not written to Mr. Connell, that Mr. Connell had never spoken to Dora about Mr. Zimbalist, and Dora had not spoken about me to Mr. Connell. Perhaps *that* would spur the Fates to beneficial action. For a week I pretended that nothing had happened; yet no letter from London arrived. Finally, as a last resort, I assumed an attitude that had several times in the past been successful in making things which I had ardently desired come to pass. I adopted a completely pessimistic outlook. I told myself that the situation looked hopeless. Mrs. Fels had not been impressed by my letter. She had easily seen through my pretensions to experience, and decided that a reply, even a negative one, was unnecessary. In any case, it would be folly on her part to take my word as to my fitness to be accompanist and companion to a rising musical star. I had been foolish to hope for a favorable outcome. It just wasn't in the cards. These things I repeated to myself constantly, while I waited and hoped for a miracle to happen.

It was now the middle of summer. What little money I had would see my family through July and August on the New Jersey farm. I required about fifty dollars for myself until the "miracle" happened, or failing that, until the return of my pupils in the fall. I could ask Dr. Lesser for another loan on his children's future lessons. But I had not yet paid off the thirty dollars I had borrowed from him during Davy's illness. Besides, should the negotiations with Mrs. Fels come to nothing (and they *must* come to nothing, I doggedly iterated, like an incantation), I would be obliged again to ask him to advance another year's tuition fee for Columbia. I suddenly remembered Mrs. Meltzer, whose husband made textiles and was very rich. Mrs. Meltzer was away for the summer at a hotel in Sea Bright. I wrote to her, asking for an advance of fifty dollars against my coaching lessons the following winter. In a few days I received a letter from Mr. Meltzer, couched in business language, and enclosing a receipt for fifty dollars which I was to sign and mail back to him. I did. And some days later he sent me a check for the amount. The legal austerity of the transaction puzzled and agitated me. I began to fear that Mr. Meltzer, for all his wealth, might demand payment of the debt at an inopportune time, haul me into court, obtain a judgment against me and demand my turning over to him whatever "assets" I possessed. My piano was, happily, safe. He could not take it from me because it would not be mine for many years. But he could take Whistler's "Mother" and the "Mona Lisa" in lieu of money! I breathed easier when it occurred to me that I could hide the pictures at Molly's or Hannah's.

I now no longer took lessons from Mr. Reeve. Aside from the heavy expense involved, I was confident that henceforth I could be safely on my own. For I had learned from him, and by experimenting, how to overcome the major technical difficulties of the classic piano repertoire. I had an ingratiating tone (everybody said that) and my curiosity about orchestral, operatic and vocal music had shown me the piano in its proper, limited perspective. The medium of expression, whether piano, violin, orchestra or voice, made, I discovered, little dif-

ference. From my extensive knowledge of music as a whole,
I deduced a norm of musical taste, a kind of unwritten moral
code. I could not formulate this code, but I knew when its
tenets were violated in performance. Shakespeare suggested
such a code for actors in his "Speak the speech, I pray you"
passage. But even Shakespeare (like myself) would be hard
put to defend his artistic credo. He could warn the actor not
"to tear a passion to tatters," but he could not tell him why
it was wrong to do so. On the concert stage and in the opera
house, singers and instrumentalists were constantly tearing
a passion to tatters and pleasing not only the "groundlings"
but the critics as well. Yet when I was asked why I thought
it wrong for Mr. Caruso to hold on to top notes, or for some
celebrated pianist to slow up and linger too fondly over a
lyric phrase, I could only maintain that it was "unmusical." At
Katz's there were tremendous discussions about "taste." Mr.
Katz himself contended that "taste" was strictly a personal
matter, that one man's "taste" was another's poison. I held
that there was an absolute "taste" which underlay the creation of the best music, and should guide the interpreter. H. L.
sided with me. H. L. applied the severest canons of "taste" to
the most celebrated artists (notwithstanding that his own playing was in the most woeful taste). Someone else remarked
that the acceptance and application of absolute taste would
rob interpretive artists of their individuality. I was glad that
the subject had been brought up; for it gave me the opening I
needed to insinuate, however obliquely, what I believed to be
the difference between taste and the cavalier, irrational treatment of music that went by the name of individuality. In the
heat of the argument I was inspired to illustrate this difference
with an example from the art of acting which was so con-
clusive as to all but silence my opponents. I went to the piano

and played the opening theme of a Chopin nocturne with the distortions of phrasing, rhythm and tempo it had undergone at the hands of a popular pianist in a recent recital. "Do you consider this in good taste?" I asked, and Mr. Katz said, "Why not, if that is the way the pianist felt it?" "Very well," I went on. "Imagine that I am a celebrated actor playing Hamlet. Suppose I deliver the Soliloquy like this: 'To*be*or *not*to *be*that isthequest ion.'" I had struck home. There was an uneasy silence. Finally Mr. Katz said lamely, "I don't see how you can compare the two. Words are *supposed* to make sense." "And music isn't?" I interrupted. "You think that Chopin played in this manner makes sense?" I had scored my point. Yet the following week, at a recital of my favorite pianist, I began to have qualms about my intransigence in the matter of taste. For the virtuoso took many liberties with Chopin that I ought to have deplored but didn't, because they seemed as natural and spontaneous as if Chopin had written them.

Such misgivings I kept to myself. But I re-examined my ideas on interpretation and concluded they were by and large valid, except in the case of exceptional performers like my favorite, whose powers of musical persuasion were so commanding as to transcend any theory. It was permissible for a Shakespeare to flout grammar and write, "the most unkindest cut of all." The poet was looking for the ultimate in emphasis, and he found it. But that single instance did not nullify the rules of grammar.

At any rate, my preoccupation with music as a whole, and my eagerness to discover a universal principle of musical interpretation, made some of the hours of that expectant summer pass quickly. I even set about arranging my day in such a way as to keep me constantly occupied, leaving me not too much time for daydreaming and speculation. It was a hot summer, and bedbugs were unusually rife. Forced to abandon my couch, I tried sleeping on the floor. But the floor was no better; and after a few sleepless nights I sought the safety of my grand piano, on which I spread a blanket, both for comfort and to avoid scratching the beautiful, shiny surface of the lid. My new bed, while not too comfortable, proved safe enough. I rose early, made my breakfast, ran down to the letter box (my heart beating loudly), tidied up the house and practiced the piano till noon. My nerves could be calmed by two kinds of music only—technical studies and the compositions of Beethoven's final period. For the first I went back to Clementi's *Gradus,* and for the second I concentrated on Beethoven's last sonata and the Variations on a Theme of Diabelli. I lost myself completely in both. Clementi offered innumerable problems to be solved, what fingering to take, rigidity or relaxation of wrists and arms, etc. They shut out for the moment all extraneous thoughts. The music of Beethoven provided an altogether different refuge and easement. While it did not banish my hopes, it reconciled me to whatever Fate might have in store for me. The Arietta of the final sonata, following without pause the agitation and turmoil of the first movement, instantly elevated my perceptions and emotions to a plane from which all earthly aspirations lost their urgency— indeed, their reason to exist. And when, at the end, I played, with what ethereal lightness my fingers could manage, the healing cascade of the scale in thirds, my heart was full to overflowing with a physical sensation of spiritual fulfillment. At that blissful moment I could contemplate with genuine indifference the London reply waiting for me in the letter box downstairs. The Diabelli Variations had an even deeper effect on me. For, unlike the sonata, where the transformation was quick, like the flip of a medal, or a sudden shift as from darkness to light, the Variations led me by imperceptible stages from jaunty reality to deep, mystical contentment. While I played the Variations and for some time after, I knew no desire, no craving that the music itself did not satisfy.

One day, on Forty-second Street, I came face to face with Edith Fallon, whom I had not seen in six months. She seemed very glad to see me, and made no mention of my failure to answer her letters. I was surprised at myself for feeling no shame for the way I had treated her. She was on her way to the Adirondacks for a month's vacation, and was taking a sleeper that very night. We went into Huyler's to talk, over an ice cream soda. Edith looked extremely attractive in her light summer clothes. I told her so, and her face grew red, and she asked what I was doing in town in the heat. She became nervous and ill at ease when I said I was spending the summer alone in New York, waiting for an important letter from London. I talked about myself and my wonderful prospect of accompanying the new great Russian violinist Zimbalist. Then I went on to my present deep involvement in the music of Beethoven, the quality of which I tried to put into words. Edith listened as intently and eagerly as she used to in the old days. Once I caught a familiar look in her eyes, and I knew for certain that her feeling for me had not changed. The look was so unequivocal that it instantly brought to my mind the scene in Meredith's *The Egoist* (which I had recently finished) in which Sir Willoughby looks into the eyes of Laetitia Dale and sees himself unmistakably there. "Do you *have* to leave tonight?" I asked her; and again a literary allusion came to mind: Mélisande's casual "Why do you go?" to Pelléas at their very first meeting. For the moment I forgot about Edith, and I lost myself in an appreciation of Meredith's genius in exposing in a single sentence the very nerve of self-

love. I was brought back by Edith's telling me that she didn't
have to leave that night, that she would stay in New York, if
I wished.

So Edith spent her month's vacation in New York. She
wrote her husband that she had decided to forgo the Adirondacks for the chance of getting a suitable part in one of the
many theatrical productions that were being cast in New
York. Edith did, in fact, look around for a play. She had found
Evanston dull, and would prefer even going on the road in
one-night stands to living in suburban idleness. I did not let
her presence interfere with my morning and afternoon oc-
cupation with music and books. She moved into a small hotel
on Eleventh Street, off Fifth Avenue. In the evenings I called
for her there, and we dined at Enrico and Paglieri's, an Italian
restaurant on West Eleventh Street. Enrico and Paglieri
served a full-course dinner with wine for fifty cents. The tables
were lit by candles and the restaurant had an atmosphere of
solvent Bohemianism. A fifty-cent dinner was not exactly
cheap. On the East Side, where I lived, one could dine just as
fillingly on twenty cents. It was at Edith's insistence that we
dined so luxuriously nightly; it was she who paid. I was, at
the moment, in no position to spend a dollar (not including
the tip) a day on a single meal. As for Edith, she could well
afford our evening meals. Her stay in the Adirondacks would
have cost her twice as much as a month in New York.

We lingered over our coffee at Enrico and Paglieri's,
smoking Turkish cigarettes which Edith bought by the hundred at Benson and Hedges' expensive tobacco shop on Fifth
Avenue, luxuriating in our sense of well-being and feeling
pleasantly conspiratorial. Edith was genuinely in love. I knew
this more by her self-conscious manner, her exclusive attention
to me at all times, alone or in company, her instant reaction

to everything I said, serious or nonsensical, her reluctance to
part with me, her absurd warnings when I left her that I must
be careful at street crossings and watch out for automobiles,
her incessant sad, rather hesitating nightly query, "What time
tomorrow?"—than by her own frequent admission. I always
had my way in everything, and because of that, and a sensation of freedom and lightheartedness I felt when I walked back
home alone at night, I reasoned that it was not love that I
had for Edith but a combination of agreeable feelings that did
not include one of dependency. I liked to be with her, she was
so pretty and well-dressed, and people looked at her, especially
on East Broadway, where a smart, elegant Christian lady was
rarely seen. I felt a kind of pride of ownership, like that of
a turfman for his prize-winning horse. But when she was not
with me I forgot her, and she never entered into my thoughts
and speculations. Sometimes, on leaving her, I walked to the
Royale Café on Second Avenue, and dropped in to have an
iced coffee. For ten cents and a nickel tip I could sit for hours
(the place never closed) and hear the gypsy fiddler Ferenc
Miklos play—with a sumptuous tone that a great artist might
envy, and a passion and abandon that he, Miklos, alone possessed—slow gypsy airs and crazily rapid czardases. Miklos also
played most creditably, at my special request, some concert
numbers that Mischa Elman had made popular in his recitals.
(I wondered why Miklos did not seek engagements on the
concert stage.) At midnight the place would fill up with the
actors and actresses from the Yiddish theater. But I no longer
gazed at them with rapture, as I used to only a few years before,
in Lorber's restaurant on Grand Street. At two or three in the
morning I would leave the Royale and walk down Second
Avenue to Houston Street, veer left to Clinton Street, and then
up to East Broadway. Impervious to the fetid, hot smells of the
sidewalks, I walked as if on clouds, my heart full of vague

ecstasies, my mind busy with ever-changing plans for the creation of operas, tragedies, poems, essays. At home, notwithstanding the lateness of the hour, I would light the gas lamp with the green china shade, and seek and find prolongation of my mental and emotional excitement in the lofty phrases of Sir Thomas Browne's *Urn Burial,* much of which I did not quite comprehend, but all of which "sounded," like some grand and generous stretch of orchestration. A single, haunting phrase like "that sad society," describing the dead, was sufficient to keep me wakeful for a long time. In the prose of Oscar Wilde and Walter Pater I found the essential elements of harmony and balance. Pater, especially, approximated the formal beauty of eighteenth-century music. I read with delight how painstakingly he manipulated words, as if they were colors of infinite gradations which had to be delicately matched. This deliberate piecing together of words excited me to emulation. I took the long, beautifully balanced, contrived opening sentence of his *The Child in the House* as my model. What in literature—except perhaps a passage from Sir Thomas Browne—could so nearly approximate the calm, pure symmetry of the opening of an adagio or andante movement in a Mozart symphony!

I pondered on the mystery of great writing, in which words were cannily selected and magically placed together to serve both the ear and the mind. Was it possible to acquire "style," that semblance of uniqueness which made each noted writer and poet identifiable? I sought out what writers had to tell about their craft. I read the essays of Leigh Hunt, Hazlitt, Stevenson, Pater. Each of them seemed to possess a special formula for style. In the light of my new knowledge I reread many great books, and these now gave me the desire to be a stylist on my own. I began essays, stories, a novel and a sonnet series; but after writing a page or two, both my inspiration and my vitality tended to ebb. What seemed original and fine-sounding one day appeared derivative and inflated the next. Yet my depressions and self-doubts were transitory, and I always returned to my writing with hope and enthusiasm.

In musical composition my efforts were rather sketchy. The themes and melodies and orchestral passages I sang to myself as I walked the streets seemed both imitative and ordinary when I played them later on the piano. And after a time I definitely abandoned musical creation, though it was a long time before I lost the habit of singing to myself, and imagining plots for operas and themes for symphonies and symphonic poems. I consoled myself for this with the thought that the great composers had left nothing more to be said in music. The later works of Beethoven were assuming terrifyingly limitless implications for me. Man could hardly probe further into the human soul, or do more to coax it into giving up its identity and merging with the forever inscrutable forces of creation. Literature, on the other hand, still seemed to me an open field. Often I felt such things, and was possessed by such intimations as I had never read of in books. Even Shakespeare had not exhausted human thoughts and emotions. He was concerned with the relation of man to man, not with man's relation to the Unknowable. Hamlet's delicate apprehensions of the world around him, wonderful as they were, left a part of me untouched, that part which Beethoven penetrated with the slow movement of the Ninth Symphony, the Arietta of the last piano sonata and the opening of the C Sharp Minor Quartet. In literature I might still have something to say, if only I could acquire a way to say it, a style. I wanted a style as deliberate and balanced as Pater's and as sensuous as Wilde's. Perhaps the combination of both would serve a nature like mine best.

MR. ZIMBALIST ARRIVES

It was the end of August, and I could no longer postpone making a realistic appraisal of my situation. Notwithstanding my regular observance of some new superstitions and my pretense of indifference to the outcome of my hopes for an engagement with Mr. Zimbalist, nothing had happened! Yet the month had passed in a fairly agreeable fashion. Thanks to Edith Fallon I had eaten regularly once a day. Now Edith had signed to go on tour with *The Concert*. Mr. Roeder had offered me my old job in the play and, urged on by Edith, I was inclined to accept it. I must have had some lingering hope of something better turning up for me than six or eight months of one-night stands, for I finally decided to remain in New York, continue my studies at Columbia and try to obtain new pupils. Edith left to spend a few weeks in Evanston with her husband before going on the road. I was alone once more, except for my brother-in-law Sergei, whom I saw occasionally at night and on Saturdays and Sundays. I practiced and read with greater intensity than ever. I began to understand why my father spent most of his time studying and restudying his holy books. It left less time for worrying about oneself.

One morning I glimpsed, through the little holes in the letterbox, a blue envelope. No letter in a blue envelope had ever arrived before. Not daring to lose time by running upstairs for the letterbox key, I attempted frantically to extract the envelope with my fingers. I succeeded only in pushing the letter farther down into the box. It was only after many unsuccessful tries that I ran to fetch the key. I opened the box and took out the mutilated letter. There on the blue envelope was a stamp with the head of George the Fifth. The London letter had come after I had given up all hope! My superstitions had worked! But my trials were not over. Was the letter good or bad? Perhaps the fateful moment called for one last desperate superstition, one final flattering sop to Fate, one last pretense of indifference. I shoved the unopened letter into my pants pocket and walked slowly and deliberately upstairs. My face burning and my hands trembling I set about making my breakfast. I ate without haste. I then washed and dried the dishes and put them away. I told myself that nothing remarkable had happened—the receipt of a letter only. The letter would have to wait until I had finished my usual morning's practicing. There were several technical matters in the Diabelli Variations which I must that very morning clean up. At twelve sharp I would shut the lid of the piano and attend to ordinary matters, such as opening the morning mail. I relied on Beethoven to absorb my mind and senses till noon. And, indeed, there were moments during that interminable stretch of time when the music possessed me exclusively. Yet some variations on which I strongly counted to make me forget the letter in my pocket failed, for the first time since I had begun working on them, to hold me fully. At last, when I had practiced so long that I thought it must be one o'clock at least, I opened the window and saw on the R. Hoe clock that it was only half-past eleven. I went back to the piano. Again I practiced a long time, and when I again looked at the clock it was time to open the letter. I saw at a glance that the letter was favorable. Right at the start Mrs. Fels, after a few words of excuse about the long delay in replying, said I seemed just the right companion for Mr. Zimbalist. The violinist would arrive in New York the last week in September and would hear me play. Mrs. Fels was hopeful—indeed, she was almost certain (she had such faith in her friend Mr. Connell's musical judgment) —that Mr. Zimbalist would like my playing. She had written the Wolfsohn Musical Bureau about me. She regretted that she would be unable to make the trip with Mr. Zimbalist. But she hoped to be in New York for the first Carnegie Hall recital. She was certain that she and I would become friends.

I read the letter many times, trying to find hidden meanings and implications in certain words and phrases. But the most optimistic interpretations could not erase the fact that I had still to satisfy Mr. Zimbalist. Until I had played for him and been accepted, it was folly for me to abandon myself to the joy that began to attack me like an ague. Yet it was impossible for me to keep the news a secret. I had to share it with someone, even if the project eventually fell through. I went over to Katz's, pledged him to secrecy and read him the letter. Mr. Katz was outright jubilant. He pooh-poohed my misgivings and said it was his considered opinion that I could hold my own with any accompanist. He did, however, advise me to make the most of the time before Mr. Zimbalist's arrival by looking through the violin repertoire. "Bone up on everything he is likely to play," Mr. Katz said earnestly, "even concertos with orchestra!" And he offered to let me take home and keep for as long as I wished any and all violin music in his store. When I left, I took with me a large bundle containing the concertos of Bach, Beethoven, Mozart, Brahms, Tschaikovsky, Mendelssohn, Bruch, Paganini, Vieuxtemps and Goldmark, the sonatas for violin and piano of Mozart, Beethoven, Brahms and Handel, and some smaller compositions favored by violinists. That night I wrote to Hannah and Molly, pledging *them* to secrecy. And Sergei, whom I also confided in, sent off a letter in Yiddish to my mother in Flemington, telling her the great news, and imploring her not to say a word about it to anyone but my father. I had little hope that my mother would keep such important tidings to herself. But since Flemington was far away and the other boarders on the farm were strangers to me, I saw no harm in her giving out hints about my rosy future. She always did, anyway, even when my future looked anything but rosy, so absolute was her faith in my talent and luck.

I set to work on the music Mr. Katz had so generously loaned me. And now the days flew. My family returned from Flemington on the first of September. My mother set about scouring the house as if to make ready for some imminent public celebration. Once, when the Flayshigs were spending the night, I had occasion to pass through the dining room, and I caught my mother telling Mrs. Flayshig that Mr. Zimbalist, with whom I had been engaged to travel all over America, was the greatest living violinist. And on Mrs. Flayshig's inquiring, in an awestricken voice, "Greater than Mischa Elman?" my mother laughed stridently and said categorically, *"Avadeh!"* (absolutely). My father was more reserved. Yet, from the respectful attitude some of his friends from the synagogue displayed toward me when they came to our house on a Saturday noon to partake of schnapps and herring, I suspected that he, too, had been unable to keep the secret. In fact, presently everybody seemed to know it—our friends and relatives, the people in the grocery and butcher shop, even the piano teacher Montana and the singer Burgo Ginsburgo, both of whom congratulated me when I met them in Katz's store.

One day my father unexpectedly asked me if it would be possible for him to hear Mischa Elman play. In shul that morning there had been a debate on the relative merits of Mischa Elman and Zimbalist. The unanimous opinion was that, while no one had yet heard Mr. Zimbalist in America, Mischa Elman was supreme and could triumphantly meet any challenger. My father said he prudently took no part in the discussion. But in view of what was about to happen to me and, obliquely, to my family, he thought he should hear Mischa Elman, so as to be in a position to make a comparison when *he* (my father delicately refrained from calling Mr. Zimbalist by name) arrived. I saw the justice of this, and I took my father down to a music store in Delancey Street which also dealt in phonograph records. Pretending that I might buy some records, I had the proprietor play two of Mischa Elman's. My father listened gravely. On the way home, he said he liked Mischa Elman's playing very much. "And how he works! What labor!" he added admiringly. "Does Mr. Zimbalist work as hard?" he asked. I said I hoped to tell him soon enough.

The day for which I had waited and longed actually arrived. I was summoned by a letter from the Wolfsohn Musical Bureau to play for Mr. Zimbalist on a certain morning at the apartment of a Mr. Rosenbaum on West 106th Street. My mother started at once to examine my meager wardrobe. My father hastily left the house. Though his face showed no emotion, I suspected he was impatient to spread the news in shul. After a close inspection of my pants, my mother announced it would be folly to appear before Mr. Zimbalist in my worn and frayed suit. "The suit shines like a looking glass," she said. "*He* will be able to see his face in it." She saw no alternative to the purchase of a new suit. I said I had no money, and I could no longer impose on the good nature of the Lessers. "I'll send your father to Beylinson for a loan. And, Semele, don't buy in Canal Street. Buy uptown in a fancy store." I agreed that the time had arrived for me to abandon the pay-in-installments clothing establishments of the East Side. I knew the very store for my new needs. Through its enormous plate-glass window in Herald Square I had seen many elegant "garments," as they were labeled. They were guaranteed to have been made from the finest "suitings." On my mother's assurance that Beylinson had never yet failed us, I went immediately to Herald Square and selected a very heavy light-blue suit (with vest) for twenty-five dollars. It fitted snugly, even a little too much so, especially when I tried sitting down, and the fitter offered to "let it out" where it was tight. But alterations might take days and I had no time to lose. I had them send the suit at once to me, C.O.D. That afternoon my father paid a visit to Mr. Beylinson at his ice cream factory and acquainted him with my dazzling prospects. Mr. Beylinson merely inquired how much I needed, opened the safe in his office, took out six five-dollar bills and handed them to my father without another word.

On the appointed day, dressed in my warm and tight-fitting new suit, I took the Broadway subway, got off at 103rd Street and walked to 106th Street. Mr. Rosenbaum's apartment was on the ninth floor of an immense corner building. A man in uniform stood at the entrance, and another man in uniform took me up in an elevator. Both men were rather standoffish and unfriendly with me, as if they had doubts that I was expected by either Mr. Zimbalist or the Rosenbaums. Yet when I got off at the ninth floor, the elevator man's behavior underwent a change. For he politely walked with me to the door of the Rosenbaum apartment and waited until a maid appeared, who said I was expected and led me in. I was shown into a huge room, from the windows of which I could see the Palisades on the other side of the Hudson. Oil paintings hung on the walls, which were covered with some rich stuff. I was very nervous, and I kept putting my perspiring hands into my trousers pockets. On a piano I saw a violin case and some music—Mr. Zimbalist's violin and his music, most certainly. Mr. Zimbalist had brought out the compositions he had in mind to test me on. But what were they? Beethoven sonatas, the Mendelssohn concerto? I was about to go to the piano and look into them and refresh my memory, when Mr. Zimbalist came into the room. He looked exactly like his pictures—very youthful, very Slavic, broad nose, high cheekbones, dark hair. He appeared completely at his ease, like a man twice his age, as he pressed my hand warmly with both his hands, and said with the thickest of Russian accents, "Excuse me, please, I did not mean to keep you vaiting. Sit down, please. I am so happy to see you. Vhat a *vahnder*ful country you live in! You have everything here. But you are not comfor*table* in this chair. Let me bring you another one," and he went across the room and brought back an overstuffed chair for me. I was overwhelmed by this reception. I had not expected a world-famous virtuoso to be so thoughtful, so kind to anybody, let alone an absolute stranger. He seemed not to think of himself at all, only of me! "No, no, it is no trahble." He waved me away when I rose to help him with the chair. "I love America already. And what pretty vooman! I walk the streets yesterday and see so many pretty vooman!" He talked without stopping, to put me at my ease, I felt, and I was grateful. "Perhaps you vould like some coffee? I tink it vould be nice to have a little coffee." He pressed a button, the maid came in, and he said to her with the same pleasant earnestness, "Excuse me, please, vould you be so kind, if it is not too much trahble, to bring perhaps some coffee." His manner with the servant was almost apologetic. I was enchanted. There were, then, great artists who were *not* temperamental, who considered other people's feelings. "You must excuse my English," he said, smiling appealingly. "I must learn to speak better. But tell me about yourself and your family." His solicitude touched me. He looked at me so earnestly and sympathetically that my diffidence and nervousness melted away. I began to tell him about my life and upbringing. He interrupted me several times. "How many brothers? Three? How very nice! Sisters? Six! No! *Vahnder*ful." I could not remember anyone who on first meeting me took so much interest in my family. I told him about Hannah and Molly and the close ties we had together. His blue eyes reflected so much sympathy and understanding that I was moved to speak openly about Hannah's loss and her frailty, her struggle with poverty, her generosity. "Oh, you will love her, I know, she is so noble," I said, overcome by emotion and the deep interest the great artist before me took in our life. Only once did Mr. Zimbalist's attention appear to wander. I was telling him about Molly and Sergei, and how the latter toiled from early morning till far into the evening for twelve dollars a week. Mr. Zimbalist surprised me by exclaiming, "*Vahnder*ful," with feeling. When I thought about it later, it seemed clear that he had misunderstood about Sergei's wages.

When the coffee things were removed, Mr. Zimbalist asked me if I knew *Scheherazade* of Rimski-Korsakov. I said I didn't. He went into his bedroom and came back with an orchestral

score of the music. He then went to the piano and began playing it. I stood near him. He read the score easily, and he played
with great facility and a beautiful tone. I was overawed and
considerably intimidated by this exhibition of musicianship
and pianism. As he played, he pointed out to me the beauty of
the themes and Rimski-Korsakov's orchestration. I asked him
if he had composed anything, and he said he'd published some
dances and a suite in the old style for violin and piano. These
he played for me on the piano. They were quite difficult. Mr.
Zimbalist was, obviously, a genius. I began to despair that my
small capabilities could ever please him. And when he suddenly said, "Shall we play a leetle?" quite as if I had a choice
in the matter, my nervousness returned in full force, though I
tried to make light of it by reminding myself that I knew very
well almost any music (except his own) he might put in front
of me. He rose and picked out a composition from the bundle
of music on the piano, then placed it on the music rack. Then,
as I sat down on the piano stool, he opened his violin case, I
sounded the A and he began tuning up. I stared at the cover
of the music in front of me. It said "A. Glazunov," and underneath, "Concerto for Violin in A Minor." I had never seen
this music! I was even unware that A. Glazunov had written
a violin concerto. All my work on the violin repertoire had
gone for nothing. I was now required to read at sight what
looked like a difficult piano part. I confessed my ignorance of
the concerto. Mr. Zimbalist sensed my unhappiness and hastened to distract me with pleasant talk. He told me he was
making his New York debut with the Philharmonic with the
Glazunov. There had been a great deal of opposition to his
choice of the concerto at the Wolfsohn Bureau. Mr. Adams,
the Bureau's proprietor, had urged him to play something safe,
like the Tschaikovsky concerto, but Zimbalist had been ada-

mant, scorning an easy triumph. Notwithstanding my agitation, I could not help a feeling of pride at being made a
confidant of a great artist's difficulties with the powerful
Wolfsohn Bureau. "Shall we try the Glazunov?" he wound
up. "Please don't worry. I know it's very difficult." I asked for
a few moments to look through the music. Mr. Zimbalist
beamed. "Of course, of course." I glanced hastily at the pages of
the concerto, trying to fathom its structure and the harmonic
scheme, while my host, fiddle in hand, walked to the farthest
window to look at the Palisades. When I had scanned the last
page, I struck my right leg toward the right leg of the piano
and touched the caster with my toe (a superstition which thus
far had never failed me). Then I called out that I was ready.
In my hasty appraisal of the form of the concerto, several things
had become clear to me—the unusual length of the opening
theme, its appearance in double-quick time in the first tutti,
the role of the accompaniment as a fast-flowing arabesque to
the slow, stately second theme. I saw that the Glazunov,
though played without pause, and containing minor devia-
tions in the sonata form—the cadenza serving as a bridge between the second and third movements—was, fundamentally,
a three-movement concerto in the classic style.

Mr. Zimbalist put the violin under his chin, beat out a preliminary measure with his bow to indicate his tempo, and
emphasized four in a bar by singing, "Puh, puh, puh . . . puh,
puh, puh . . . puh, puh, puh . . . puh, puh, puh. At the last
quarter beat, he began to play. The depth, luster and purity of
his tone, heard at such close proximity, was so startling that I
instantly realized I must not savor these things but give all my
attention to the hazards of the concerto, or disaster would
ensue. (Later, in recalling that moment, I saw a certain similarity between my situation and that of Ulysses when, to with-

stand the blandishments of the Sirens, he had himself lashed to the mast of his ship.) I placed all my musical faculties on the alert. Almost at once I felt myself dominated by a musical personality, a musical *individualist* who bent the music to his pleasure. The music was Mr. Zimbalist's vehicle, and he was complete master over it. The Glazunov sounded as if the violinist had written it for himself, and it couldn't possibly suit any other violinist. He played it with the utmost freedom, but the kind of freedom that had been decided on long in advance. I tried to anticipate what he would do. I disregarded passages in my haste to keep abreast of him. The most difficult moments for me were the slow, lyric parts of the concerto, for Mr. Zimbalist had an uncanny control of his bow, which he drew across a string slowly, endlessly, without a tremor, until he reached the frog, at which point there came no rasp of string against wood, but all sounded smooth as silk, and the bow began its slow, deliberate downward journey. At those perilous moments it was difficult for me to breathe. Several times during a long-drawn-out, seemingly endless note, I must have appeared confused, for Mr. Zimbalist beat time for me by nodding his head violently. I listened to the beautiful cadenza with only half an ear, which heard and wondered at the ease of the double-stopping, the impeccable intonation, the technical mastery, while the other half anticipated the complexities of the Rondo which was soon to follow. We finished together, and my ordeal was at an end. I felt I had done very well under the circumstances, and I was pleased, though not surprised, when Mr. Zimbalist said, "*Vahnder*ful; are you sure you never saw the concerto before?" Then and there he engaged me for the tour. And as he shook my hand, he said that the Wolfsohn Bureau would attend to the "arrangements." I was hardly prepared for so hasty a decision. I could not speak for joy, and I

wanted to cry. In a single morning my troubled world had
changed into something new and rare. I looked with tear-
dimmed eyes at the great virtuoso, only three months older
than I but many times my age as an artist and as a man of the
world. This blue-eyed, slender, Jewish youth with the Slavic
face, lifted by his art above me, as above everyone else, would
henceforth be my musical idol and, perhaps, my friend. If, because of his eminence, I could never have with him the intimate
relationship I had with H. L., I would still be forever grateful
for the privilege of even restricted intimacy. I could never
attain his stature as an artist. But I could be his musical disciple.
I could try to emulate his unusual qualities as a man, his
benevolent sophistication, his social ease, his charm and his
exquisite manners.

We played more; and now I found myself in safer waters. Mr.
Zimbalist's first Carnegie Hall recital program contained pieces
I knew well, or had studied in preparation for this very audition. It had also, however, a new and tricky suite by an Englishman named Edwin York Bowen. This suite, and some other
compositions that were new to me, I was given to take home
and practice. There still remained a fortnight before the
recital. We would begin rehearsing on Monday in the Prince
George Hotel on East Twenty-eighth Street, where the Wolfsohn Bureau had engaged a suite for him. (He explained that
his present hosts, the Rosenbaums, were friends of Mrs. Fels,
who had kindly put him up until his suite at the hotel could be
got ready.)

When we finished playing, Mr. Zimbalist graciously invited me to lunch. He had, he told me, on his walk the preceding day, come upon a "*vahnder*ful" restaurant, all white tile
on the inside, which looked inviting. It was quite a distance
downtown, on Fifty-ninth Street (he had made a note of the

street). We walked down Broadway to Fifty-ninth Street. Mr. Zimbalist stopped frequently to gaze at store windows, especially of haberdasheries. In the window of one there was a display of silk shirts in beautiful, lurid colors. Zimbalist was much taken with them, and we went into the shop and he purchased three shirts in pink, blue and mauve at the considerable price of five dollars apiece. He was very communicative as we walked. He appeared to be interested in everything, and his knowledge of the countries of the world and their national characteristics astonished me. Sheer size aroused his enthusiasm. He quoted population figures in a dramatic tone that always made me say with admiring incredulity, "You don't say so!" He would stop short and fix me with his blue eyes. "Now, vhat do you tink is the popoolation of Japan?" I shook my head. "No, really! Vhat do you tink? Make a guess." I had no idea. But he looked so eager for me to underestimate the population of Japan so that he might overwhelm me with some enormous figure that I hazarded, "Twenty million." He gave me an enchanting smile. "Twenty millions? My dear friend, Japan has a *hundreds* millions!" I expressed disbelief and he looked delighted. I was very happy that I could so easily afford him pleasure. By first asking me a question which I was unable to answer, he imparted to me on that walk many items of curious information which seemed most vital at the moment, though on reflection, later, I couldn't quite see their connection with art. "Do you realize, Mr. Chotzinoff, that the Ukraine grows more vheat than the rest of the world—even America! Do you know how many bushels of vheat the Ukraine sends out? Vell, how much do you tink? A hundred tousand bushels? Two hundred tousands? Say what you tink." I said two hundred thousand. "*Tree* millions!" he burst out triumphantly, and waited for the look of wonder on my face which he expected, and got. When he had exhausted the products of the earth, he turned to the stars. "You have read Flammarion?" he inquired, and I was happy that I hadn't, for he would have been disappointed if I had. "You must read Flammarion. You have no idea vhat a marvelous and strange world is in the sky, how many millions—vhat do I say, millions!—*trillions . . . hundreds* of trillions stars and planets!"

I marveled at the vastness and complexity of the planetary system. But I was more interested in my artist companion, his origins and upbringing, and I politely and rather craftily (I thought) steered him into revelations about himself. I learned that his father was a band leader in Rostov-on-Don, Zimbalist's birthplace. At the age of twelve, Elfrem had been sent to the St. Petersburg Conservatory to study with Professor Leopold Auer. Mischa Elman was a fellow pupil (I was awed at the very thought of a class which could boast of two such towering musical figures). At this point Zimbalist related how Professor Auer had taken him and Elman to lunch at the palace of a grand duke, and how young Elman had drunk the water in the fingerbowl in the mistaken belief that it was cold soup. I could honestly laugh at this story, for I had been initiated into the mystery of fingerbowls by Edith Fallon once at the Claremont Restaurant. As Mr. Zimbalist described Professor Auer, the great pedagogue reminded me of Mr. Sam Franko. It seemed that Professor Auer had a terrible temper and was feared by all his pupils. "The first time I played for him he was very nice. He gave me the music of a new concerto to learn. When I came to the class the next week, I was a little afraid, because I had not practiced much. I put the music on the stand and played the first movement. When I finished, the Professor, without a word, lifted the stand and the music, opened the door and threw both out in the cor-

ridor. Then he took me by the collar and threw *me* out too!"
I gasped at the Professor's temerity in manhandling one of the
greatest violinists (indeed, since that very morning I considered
Zimbalist *the* greatest violinist) in the world. But Zimbalist
laughed at the recollection. "Believe me, after that I took care
to practice." "Was Auer a great teacher?" I asked, and Zimbalist replied gravely, "Yes. A very great teacher."

I was fascinated by such talk, and I kept asking pertinent and
provocative questions. I was astonished to hear that the twelve-
year-old Zimbalist had occupied one of the first chairs in the
Marinsky Theater orchestra, and that he used to play in string
quartets at the house of Rimski-Korsakov. Not only had Zimbalist been an intimate of Rimski-Korsakov, but he knew all
the celebrated musicians of Europe. He made his debut at the
age of seventeen in the Tschaikovsky concerto, with the Berlin
Philharmonic under Arthur Nikisch. The audience clamored
for an encore, and Zimbalist played a movement of a Bach
partita. "Vhen I returned to the artists' room, Nikisch took my
violin and played a few bars of vhat I had just played, but so
scratchy and heavy and out of tune that I was puzzled. Nikisch
gave me back my violin and said, laughing, '*So hat Joachim
gekrazt*' (Joachim scraped like that)." "What?" I exclaimed.
"The great Joachim *scratched?*" Zimbalist explained that
Joachim must have been pretty old when Nikisch heard him.
"But you know, vhen a great artist gets older and does not
play vell any more, people are afraid to say so, and they keep
on telling themselves and everybody else, 'Isn't he *vahnder*ful!
Isn't he marvelous!' It's like the songs of Schubert. Schubert
composed many beautiful songs. But he composed some not
so good. But people are afraid to say so. So if Schubert writes
a song called 'Der Tisch' everybody says, 'isn't "Der Tisch"
*vahnder*ful,' though the words of 'Der Tisch' are ordinary and

the music is ordinary too." I was relieved to hear this. I had never dared to admit to myself that the great composers (and the great writers and poets too) could be vulnerable. I thought of Beethoven's universally admired Mass in D, which I never dared confess I did not like. In the light of what I had just heard, I was emboldened to confess my dislike of Beethoven's Mass. Zimbalist, unfortunately having never heard the composition, was unable to confirm me in my adverse opinion. But in the course of our conversation about composers, he dismissed the music of Debussy as just "French eau de cologne," a verdict which shocked and pained me, but which I had not the courage to oppose. Besides, a musician of genius like Zimbalist might be right! It was quite possible that I had all along been in error about *Pelléas*.

Presently we came to Fifty-ninth Street. Mr. Zimbalist led me unerringly to Childs Restaurant, and pointed to it with pride. We stood in front of it quite awhile, watching through the plate-glass window the frying of griddle cakes. Mr. Zimbalist became absorbed in this operation. We finally entered and sat down at a long table. Mr. Zimbalist called my attention to the splendor of the place and the white tiling on the walls. Nowhere else, he told me, had he encountered a restaurant so sumptuous. He asked me to guess the number of tiles that went to cover the walls. I now felt myself an adept at this game, and I glibly understated the number, whereupon he said he would not be surprised to learn that the tiles ran into the "tousands." Once again I was charmed by his manners. He ordered his lunch with many apologies to the waitress: "Would it be too much trahble to . . . ? Tank you *so* much. . . . So *sorry*. . . . I vahnder if I could trahble you for a spoon," etc. The waitress beamed. I made a mental note of his behavior with a view to imitating it—not, of course, in his presence, but when I should find myself in other company.

After lunch we walked to the Wolfsohn Bureau offices on Thirty-fourth Street. I was introduced to Mr. Adams, the proprietor, who led me into his room and gave me a date book in which were entered all of Mr. Zimbalist's engagements for the tour. I was to be paid thirty dollars per recital. The engagements were about evenly divided between orchestral dates and recitals. Mr. Adams leafed through the date book and figured out that I would earn approximately sixty dollars a week. This was almost double what Mr. Belasco had paid me. But Mr. Adams pointed out that I would have to pay my living expenses on the road. At the moment I wouldn't have cared if I had to pay my railroad fares as well, I was so overcome by the great change in my situation. Here I was, an obscure East Side youth, hobnobbing with the president of the powerful Wolfsohn Musical Bureau and making arrangements to be the accompanist and companion of one of the world's great violinists—indeed, the greatest! The burden of my happiness was too much for me to bear alone. I parted from Mr. Zimbalist and Mr. Adams (they had business to discuss). Too agitated to wait for the elevator, I ran down the ten flights of stairs. An I.T.O.A. cab stood at the curb. I felt in my pocket. I had sixty-five cents, enough for the ride downtown. I felt no remorse at my extravagance. I jumped into the cab and gave the driver Dr. Lesser's address. My first impulse had been to drive home, but I realized that once I had broken the great news to my family, I would long for the unbiased adulation of my friends. Now I sat on the end of the cab seat and gave myself up to thoughts of the astonishment and delight I would read in Mrs. Lesser's face. At the same time my eyes followed anxiously the changing numbers on the cab meter. I had miscalculated the cost of the ride. Long before we stopped at the Lesser house, the meter registered sixty-five cents. But I was not alarmed. I would borrow a quarter at the Lessers'. With the prospect of averaging sixty dollars a week until the following April, I felt I need have no qualms about borrowing small, or even large, sums. I asked the driver to wait, and I ran up the flight of stairs to Dr. Lesser's office. Without any explanation, I asked the doctor, who was treating a patient, whether he happened to have a quarter on him. He gave me a quarter and I ran downstairs and paid off the driver. As I did so, I looked up at the doctor's apartment. The doctor and his wife were watching me from their parlor window. To their knowledge I had never before taken a taxi by myself.

MY MOTHER RIDES
ON THE SABBATH

On Monday I visited Zimbalist at the Prince George. He had a small suite, but a cozy one. An upright piano had been placed in the hall that separated the bedroom and parlor. Zimbalist was unpacking. I asked if I might help, and I was made happy by his saying, "*Vould* you be so kind?" As we unpacked the wardrobe trunk, he remarked that he and I were the same height, and asked me to try on his full-dress coat. The coat fitted me perfectly. Then he asked me simply, as if it were the most ordinary thing in the world, if I "vould be so kind" as to accept a full-dress and an afternoon outfit, as a gift, explaining that he had taken the precaution of ordering duplicates of his evening and afternoon clothes. He also presented me with a pair of patent-leather pumps, which were just my size, a pair of suspenders and two pairs of heavy silk socks. I wondered how he knew I was in need of the things he gave me. I had thought it best not to tell him that I had only that morning arranged tentatively for the rental, on a monthly basis, of a full-dress and a cutaway for evening and afternoon concerts. I could think of no reason for refusing those lavish gifts. And when Zimbalist said my acceptance would make him happy, I could not find the proper words to let him know how much I appreciated his tact in such a delicate matter.

The telephone rang frequently and Zimbalist answered it in a way that left no doubt of his pleasure at speaking to whoever was on the line. Once, when he stepped out of the room for a moment, I answered the ring. "Do you know a Mr. Davis?" I called out to Zimbalist. "He wants to speak to you." "No, I don't," Zimbalist said as I handed him the receiver. But he greeted Mr. Davis so cordially that I thought he must have suddenly remembered that he did know Mr. Davis very well indeed. All the same, it seemed to me not consonant with the dignity of a great artist to be available to any stranger on the telephone. I also felt a bit jealous. His accessibility somehow minimized my own standing with him. I wanted to be in the position of intermediary between him and the outside world. I was sure that's what Mrs. Fels had in mind.

The telephone and the doorbell rang constantly. Bellboys delivered letters, telegrams and packages. I boldly signed Zimbalist's name (with his permission, and a smiling "If it's not too much trahble") to receipts, and tore off the wrappings of bundles. I conveyed the contents of the trunk and valises to closets and bureaus. Never had I touched so many shirts, ties and handkerchiefs. The socks alone ran into the dozens. One small leather box was filled to the brim with cuff links, studs and vest buttons in gold and other metals, some ornamented with pearls, undoubtedly real. Yet Zimbalist betrayed no pride of ownership. Nor did he lock up any of his treasures, whose number and quality I made a mental note of, to retail at home and at Katz's.

Visitors appeared. A heavily pockmarked man—he was the very same Davis who had telephoned—came to offer his services as personal representative, claiming that only a man so experienced in artists' relations with the press and public as himself could keep Mr. Zimbalist from becoming a prey to managerial greed and newspaper misrepresentation. The man was noisily passionate and superficially convincing. His insincerity and charlatanism were transparent even to me. To my dismay, the violinist appeared impressed, for when the man begged for a trial engagement, Zimbalist took him on.

Mr. Davis had hardly left when another visitor was announced. This was the famous editor of the *Jewish Daily Forward,* Abraham Cahan. Mr. Cahan was one of the notables of the East Side. I had often seen him enter the *Forward* offices, but I had never spoken to him. He came to interview Mr. Zimbalist for his paper. My pleasure at finally being presented to the great editor was dampened by Zimbalist's failure to mention my name. I was simply introduced as "my accompanist." However, I soon forgot this curious lapse in Mr. Zimbalist's generally impeccable social behavior in the discussion of political and literary values that ensued. At first Zimbalist gave Mr. Cahan a résumé of his life, revealing details which were new to me. Both Mr. Cahan and I were charmed with his vivid description of the part he had played in the 1905 revolution. Filled with revolutionary ardor, he had addressed a meeting of fellow students at the St. Petersburg Conservatory. For this he was promptly expelled from the Conservatory. Months later, through the influence and interposition of Professor Auer and a musical grand duke, he was forgiven and readmitted.

Mr. Cahan inquired into Zimbalist's literary tastes. He expressed pleasure when Zimbalist told him Dostoevski was his favorite author, for he too admired Dostoevski above all other writers. They went into detail about Dostoevski's greatness. Hearing this, I summoned the courage to speak up, at first hesitatingly, then with gathering assurance. My favorite among

Russian authors was Turgenev, who had not even been men-
tioned. Only Tolstoi had been considered as a possible rival to
Dostoevski. Both editor and violinist categorically agreed that
The Brothers Karamazov was the deepest and loftiest expression of the Russian soul. When I pleaded for Turgenev my
opponents were greatly surprised at my boldness and temerity.
They listened attentively, for I was able to quote incidents and
name personages not only from Turgenev's novels but from
Tolstoi *and* Dostoevski as well. Nevertheless, I was voted down.
Yet I saw I had impressed both men with my detailed knowledge of Russian writers. And when Mr. Cahan rose to go and
shook my hand, I was gratified when he said, "I didn't catch
your name . . . ?"

At lunchtime Zimbalist invited me to a "little place" he
had discovered on his walks in the neighborhood, where, he
said, one sat on a high stool and ate from the counter. "Little
places," I soon learned, held the fascination for him that big
places had for me. This little place was unusually small and intimate, rather airless and quite cheap. When we returned to the
hotel, we found many people waiting to see Zimbalist—photog-
raphers, parents with children carrying violin cases, and a
delegation from a Jewish charity organization come to ask
Zimbalist to play a benefit concert. I felt very important as I
interviewed them first, while Zimbalist retired to his bedroom.
Already, I reflected, I was beginning to measure up to Mrs.
Fels's specifications.

From that day on, I lived only to serve Zimbalist. I spent all
day at the Prince George. We ate our meals at "little places,"
took walks and called at the Wolfsohn Bureau. Some nights
Efrem (we were now on a first-name basis) had dinner engagements. I remained in the hotel, sent out his clothes to be
pressed, arranged for his laundry, or practiced the piano. I was

made happy when he offered me the couch in the living room whenever it grew too late to go home. In the morning I enjoyed the luxury of ordering up breakfast. Only one thing marred my happiness. Efrem showed no inclination to practice the violin or rehearse with me. His debut with the Philharmonic was drawing near. Yet he had not, to my knowledge, taken his violin again from its case since the day I first met him (except at his American debut with the Boston Symphony). I spent the night before his Philharmonic rehearsal at the Prince George. He was due at Carnegie Hall at ten in the morning. I was up very early and expected that he, too, would be up betimes to have breakfast, dress and practice an hour or so. I listened at his door frequently until nine o'clock. Then, alarmed that he would be late for rehearsal, I woke him up. He appeared to be quite unconcerned at the lateness of the hour, and I could see no trace of nervousness. He took his bath (he took a bath every morning!), dressed leisurely, and we left the hotel, I proudly carrying his violin (he said, "Please don't bother," but I said it would be a pleasure, which it was). Not a note had he played, and I wondered at his confidence. I felt very privileged as we entered a Carnegie Hall darkened except for the stage, where the orchestra was rehearsing under its new conductor, Josef Stransky. Very calmly Efrem opened his violin case, tuned his violin and walked out into the corridor. Soon I heard bits of the Glazunov. In a few minutes he returned to the hall. Mr. Stransky had stopped conducting and was peering into the auditorium, looking for the soloist. Efrem walked composedly onto the stage, shook hands with the conductor with extraordinary affability, while the orchestra greeted him with handclapping and the beating of bows on stands. I sat down near the stage where I could watch him at the closest range. Never had I seen any artist so cool. At a nod from him, Mr. Stransky started the

Glazunov, and almost at once Efrem's pure, deep, silky tone
began to float over the tawny triplets of the horns. He played
with complete absorption, as if he were quite alone in the hall,
with no one looking at him. His bow gave out not the slightest
sound of friction as it sailed on the strings. The fingers of his
left hand moved effortlessly up and down, even into the highest
reaches of the E string, in every gradation of pace, in the most
hazardous passages, now spreading out into complicated chords
or barely touching the strings as his bow released fluty sounds
that had no apparent connection with the strings at all, like
lovely, incorporeal soap bubbles that detach themselves from
a pipe and float away. Frequently the orchestra broke the spell
by rushing ahead of Efrem, lagging behind him or losing its
place. At those times Mr. Stransky was apologetic, and Efrem,
unperturbed, beamed at him and asked if it would be too much
trouble to go back to—and he pointed with his bow to a place
in the open score on the conductor's stand. Mr. Stransky encountered many perilous moments in the concerto; and at the
end I had to admit to myself that the orchestral accompaniment
had been on a lower plane than I had expected it to be. But
Efrem seemed quite pleased as he shook hands with the concert-
master, bowed to the orchestra and thanked Mr. Stransky pro-
fusely. I did not dare voice my opinion as we walked back to
the hotel. But when we stopped at a self-service "little place"
for lunch, I asked Efrem what he thought of the new conductor.
He gave me a knowing look, but did not reply.

At home, at the Lessers', at the Kovners', at Katz's, I was
bombarded with questions about the personality and habits of
the new Russian violinist. I was not only happy to enlighten my
questioners; I myself reveled in the marvels I related, enlarged
on the details and most likely permitted myself a good deal of
latitude in the stories I told. I contrasted Zimbalist's elegance

with his simplicity, citing the "little places" which he patron-
ized, when he could well afford to have all his meals in the
dining room of the Prince George Hotel. His fabulous manners,
his ease with strangers, his kindness and generosity (I was not
ashamed to tell about the evening and afternoon outfits he had
given me—indeed, I was soon adding imaginary supplementary
gifts of shirts, collars and ties), his naïveté, the childish pleasure
he took in confounding me with astronomical figures relating
to Russian exports, the world population and the starry heavens
—these were my constant subjects. My friends were as eager to
hear about Zimbalist as I was to talk about him. Mrs. Kovner
alone among them sometimes asked a question that had a touch
of flippancy, such as, "Does he eat the same kind of eggs that
we eat?" My mother was impatient to entertain Efrem. I told
her I intended to wait for the arrival of Mr. and Mrs. Fels. We
would then give a grand dinner for the violinist and his rich
patrons.

I spent all of Thursday, the day of Zimbalist's New York
debut with the Philharmonic, at the Prince George. I expected
Efrem would want to run through the Glazunov with me. But
the day passed like any other. We had visitors, went out to lunch
in a little place and took a long walk. Later, he played on the
piano the beginning of a cello concerto he was composing. No
one could have guessed that day that he was a violinist at all, let
alone one who was that evening to make an important debut. It
was only after he put on his full dress that he took out his violin,
examined the strings, rubbed them down with a silk handkerchief, and played a few scales and some of the more difficult
passages of the concerto. Not the slightest trace of nervousness
could I read on his face or in his movements. My own nervousness was extreme, and I repeatedly looked at the clock and
urged him to hurry. He reminded me that Mr. Stransky had

first to play a symphony, and that there was therefore no need to rush. When we arrived in Carnegie Hall, Mr. Stransky was in the middle of Beethoven's Eighth Symphony. Efrem leisurely took out his violin and tuned it from the sounds of the orchestra. Once again he played a few passages at random. When the time arrived for him to go out on the stage, I left him and ran into the hall, where I joined the standees in the rear. I felt agitated and exalted when I saw him come out on the stage and bow to the great applause that greeted him. I was fervently conscious of my own extraordinary position—the friend and confidant of a great artist. I looked at the unsuspecting people standing near me. How surprised they would be to learn that I had spent the entire day with the magnetic, poised youth on the stage, that he had let me carry his beautiful Stradivarius from the hotel to the hall, and that in all probability I was the only person in the vast audience whose presence he was conscious of at that moment. How piquant, that to these people I was just another standee! Yet it was possible that they could read in my face some connection between me and the artist on the stage. I tried to look self-conscious. I could not keep my mind on the performance for any length of time. I kept looking around me, or peering out at the people in the hall and in the boxes. I spotted several well-known musicians—Walter Damrosch of the New York Symphony, Arturo Toscanini of the Metropolitan, the young soprano Alma Gluck and the famous opera star Emmy Destinn. I was not surprised to find Miss Destinn at the concert, for in an interview in a morning paper Mr. Zimbalist had stated that Miss Destinn (whom he had never met) was his favorite soprano, and that her voice had the quality of a Stradivarius violin. Whereupon Miss Destinn, out of gratitude, had sent him two dozen red roses with long stems.

When Efrem reached the cadenza I forced myself to give

my complete attention to it. It was so difficult that I was certain the success of the debut depended greatly on it. It came off even more beautifully than I had expected. When it was over and the orchestra swung brassily into the final Rondo, while the audience, relieved of tension, relaxed noisily, as it generally does after cadenzas, I bent my ears to the standees near me to catch their comments. They were, to my great joy, enthusiastic. The end of the concerto was greeted with tumultuous applause. I ran backstage and stood in the wing, as Efrem went out again and again to bow. Once, when he returned, he handed me his violin. Several times he grasped Mr. Stransky's hand with both of his, led him to the front of the stage, and bowed to him and then to the audience. I knew I was witnessing a triumph. And when Efrem and Mr. Stransky finally went up to the artists' room, people began pouring in in such numbers as hardly to leave room for the two performers. Mr. Katz pushed his way in and also, to my displeasure, Sol Rashkin, whom I had not seen since we played together in Kiamesha Lake. Mr. Katz pronounced Zimbalist a noble virtuoso and asked to be introduced to him. This I did, and Efrem greeted him as warmly as if he had unexpectedly come upon a long-lost friend. Mr. Katz was touched to tears by this reception, and I whispered in his ear, "He is not only a great artist but a wonderful man." Mr. Katz then offered to take me to Childs for some wheat cakes and coffee. I thanked him and told him I would probably have to have supper with Zimbalist. "Much better, much better," Mr. Katz exclaimed as he left the green room. I remained near Efrem, who was greeting enthusiastic strangers with overwhelming, though impartial, warmth. A thin, tall, aristocratic man introduced himself to Efrem and they conversed for some time. I caught his name—Rawlins Cottenet—and remembered seeing it listed in the Metropolitan Opera House programs as a member of the board of directors. Notables milled about or stood in line waiting to greet Efrem. I heard magic names—Franz Kneisel, Alexander Lambert (the celebrated pianist and teacher) and Frederick Steinway. Efrem did not introduce me to any of them, though I stood at his elbow. I knew I would get to know them in time. At the moment I felt intoxicated by Efrem's success, and I smiled warmly at the people he greeted, as if he and I were jointly responsible for the excellence of the debut.

At last the crowd thinned out and we were ready to leave. Efrem and Mr. Stransky again felicitated each other and said good-bye. I took the violin case, and we left by the stage door. There a number of young people stood waiting for a last glimpse of the great violinist. They applauded as we got into a cab and Efrem, beaming, bowed to right and left. On the way to the Prince George, Efrem asked me what I knew about some of the celebrities who had introduced themselves to him in the green room, and I told him what facts I knew and what gossip I remembered. We went up to Efrem's apartment. I was waiting for him to invite me to have supper with him in the beautiful, dark-paneled dining room downstairs. But when he had changed his shirt and collar, he said calmly that he had accepted Mr. Cottenet's invitation to have supper at Sherry's. The keenness of my disappointment must have been reflected in my face, for Efrem added that he would not stay away long. He suggested that I go down to the dining room, have supper and sign his name to the bill. He would try to join me for coffee. We then went downstairs. He got into a cab and I went into the paneled dining room. It was late, and I was the only one there. I ordered a Spanish omelet (for its exotic name) and a glass of beer. I lingered over my supper, and watched the door for

Efrem. At one o'clock I called for the check, boldly signed "Efrem Zimbalist," left a dime for a tip and went upstairs. It was two-thirty when Efrem returned. He seemed very elated. He said Mr. Cottenet was a charming and cultured man. He had been invited to dine at Cottenet's house in Murray Hill the following day. Mr. Cottenet represented the Vanderbilt interests at the Metropolitan. In fact, he had already arranged a "private" for Efrem at Mrs. Vanderbilt's. Mr. Cottenet was also a composer. He had written a piece for the violin called "Chanson Meditation," which he was sending to the hotel. I was envious of Mr. Cottenet, as Efrem continued to tell me about him and his place in "society." It was clear to me that Efrem was being "taken up" by Mr. Cottenet, perhaps so exclusively as to shut me out, except as one who would always be around to hear about the charms of social life which he was not permitted to share. I went to bed on the living-room couch in a state of depression. However, at breakfast the next morning I forgot Mr. Cottenet and the implications of his entry into Efrem's life, as I read in the papers the wonderful reviews of Efrem's debut. And when I next thought of Mr. Cottenet, it was quite without bitterness. I felt that, for my part, any association, however limited, with an artist and a personality like Zimbalist was something to be grateful for.

We started to rehearse the programs for three New York recitals, and for a joint concert in nearby Union City with Alma Gluck, which preceded the first Carnegie Hall recital by a few days. We began with the Sonata in E Major by Handel. To my great astonishment, I found the sonata, which looked so simple, more difficult to play than the Glazunov concerto. The slow parts, especially, baffled me. Efrem's phenomenal control of the bow permitted him to draw out a phrase or a note to its utmost extent. I tried to "breathe" with the violin, to anticipate the changes of bow, but I found myself either behind Efrem or ahead of him. As he drew out an interminable note, he left me helpless, trying to guess at the tempo he had in mind. And now he began to show signs of impatience at my failure to synchronize the piano with the violin, and this in turn increased my nervousness. The same thing happened in Bruch's *Scottish Fantasy,* where I floundered around under Efrem's inhumanly slow lyricism. I felt easier in the fast parts. And I breathed a sigh of relief when the rehearsal came to an end.

We went to Union City by ferry and train. It was very exciting to be going to my first concert with Efrem. But it was with some trepidation that I looked ahead to the Handel sonata which opened the program. As we walked through the day coach of the train, we passed Miss Gluck and a lady companion, who were seated near the door. In back of them sat Mr. Rosenstein, Miss Gluck's celebrated accompanist. We took seats farther up the coach and disposed ourselves for the short ride to Union City. Efrem read his afternoon paper for a while, and then asked me if I had noticed the pretty woman in the forward part of the car. "That was Alma Gluck," I said. "Very pretty for a singer," he commented, and asked if I could tell him something about her. I told him Miss Gluck's romantic story. She had been an East Side stenographer who had married a Mr. Glick, also of the East Side, by whom she had a daughter. Mr. Glick had encouraged his wife to study voice. She had sung for Mr. Gatti-Casazza and Mr. Toscanini, who had engaged her for the Metropolitan. She had made a sensational debut as Sophie in Massenet's *Werther* two years ago, and had since become a popular concert artist. When I finished my story, he said, "Do you think she would mind if I went up and spoke to her?" I was sure she wouldn't. He got up and walked over to Miss Gluck. I saw him bow with extravagant politeness. Miss Gluck's lady companion rose and joined Mr. Rosenstein. Efrem, after many protestations, sat down next to Miss Gluck and remained there until we arrived at Union City. There we were met by the local manager. He put Miss Gluck, her companion, Mr. Rosenstein and Efrem in one automobile. He and I rode in another. We drove to a nondescript little hotel, dressed and went to the theater. I asked Efrem, not without a pang of jealousy, what he thought of Miss Gluck. "Very pretty, very pretty," he said. When we arrived at the theater we found Miss Gluck already there. She looked tall and radiant in a white satin gown, her hair in a braid, like a chaplet, around her head, her hands encased in long white gloves, in one hand a small fan. I had never seen any woman as beautiful and stately as Miss Gluck.

Efrem and I opened the concert. I sat down at the piano, sounded the A, and accomplished my superstition of touching the leg of the piano with my right foot. The Handel went fairly well on my part. Miss Gluck came next, with a group of old Italian songs. Efrem and I watched and listened from the wings. Miss Gluck's voice was phenomenal, I thought, for its velvety quality, its purity and a certain liquid sensuousness. But more remarkable was the quality of intimacy in her singing. Though she looked out into the theater, she gave me the feeling that she was singing to and for me alone. The audience must have had the same feeling, for it applauded her ecstatically, and recalled her many times. In the intermission, Efrem disappeared into her dressing room. On the train going back to New York they sat together, and on the ferry they wandered off to the railing and looked out at the water and the New York skyline. In New York, Efrem did not ask me to accompany him to the Prince George, as I had hoped. He and Miss Gluck got into a cab and rode away. Depression overcame me, as when Efrem first talked to me about Mr. Cottenet. My hold on Efrem seemed to become more tenuous with each passing day. I was obliged to console myself with the success, or at least with the nonfailure, of my first public appearance with one of the world's most eminent artists. At home I gave a glowing account of my part in the concert, Efrem's beautiful playing, Miss Gluck's radiant appearance and intimate artistry. I failed to mention that Efrem never asked me to take a bow with him. I felt that omission keenly, all the more as I had seen Miss Gluck motion *her* accompanist, at the end of a group of songs, to rise and bow to the audience. I lay awake a long time that night, nursing this disappointment and a foreboding of the rapid loosening of the strong ties I thought I had established with Zimbalist.

My forebodings were well-founded. Miss Gluck seemed to take most of Efrem's time, especially evenings. The night following their first meeting, Efrem took her out to dinner. Earlier in the day we rehearsed the Carnegie Hall program. I had a premonition that he had made an engagement for the evening, but in the forlorn hope that he hadn't, I suggested having a bite in some "little place." It was then that he told me about his date with Miss Gluck. His preparations were elaborate, as before a concert. He sat for a long time in a hot bath, and then put on full evening dress. He had me telephone downstairs for a private car and chauffeur. I saw him into the car, and went disconsolately home. The next afternoon we rehearsed again. He told me that Miss Gluck and he had had a delightful evening. When he called for her at her apartment, she had looked, in a low-cut evening gown and fur wrap, even more radiant than at the Union City concert. They had then driven to Childs on Fifty-ninth Street. As he had expected, Miss Gluck was very impressed with the original features of the restaurant. Outside they had watched the man behind the plate-glass window tossing buckwheat cakes. Inside, Miss Gluck had marveled at the profusion of white tiles, and at the vast number of diners present. After that they went to the Prince George, where Efrem played the piano and introduced her to several arias from the little-known operas of Rimski-Korsakov. She had been much taken with a "Song of India" from the opera *Sadko,* and Luba's aria from *The Czar's Bride,* and she planned to put them on her programs.

Mr. Cottenet also took a good deal of Efrem's time. At Cottenet's house, or through him, Efrem met the socially elite of New York and got to know them intimately. Efrem talked to me about the Vanderbilts, the Whites, the Burdens and other personages I had come to know through the society columns of the *New York Journal,* as familiarly as I talked about my East Side friends. Mr. Cottenet came through not only with the "private" at Mrs. Vanderbilt's he had promised Efrem, but also with one at Mrs. Burden's and one at Mrs. Mills's. Cottenet would drop in of a morning at the Prince George to hear us rehearse, and then take Efrem out to lunch. Sometimes he invited me too. In spite of my jealousy of him, I grew to like him very much. He was that rarity among American men, the continental type. He represented the charm of culture, and he was supported by those members of a rich social stratum who wished to achieve the sophistication and emotional security of its French, English and Italian counterparts. Mr. Cottenet, steeped in European culture, served as a bridge between the two worlds. In art and in music New York society accepted him as arbiter. He divided his summers between Venice and Newport. It was he who had alerted the Metropolitan Opera to Toscanini, whom he had heard conduct at La Scala. He was a friend of Josef Hofmann and Fritz Kreisler, and was on an intimate footing with Caruso and all the great stars of the Metropolitan. He intrigued Efrem and amused me with social

gossip of an intimate nature. He knew who in New York's ultimate social circle was about to seek a divorce and who was
soon to marry. He brought us details of the negotiations going
on at that very moment for an alliance between the young
daughter of one of America's richest families with an important
foreign nobleman. He told us with relish about the exorbitant
financial demands of the family of the groom, and the hesitancy
of the young lady's mother to entrust her daughter to a for-
eigner, news of whose addiction to certain unconventional
amorous practices had reached her ears. Listening, I felt as if
I myself were part of that charmed circle. I searched the newspapers to find out more about the ativities of the splendid families with whom, through Mr. Cottenet, I felt I was on
a certain footing. Dazzled by their wealth and prestige, I now
only seldom thought of the poor, or flouted the rich, as I used
to in those faraway days when I read Jack London's *The People
of the Abyss* and quarreled with Madame Franko over my refusal to wear white tie and tails for my introduction to German-
Jewish society. I was eager to see society at close range at the
"privates" Efrem and I penciled in in our date books.

Efrem's first Carnegie Hall recital, on a Saturday afternoon,
was now only a matter of days away. Efrem gave me a lower-
tier box for my family. I invited Hannah and her husband,
Jake, Molly and Sergei. My father and mother were automati-
cally ruled out, for pious Jews did not ride on the Sabbath. Indeed, my playing the piano on the Sabbath was also considered
a desecration by my father, but he had long since adjusted himself to my nonobservance of orthodox practices. The box held
eight seats, and I was about to distribute the remaining four
to friends when Molly made the startling suggestion that our
mother should be induced to attend the recital. Though my
mother's piety was not to be compared in intensity with my

father's, she had never to my knowledge broken any of the Sabbath laws. I laughed at the very idea. But Molly maintained that my mother regarded this concert as the culmination of her hopes and dreams for me, and that her desire to be present would override her religious scruples. Of course, she would have to go secretly, incognito. That could be arranged. And to that end the box at Carnegie Hall would admirably lend itself. She could sit unseen in the little vestibule between the box and the corridor, and nobody would be the wiser. Molly undertook to sound her out. She brought back an astounding report of the interview. Far from showing displeasure or even surprise at Molly's suggestion, my mother had eagerly embraced it, saying fervently, "God will understand, but Mayshe Baer"—my father —"must never know."

My mother's momentous decision to break the Sabbath law for the first time in her life (and it was to be the only time) and the risks it involved helped to take my mind off the perils, for me, of the Carnegie Hall recital. Molly and I carefully planned the conspiracy. It was to be a costly venture, requiring a taxicab to and from the hall, since the subway was too public, and some acquaintance might recognize her. Molly was to telephone an I.T.O.A. taxi to be at the corner of Water and Jefferson Streets punctually at a quarter after two on Saturday. Water Street was predominantly Christian, and there was no likelihood of her being seen by friends or neighbors. The taxi would arrive at Carnegie Hall *after* the recital had started and all the people were in. A little before the end of the program, Molly and my mother would leave the hall and return to Water Street in another I.T.O.A. taxi, which would be waiting for them. My mother would tell my father that she was going to spend an hour or so on a bench in Jackson Street Park, where the air from the East River was, in the early autumn, held to be health-

ful and bracing. In all probability he wouldn't even notice her
absence, for it would coincide with his customary Sabbath-
afternoon nap.

When I went to bed Friday night and put out the light,
there instantly rose before me a brightly lighted Carnegie Hall
filled not only with my family and friends but with the most
famous musicians and music teachers in America. Except for
Efrem, I was alone on that vast stage. Opera glasses were being
trained on me, and I anticipated the surprise of the viewers
as my frightened face waxed larger and larger in front of them.
I reached out for the matches on the table and lit the gas. It was
reassuring to see my beautiful piano and the ebony music cabinet near it. Whistler's "Mother"'s sepia profile radiated calm
and serenity. For a while I lost myself in the fathomless look
of the "Mona Lisa" on the opposite wall. I was well aware that
only art could divert my thoughts and emotions to a counter-
feit world that held no terrors. I regretted that I had been so
foolish as to abandon the study of Hebrew. If I hadn't, I should
now be deep in the Psalms, as oblivious of reality as my father
was when he chanted softly to himself the songs of David or
Solomon. Indeed, I presently heard in my mind the Twenty-
third Psalm in the sentimental two-part harmony of an arrangement we used in P. S. No. 2, and I recognized my own
childish contralto singing the counterpoint. I remembered my
musical, fascinating, yet cruel, schoolteacher Mr. Strassmeier,
whose performance of "The Mosquito Parade," to which we
marched into assembly each morning, inspired in me the ambition to become a pianist. Perhaps he would be in the audience
tomorrow! I shouldn't mind his being there. If all went well,
he would be happy to realize what he had unwittingly wrought.
Yet if all did not go well . . . ! To banish the thought, I read
Milton's *Areopagitica,* whose lofty images always sent shivers

down my spine. Before, bleary-eyed and exhausted, I again put out the light, I had read many noble passages in prose and poetry. Words and phrases echoed and fused together in my mind, but at length oblivion overcame me. I slept dreamlessly, and so late that my mother felt obliged to wake me. I dressed (for the first time I put on my cutaway) and took the subway to the Prince George, where Efrem and I played through some of the trickier passages in the program. At two o'clock, Mr. Copley of the Wolfsohn Bureau arrived to escort us to Carnegie Hall. At the stage entrance I found Miklos, the gypsy violinist, and several piano students, frequenters of Katz's music store. Miklos asked if he might turn pages for me. If he had been a pianist I would have said no. But I had little to fear from the proximity of a gypsy fiddler, and I assented and took him in with me. The piano students begged me to pass them through. I told them I would send Mr. Copley out presently to attend to them. But when I appealed to Mr. Copley, he reminded me that tickets were to be had at the box office. I sent Miklos out to tell them the bad news. Secretly I was relieved that they could not get in.

Efrem behaved as calmly as he had in the theater in Union City. He tested his violin and changed a string. He played a few scales slowly, then put his violin back in its case. I stood at the window and tried to concentrate on the automobiles, taxicabs and occasional carriages which drew up at the stage entrance. My hands were wet, and I kept putting them into my trousers pockets to dry. Yet the moment my fingers were exposed to the air, they began to perspire again. At last Mr. Copley appeared and told us it was time to begin. I followed Efrem onto the stage. Miklos, carrying the music, followed me. The applause was deafening. The distance from the stage door to the piano, which had looked small, now looked quite long. My walk across

the stage in full view of everybody in the hall proved an unexpected, interminable ordeal. As I walked, I felt the boards underneath my feet tremble, and I heard the faint rumble of a train.
I remembered that the subway ran right underneath Carnegie
Hall. At last I gained the piano seat. My one thought now was
to go through with the indispensable superstition of touching
the piano leg without attracting the attention of the audience.
Efrem was still acknowledging the applause. Under cover of
adjusting the piano stool by turning the knobs on either side,
I warily felt for the piano leg with my foot. It was nowhere
within reach! After several unsuccessful attempts, I slumped
down in my seat, stretched my leg out full length and boldly
made contact with the elusive leg of the piano. That done, I
sounded the A. Efrem waited for utter silence, then nodded to
me. We should have started together, but I followed with my
chord a fraction of a second later. This mishap brought back
my nervousness in full force. My hands felt sticky and cold,
the action of the piano keys was extraordinarily light, respond-
ing with startling loudness to the merest touch. Then, too, Miklos behaved strangely. He kept watching Efrem instead of the
music on the piano. Several times I was obliged hastily to turn
a page myself. The Handel over, I began to fear the Bruch
Scottish Fantasy, which came next. It was full of arpeggios and
octaves. As we returned to the stage for the Bruch, I made a
desperate resolve. Rather than court disaster and shame by attempting to play, in the nervous state I was in, the difficult
passages as written, I would instead reduce the arpeggios to
their harmonic foundation and play the octaves as single notes.
The decision itself relieved my anxiety to such an extent that
as the difficulties loomed up, they did not seem altogether in-
surmountable. I attacked some of them boldly and came through
unscathed. However, a good part of my performance was im-

provisational, and the octaves I eschewed altogether. The ordeal was over at last, and we retired backstage, where I told Efrem about my nervousness and the fears that had obliged me to take the safer course. Efrem was sympathetic and told me not to worry. Thereupon I lost all nervousness, and I played the rest of the program as written. During the encores I felt so relaxed that for the first time I could look out boldly into the auditorium, not caring what faces I recognized. And when there came a rush of people down the aisles, I recognized many, and even smiled at them. At the very end Efrem took me out to bow with him, and I thought I detected a swelling in the volume of applause. I ached from the waves of pure happiness that kept sweeping over me. When we reached the green room, it was already bursting with people. Strangers shook my hand and congratulated me. Everybody who had ever been in Katz's music store was there. Mr. Katz, with tears in his eyes, embraced me warmly, then stepped aside, "to give other people a chance." Suddenly Madame Franko stood before me and pressed my hand and said she was proud of me. I turned away in anger. She had made no attempt to see me since she had turned me out of her house. She was now attempting to claim me in my hour of triumph, and to bask in my success! A moment later I forgot her in the press of important musicians who, having finished talking to Efrem, came over to speak to me: Miss Gluck, Alexander Lambert, Mr. Kneisel, and most flattering of all, the great pianist Rafael Joseffy. I was praised for my tone, the delicacy of my adjustment to the violin and my musicality in general. I did not forget to thank Miklos for turning pages, or at any rate attempting to turn them. I jokingly asked him why he had hesitated so often when turning, expecting that he would say he had been too absorbed in Zimbalist's playing to pay much attention to me. Instead, his pockmarked face reddening, he confessed that he had never learned to read music! He had asked to be a page turner only that he might hear Zimbalist at close range. I felt too happy to resent the deception. Now a tiny white-haired middle-aged lady, a miniature woman, so small that I thought for a moment she must be a child, advanced and gave me her hand. "I am Mary Fels. We arrived two hours ago, just in time for the concert," she said softly and poutingly, in a voice that seemed exactly proportioned to her height and appearance. I pressed her hands in gratitude and told her I owed everything to her. She beckoned to a little bald man, so exactly her miniature size as to pass for her twin brother. It was her husband, Joseph Fels. Unlike his wife, the quality of whose voice implied vague yet meaningful things, Mr. Fels spoke sharply and to the point. He said nothing about the concert or my playing, but asked me if there had been a good sale of tickets. Mrs. Fels told me not to mind him, that he knew little about music. Then she said we must soon meet quietly and have a talk. I boldly asked her if she and Mr. Fels would come to dinner at my house. I would, of course, invite Efrem too, I hastened to add. Then and there we set a date. Mr. Fels wrote it down in a little book he took out of a pocket.

The Felses took Efrem in tow, and I went home alone by subway. Molly managed to convey to me by signs and whispers that my mother had attended the concert, that nothing had gone amiss and my father had no suspicion whatever. The house was full of friends who had been at the concert. There was also a distant relation from Waterbury whom I hadn't seen in years. He told me he had made a special trip to New York to hear me at Carnegie Hall and to put before me a number of life-insurance propositions with the Prudential Insurance Company, which he represented. He realized, he said, that this was hardly the moment to discuss business, and he was prepared to spend several days with us. I was flattered by his assumption that I would be earning enough to pay the heavy premium of a life-insurance policy. But unfortunately for him, I belonged to that class of Jews, in those days quite numerous, who believed that a life-insurance policy always resulted in the speedy death of the insured. Life insurance, my mother held, was for insensitive Christians only. It was a superstition our whole family shared. Therefore our cousin was made to realize that his trip to New York had been for nothing. However, he made up for his disappointment by staying two days with us at no further cost to himself, and making a trip to the Statue of Liberty on Sunday.

My reception at home was very gratifying. My cutaway, stiff shirt and wing collar, my starched cuffs sticking out several inches from my sleeves, the studied air with which I parted the tails of my coat whenever I sat down, made a great impression on everyone. The only things lacking were a pearl pin for my cravat and a watch chain across my vest. I had little doubt that I should acquire them in time. My mother said shamelessly, in a loud voice, that it was a pity recitals had to take place on the Sabbath, when good Jews were unable to attend. I said nothing about my nervousness during the first half of the recital and pretended I was confident from the first. Then I spoke about Mr. and Mrs. Fels, creating a sensation when I said offhandedly that they *and* Mr. Zimbalist had accepted an invitation to dine at my house. However, I cannily did not reveal the date. I had not forgotten the dinner I gave for Professor and Mrs. Mason, when the Flayshigs and their twin little boys arrived unexpectedly, with disastrous results.

That night when I undressed and got into bed, my mother came to me in the dark, and hugged and kissed me and wept for joy. She told me that when she saw me come out on the stage of Carnegie Hall, she knew complete fulfillment for the first

time in her life—everything she had ever hoped for had come
to pass. Now she had nothing more to live for except to see
me married and the father of a son like me. As for her breaking
the Sabbath law, she was confident that the Deity would not
overlook the exceptional nature of her case. If it was permissible
in the sight of God for an ailing Jew, even for a paragon of
piety like a rabbi, to eat on Yom Kippur (and it *was* permissible;
both her father and mine had vouched for it), there must surely
be some provision in Heaven for a mother who yearned to see
with her own eyes the public triumph of her only son. I asked
her what she would do if my father found out and accused her
to her face. "I would deny it," she said indignantly.

"DARLING"

〰️ The reviews of the recital all contained laudatory comments about my playing. I bought three copies of each paper and gave a set each to Hannah, Molly and my mother. My mother put hers in an empty glass jar, which she placed on the dining-room mantel, like an ornament. In that position the clippings were exposed to the eye and were within easy reach for showing to inquiring visitors. From the Yiddish reviews she read aloud those lines that pertained to me, omitting all the long paragraphs about Zimbalist. It seemed to me that everybody on the East Side had read the reviews, especially the one in the *Forward*. I was conscious of being looked at in the streets and pointed to. I felt the glow of being thought exceptional. I noted subtle changes in the attitude of the colleagues I met at Katz's. The haughty Beniamino Burgo now tipped his fedora hat to me, and Sol Rashkin was not nearly so aggressively hostile as he used to be. I. Jacobs, whose friendliness and generosity never could quite conceal a genial feeling of superiority, treated me like an absolute equal. In discussing pianistic problems, he now said "we pianists," thus placing me solidly in the circle

of acknowledged virtuosos in which he had always regarded
himself as a member. Even Mr. Katz showed a deference toward me I had not noticed before. My indebtedness to him
amounted to seven and a half dollars. On receiving my first
check from Efrem, I decided to pay Mr. Katz in full. When I
put the money down on the counter, Mr. Katz blushed, and
stammered, "What's the hurry? What's the idea of paying up
like this? Don't let it go to your head." I guessed what he meant
by "it." "Let it be like old times. I want you always to keep
owing me something. It's more friendly. I'll take five dollars.
You'll owe me the rest." To please him I took back the two and
a half dollars and, in addition, bought some music, which he
smilingly charged to me. But the final proof of my new standing
among East Side musicians came from Ivan Tschirsky, the famous piano teacher and composer, who had given me an audition
once, but had refused to teach me for less than his fee of two
dollars a lesson, which I was unable to meet. One day after
Efrem's recital I was in Katz's store when he and Montana came
in together. Although he had seen me only once in his life,
Tschirsky embraced me warmly. Then, flinging backward his
leonine head (he gave out that he was the illegitimate son of
Anton Rubenstein, and he actually resembled the great pianist),
he said over his shoulder to Montana, "Forgive this display of
emotion over an old pupil." I was too dumfounded by this
shameless prevarication to refute it.

True to her promise, Mrs. Fels invited me to have tea alone
with her in the tearoom of the Prince George. The tearoom
of the Prince George was a cavernous place so dimly lit that I
could not at first make out the faces or the figures of the people
in it. It was full of little low round tables, on each of which
stood a small candle covered by a conical silk-lined brass shade
with long beaded fringes. Bumping against shadowy figures,

I finally found Mrs. Fels. I would have missed her altogether
had she not caught at my sleeve as I was about to pass her. As
I grew accustomed to the dimness of the room, I made out more
clearly the faces of couples around me. The tearoom was obviously a trysting place, and offered the nearest thing to pri-
vacy in a public place. It was ideal for lovers. Husbands and
wives sitting at different tables might very well not be aware of
each other's presence. It occured to me to invite Mrs. Lesser to
have tea with me there. Or Edith Fallon, when she happened
to be in New York.

Mrs. Fels asked me how I was getting along with Efrem and
what estimate I had formed of his character. I told her in all
honesty that he was the most fascinating person I had ever
known, and Mrs. Fels said he was fascinating indeed. One must,
however, she added, beware of his charm, for he was prone to
take the people who loved him for granted. She told me the
story of how she first met him. Efrem had come to tea to her
house in Regent's Park, "and stayed four years," she said laugh-
ingly. Both she and Mr. Fels had taken a great interest in him.
They had given him a home, bought him a Stradivarius and
directed his career. Mrs. Fels then told me to my face that I
looked like a good man, and that she expected me to have the
best influence on her protégé. But I must not let him hurt me,
and she hoped I would confide in her. I asked her questions
about London, which, because of this new connection with an
actual resident, was now closer to my heart than ever before.
Mrs. Fels spoke about the charm of Regent's Park, and the
notables who frequently gathered in her house. Her friends
included H. G. Wells and George Bernard Shaw. I revered
both authors, especially Shaw. Mrs. Fels said that when I came
to London, I should meet Mr. Shaw at tea. The idea of having
tea with G. B. S. in London made me forget for the moment

both Efrem and Mrs. Fels. What could I say to him? Perhaps I could summon the courage to ask him why he had permitted Candida, the lovely heroine of his play of that name, to choose to remain with her dull husband, instead of going away with the fascinating, insolent young poet Marchbanks (whom, according to Edith Fallon, I resembled). Should Shaw then reiterate the reason Candida herself gives in the play—namely, that her clergyman husband needed her more than the poet did—I would be bold enough to ask in what way the satisfaction of the needs of an ordinary clergyman would benefit the world. Whereas (I would point out) if her running away with March-banks would result in his creation of a single perfect sonnet, the world would be the gainer. Mrs. Fels brought back my wandering thoughts by pouring out another cup for me and offering me some ladyfingers on a plate.

No unexpected visitors arrived the night the Felses and Efrem came down to East Broadway to dinner. My mother was for buying a new white damask tablecloth in honor of the distinguished guests. But I had found out that, notwithstanding their great wealth, the Felses were simple people, even parsimonious, who rode in streetcars, on the elevated and in subways, like ourselves, though it was true that Mr. Fels gave large sums to the Single Tax Movement. I decided that our old tablecloth would do well enough. I did, however, place a new candle and a full box of matches on the seat in the toilet in the hall.

Except for a slight "incident" during the introductions, the evening was to develop into a brilliant success. When Mr. Fels removed his hat, my nephew Walt Whitman, who, though only four, was almost as tall as the industrialist, put his finger on the visitor's bald head and said, "What happened to his hair?" Mr. Fels fortunately met this inquiry facetiously, and so saved us from embarrassment. The guests praised the food and ate well. Efrem said he hadn't eaten blintzes since he left his home in Rostov ten years previously. As I expected, Efrem quite charmed my family. He showed great interest in Molly, and drew her out on the problem of rearing children. He spoke Russian with my brother-in-law Sergei, and they exchanged reminiscences of the 1905 revolution. After dinner, Mr. Fels, at no one's suggestion, launched into the theory of the single tax, addressing himself impartially to my mother, my father and me, in turn. My father and mother neither spoke nor understood English. My father listened to Mr. Fels with a solemn air, but kept his eyes on the floor. My mother, relishing the novelty of being addressed directly by the rich owner of the nation's leading soap, looked him straight in the eyes and gave him, each time he paused for breath, a charming smile, her parted lips showing off her dazzling white false teeth. I was too worried about what Walt Whitman might say or do next to give all my attention to Mr. Fels. I gathered dimly that taxation of idle land would somehow do away with poverty. "And also," said Mr. Fels tactlessly, "with slums like these," and he waved his hand around the room and toward the windows. Having expounded the theory of the single tax, Mr. Fels fell silent, and my mother, who always interpreted silence at a gathering as a reflection on the resourcefulness of the host or hostess, asked me in Yiddish to ask Mr. Fels in English if his soap was selling well. This inquiry set Mr. Fels off on the subject of advertising. He spoke vehemently, as if he had learned that my father, my mother and I were opposed to advertising. "They said I spent too much money advertising Fels-Naphtha," he exclaimed with scorn, "so I cut out all advertising for a period of six months. And you know what happened? Let me tell you." He fixed my father with his eyes. "The sales fell off by a third. By a third, mind you, or by just enough to kill the margin of profits." My father began to show signs of discomfort. I drew Mr. Fels's attention to myself by exclaiming, "You don't say so!" He turned to me, and my father, much relieved, lifted his yarmulke and with his other hand wiped the perspiration from his head. "Mary," Mr. Fels continued, pointing a backward thumb at his wife, "Mary laughs at me when I tell her that the concert business needs advertising as much as soap does. Now, I saw this proved the other day at Efrem's recital. Efrem is as good a fiddler as any. I don't know anything about music, but that's what the experts say, and they say he is one of the best. The house should have been sold out. But it wasn't. And why? Because his silly agent doesn't believe in advertising. Why, I would have had two dozen sandwich men carrying placards six feet high with the words 'Zimbalist, the King of Violinists,' parading for weeks up and down Fifty-seventh Street." "Oh, keep quiet, Joe," Mary Fels said in a quiet, honeyed voice; and to me, "Pay no attention to Joe." Then she bent over and in my ear whispered, "Joe has a great heart, but he doesn't understand the things you and I understand." Mr. Fels rose and began looking around him. I guessed what he wanted and I was prepared. "Would you like to wash your hands?" I said cordially. This euphemism was one of the "social" phrases Edith Fallon had taught me, but so far I had had no occasion to use it. As I expected, Mr. Fels said forthrightly, "Yes, I would." I said, "Follow me, please," and I led him out into the hall and into the toilet. I struck a match, lit the candle and shut the door on him.

The dinner party made history in the neighborhood. Even more than my debut at Carnegie Hall, even more than my association with Zimbalist, the presence of Joseph Fels in our house lifted the social standing of my parents to a point where it could climb no higher. My father's position in shul was greatly enhanced. He received enough invitations to partake of herring and schnapps on Sabbath noon to last him a year of Saturdays. Absolute strangers called on my mother and invited her for tea and cake. My mother received them warmly and talked freely about "our friends the Fels-Naphthas." And when a shipment of thirty-six cakes of Fels-Naphtha soap arrived one day as a gift from Mr. Fels, my mother put the opened carton in the parlor, on display to all callers.

I myself found a more romantic satisfaction in the splendors of the great houses Efrem and I now frequently played in. Before we left on a tour of the West early in December, we had played four or five "privates" in New York and nearby fashionable places like Morristown, New Jersey. Now I came face to face with such wealth and elegance as I had not thought existed. In Morristown the wife of an old retired general arranged a surprise birthday celebration for her husband in the form of a huge musical entertainment. The artists and ensembles the old lady engaged included Alma Gluck, Louise Homer, the famous contralto, Clement, the French tenor, Pasquale Amato, the baritone, Efrem Zimbalist and the entire Metropolitan Opera House chorus and orchestra! We traveled to Morristown in a special train. And when we arrived at the general's mansion on the outskirts of Morristown, we were told not to make any noise until the general, who was taking his customary after-dinner nap, should awake and be led downstairs to the great suite of drawing rooms, there to be surprised by the largest assembly of musical forces ever to perform in a private house. We were, accordingly, all silent as mice. When the general was led in by his wife, I expected him to collapse with surprise and joy at the spectacle that faced him. But far from collapsing, he showed no emotion whatever, as if he were quite used, on coming downstairs after his nap, to find the massed forces of the Metropolitan

Opera House in his drawing room. Notwithstanding the large
number of soloists, the program was a short one, because the
old general retired early. The entertainment was over in about
an hour, and the general went to bed. Then came a late supper
for the artists and the guests, after which we were transported in
many motorbuses and cars to the railroad station, where the
private train was waiting for us. In the train there was much
speculation about the probable cost of the extraordinary surprise
party. It was said that the flowers alone would run into thou-
sands of dollars. One wag said that the real surprise for the
general would come with the bill.

I remember even more vividly our first New York "private"
at the home of Mrs. Ogden Mills, a society "leader" of those
days. The artists were Zimbalist and Georgette Leblanc, the wife
of the Belgian poet and writer Maurice Maeterlinck. Efrem
opened the program with a group of small pieces. Then a
thronelike chair was brought in and placed on a platform. I was
very eager to hear Madame Leblanc sing, for she was reputed to
be the rival of Mary Garden. I took up a position at the door
leading to the library, which was our retiring room. Seeing me
standing up, a lady in the audience beckoned to me and pointed
to a vacant chair next to her. I walked across the room in full
view of everybody and sat down next to the lady who had
beckoned to me. She was middle-aged but still very beautiful.
She wore a crinkly, voluminous satin dress and carried a fan
of large white feathers. She complimented me on my accompaniment and I thanked her and said she looked like a Gibson
girl. She laughed and said she *was* a Gibson girl. She was Mrs.
Charles Dana Gibson, the artist's wife and the model for the
Gibson girl. "But I am a ruin now," she added genially. "Oh,
look," she said as Madame Leblanc walked slowly into the
room, stepped up on the dais and sat down heavily on the

thronelike chair. Madame Leblanc was hefty. She wore a low-cut gown which exposed a considerable bosom. But all eyes were turned to her forehead, in the middle of which rested a large diamond attached to her head by a delicate, almost invisible, chain. Mrs. Gibson, after a close look, said, "Goodness sakes alive! Did you ever . . . ?" and gave me a knowing wink. Madame Leblanc began a song in French. She sang through her nose, solemnly, in an exaggerated, affected manner. I could not resist laughing. Mrs. Gibson leaned toward me and whispered, "Did you ever hear anything so funny?" and she spread out her fan and held it in such a way as to conceal our heads from the people around us. So shielded, we both laughed as noiselessly as possible all during Madame Leblanc's number. Later, at supper in the dining room, we renewed our conversation. Mrs. Gibson pointed out several ladies and gossiped about them in an intimate, earthy way. I saw Mrs. Gibson frequently that winter at "privates." She always greeted me heartily, and talked freely about herself and the people around her; not maliciously, but realistically. In this way I came to know the history and peculiarities of many society figures.

The "privates" we played were generally preceded by a select dinner party, and Efrem was often invited to dine. I, never. At around ten o'clock, the nondining guests would begin to arrive. I came at that hour, carrying Efrem's violin and the music. I remember with what emotion I entered the great vestibule of the Vanderbilt house on Fifth Avenue and Fifty-second Street. This was the very house in which Consuelo Vanderbilt had married the Duke of Marlborough. I had read about that international marriage in the *New York American* or *Journal* when I was a small boy. Since then I had often stopped to admire the great iron gates which led into the driveway. (In the periods when I turned to socialism, I had gazed at these gates with

scorn and distaste.) Now I was actually inside the famous house.
A splendid-looking man in knee breeches and a gaily colored
cutaway took my hat and coat. At the same moment a party of
ladies and gentlemen in evening dress came out of the dining
room and made for the salon across the hall. Efrem was among
them, chatting and bowing and making himself agreeable. He
seemed to have been born to the grandeur around him, and to
this charmed, exclusive circle. Mr. Cottenet, also of the party,
waved a friendly hand to me as he passed me. When Efrem and
I came out to play, we found the most numerous assembly of
guests we had yet seen at any "private," except for the Morristown surprise party. I looked for and found Mrs. Gibson, who
saw me and shook her fan in my direction. In the dining room
at supper, I stood about alone until Mrs. Gibson mercifully
joined me. Efrem went around the room greeting the many
people he knew. Mrs. Gibson introduced me to several ladies
who stopped to chat with her, among them the hostess, Mrs.
Vanderbilt, a tall, thin, straight-backed old woman. For some
mysterious reason, I had expected Mrs. Vanderbilt to speak with
an affectation of accent or elegance. None of the society women
I had so far met had any affectations. They appeared to be quite
unaware of their glittering surroundings, their gowns and their
jewels. Indeed, the voices of many of them had a plebeian,
hearty quality, and I heard frequent mistakes in grammar. One
beautiful and magnificently dressed lady spoke like a Negress,
with soft, honeyed intonation, discarding all *g*'s, as if there was
no such letter in the language. I had fully expected that the
ladies and gentlemen in American society would assume a British accent and converse in witty paradox, like the lords and
ladies in the plays of Oscar Wilde, and I was disappointed that
they didn't. Yet I was secretly glad of it, for it made social inter-
course between us easy. Even Efrem's demeanor seemed to me

overpolite and overrefined, compared with the naturalistic behavior of American society men. This confused me. I wanted to be like Efrem in every respect; yet his manners went quite beyond the social requirements of the American elite.

The "privates" given by wealthy Jews were on a different social and musical plane. We played at the homes of Mr. and Mrs. Jacob Schiff and Mr. and Mrs. Adolph Lewisohn. I had not seen Jacob Schiff since the memorable Sunday, four or five years before, when he came down to the Educational Alliance. His house on Seventy-eighth Street was rich, though not as imposing as Mrs. Vanderbilt's. Mr. Schiff wore a wide red ribbon like a sash across his stiff shirt, and was as impersonal as I remembered him at our only other meeting. But the Jewish guests, of which there was a majority, were as warm and friendly and uninhibited as any Jews on the East Side. I noticed that while their manners and personalities underwent a change in the presence of Christians, they were altogether natural among themselves. It was as if they (I among them) were all members of the same convivial club. Nothing stood between them. They behaved like people on East Broadway. It was the same in the palatial house of Adolph Lewisohn. Though I envied the authority and the sense of easy power reflected in the behavior of the elite Christians and wanted to be welcomed among them like Efrem, I was happier among rich Jews, where I was altogether at my ease. People came up to me of their own accord and spoke to me pleasantly. They talked about music knowingly, they applauded the playing and singing of the artists vociferously. Indeed, they appeared to look upon art with the awe and respect poor and uneducated Jews felt for rabbis and Talmudic students. And their taste in music was of a higher order than that of Christians on the same economic level. The Jews who gave musical "privates" themselves took

a hand in the programs. The Christians engaged the most popular or fashionable artists and merely stipulated the length of
time for the programs, so that the ensuing supper should take
place at a given hour. It flattered Miss Gluck, who with
Zimbalist and Amato were the artists engaged for the Lewisohn
"private," to be requested by Mrs. Lewisohn to include "Depuis
le jour" from *Louise* among her numbers, and it pleased her
and Amato to be asked to sing the duet "La ci darem la mano"
from *Don Giovanni*. Applause at the Lewisohns' was hearty
and demonstrative, unlike the polite handclapping at Mrs.
Vanderbilt's and Mrs. Mills's. I saw that artists had a better
time at the musicales given by Jews. Yet, curiously enough, I
brought home tales mostly of the Christian musicales and
suppers, not of the concerts in Jewish houses. (The exception
was Jacob Schiff's. Jacob Schiff was, for us, the venerated
symbol of Jewish leadership, and my father was avid to hear
everything about him and his house.) I held the family spellbound with my descriptions of the grandeur of the Vanderbilts,
the Whites, the Millses, the Goulds. Sometimes I wondered
whether I really should have liked to be born a wealthy, elite
Christian. I saw myself a Vanderbilt or a Gould, and lost myself in a daydream of belonging to the international set, deferred to by a Rawlins Cottenet and by Efrem. Yet I was certain
I should also want to possess my Jewish awareness, sympathies,
the Jewish appreciation of the relativeness of everything. Perhaps to be born a Daniel Deronda would be ideal—a Jew
brought up until manhood as a wealthy and patrician Christian,
somehow sensing his difference, his superiority, and at last dis-
covering to his satisfaction the source of that strangeness and
superiority. But of one thing I was always sure: it was pleasant
to return to East Broadway and to my soul-satisfying front
room. Once there, I no longer indulged in daydreams of wealth

and exclusiveness, either as Jew or as Christian. When I thought of moving away, it was not to some exclusive neighborhood, but to a country suburb, Staten Island perhaps, someplace with trees and a lawn. Talk of the country deeply disturbed my father. "This Staten Island," he once asked me. "Does it have a shul?" I said I didn't know if it had a synagogue, but I was sure it had plenty of trees. My father smiled ruefully. "I would rather see a few beards than a whole forest of trees," he said.

In the meantime the gifted and charming Efrem was more than ever occupied with social activities. I had glimpses of fascinating people who visited him at the Prince George. One afternoon the lovely Russian ballerina Lydia Lopoukhova came to have tea with Efrem while I was with him. She spoke hardly any English. She looked like a chubby little girl—she was only sixteen or seventeen. Her manner was so frank and natural, her laughter so innocent and touching that she seemed to me to have stepped out of a novel by Turgenev or Tolstoi's *Childhood, Boyhood, Youth*. I did not see her again.

I did get to know Alma Gluck fairly well. She and Efrem had several joint concerts, and she came frequently to the Prince George when I was there. Her daughter, Abigail, then about nine, had been put to school in a convent at Peekskill. To give Abigail a treat, Miss Gluck, Efrem and I journeyed one day to the convent and gave the students and sisters a small recital. Miss Gluck had asked me to play for her, and arranged for a rehearsal at her apartment. She received me in a suit, and a hat with a single long feather. We went through the songs she was to sing at the convent. A maid brought in tea on a silver tray, and Miss Gluck asked me how many lumps, and poured the tea naturally, quite as if she had not been brought up, like me, in poverty. She looked as beautiful and radiant in street clothes as she did in evening dress. We talked about music. I asked her whether she hoped someday to sing the Wagner heroines. I said she sang Mozart and Rossini and Verdi and Charpentier beautifully, but I was sure that kind of music couldn't quite satisfy a true artist. Miss Gluck laughed and said she did not think she was cut out for Brünnhilde or Isolde, and I asked her if she was deterred by the vocal difficulties of the roles. At that she rose, went to the piano and struck the G, twelve notes above middle C. She then burst into "Jo-ho-to-ho," Brünnhilde's battle cry, with such brilliance, accuracy, vocal ease and beauty of tone as I had never heard at the Metropolitan. I was dumbfounded and abashed. She sat down again and poured herself another cup of tea. "I find Mozart and Rossini more difficult," she said, smiling. It took me several years to understand why.

It was easy for me to understand Miss Gluck's attraction for Efrem and, of course, his for her. The two were talked about everywhere. Down at the Irving Place Theater a German operetta called *Alma, wo wohnst du?* (Alma, Where Do You Live?) was enjoying a long run. Presently a story went the rounds to the effect that someone had banteringly inquired of Miss Gluck, "Alma, *wo wohnst du?*" and that she had without hesitation replied, *"Wo Zimbal-ist."* News of the romance of the violinist and singer had even reached the East Side. The question of their eventual marriage was often debated in my own house. My mother, brushing aside the question of divorce as of little account, was for the marriage, but with a reservation about the chances of happiness where a wife is older than a husband. (Miss Gluck was a few years older than Zimbalist.) My father, on the contrary, held that a marriage was all the better, certainly safer, for the wife's being older than the husband. It kept, he said, the woman from the temptations of youth. Yet he was against the alliance on the less controversial grounds of the injustice to Mr. Glick, who had married Alma when she was a penniless girl, had paid for her singing lessons, fostered her career, and was now to be rewarded for his pains by being asked for a divorce. My own feelings were altogether personal. Viewed dispassionately, such a union between two great and attractive artists was ideal. But, except publicly, I was unable to take a dispassionate view. I had through Efrem been offered a glimpse of the beautiful, exciting world of top musical art. And as Efrem's companion and confidant I could in time become an established part of it. Efrem's marriage would at best relegate me to the position of a musical appendage, and the time was past when that alone could satisfy me. Mrs. Fels, in a well-modulated burst of confidence, told me that she trusted Efrem not to do anything foolish. She also had faith in my good sense; I must not underestimate my influence with him; together, she and I must do everything in our power for the benefit of his career and his own ultimate good. In justice to Efrem, I reminded Mrs. Fels of the extraordinary attractiveness of Miss Gluck and the added glamour of her artistry. Mrs. Fels said she was quite aware of everything. She then began to speak about me. She said many complimentary things, such as that I had lived up to her expectations, that I was sensitive and cultured. She then asked me if I would care to go to London in the late spring and be her secretary. This was a breathtaking proposition—to be in London, renew my childhood memories of it and live in the house of Mrs. Fels where I would meet G. B. S. and other world-famous writers! But then Mrs. Fels spoke of the "arrangements," and the vision of an exciting London life began to recede before the practical drawbacks of her offer. For Mrs. Fels mentioned a salary of ten dollars a week and my keep, and I wondered how my family on East Broadway could live on so small a sum. She was also to pay my passage to London. We would sail on the same boat, but for economy I would go second class. This in itself was depressing. I should know no one in second class. However, I really would not have minded even the steerage, if the salary were larger. Mrs. Fels asked me to think it over, as there was plenty of time, and I told her I would discuss it at home. But I knew then that I would not deprive my family of the security and comfort I had provided for them in the last two years, and I then and there resolutely put the idea from me.

Our colloquy took place on the Twentieth Century Limited to Chicago, the first stop on a cross-country tour Efrem was making. Mrs. Fels was to return to New York after the Chicago recital. Efrem had retired early to his berth, and Mrs. Fels and I sat in the darkened car in a section that had not yet been made up. We were traveling in a blizzard. The windows of the car were covered with frost. Large flakes dashed against the panes and splattered open and stuck like torn, wet pieces of paper. The train stopped for a while at Buffalo. There were faint echoing shouts from the station, a clanging of iron as the door of the car was flung open. The rumbling of wheels stopped, and we heard instead the loud hiss of the steam in the overheated car. This was my first long trip, and I felt mystery and excitement all around me. The darkened car, the shadowy, enigmatic, gray-haired, diminutive figure of Mary Fels opposite me, the thought of the vague conspiracy in which we were both involved, were exhilarating and at the same time oppressive. I remembered the train ride of Anna Karenina from Moscow to St. Petersburg, Anna sitting huddled up in furs, the station stop with the cries and noises from the platform (resembling our stop in Buffalo), the meeting with Vronsky in the corridor, the flurry of snow, the heat, the cold, and above all the romance of the wild forces of nature orchestrating the equally uncontrollable forces of love and desire in Anna and

Vronsky. Though the tremendous speed of the train made me feel slightly nauseated, I felt a sense of achievement in riding on the celebrated train. The names of the cities we passed or stopped at strung themselves in my mind like Whitman's catalog of American towns, the mere enumeration of which, even without meter and rhythm, generated musical overtones. I was speeding over America to play in fascinating places, in Chicago (would I find Chicago a huge stockyard inhabited by cruelly treated and starved Polish laborers, as I remembered reading in my childhood in Upton Sinclair's *The Jungle,* or the sprawling shanty town of sordid passions and moneygrubbing, as in the books of Theodore Dreiser?), in Colorado Springs, in Los Angeles, in San Francisco. (Perhaps I would see that peak in Darien upon which Cortez stood *silent!*) I was constantly aware of the vastness of the land as we ground over it, unlike the gentlemen I had seen and heard in the washroom and in the dining car, who all appeared to be their usual insensitive business selves *in transit.* I, on the contrary, was living in the moment. I exulted in the storm that shrieked around the tightly knit, impenetrable train, ran ahead of it and lay in wait, pursued it relentlessly, as if expecting to find a weakness in the plunging iron and steel, then to breach it and demolish it. Indeed, there were occasional howls and shrieks from the train as if it had been mortally hurt. At one moment I was on the side of the train; at another I favored the storm. Mrs. Fels had retired to her berth, leaving me, as she no doubt imagined, to speculate on the problem of Efrem Zimbalist and my prospects in London. Even when I grew tired and went to bed, I raised the shade of my window and watched the storm. It seemed only a moment later when I felt a pulling at my blanket and heard the porter say we would be in Chicago in an hour.

Chicago, from my window in the Auditorium Hotel, was a

vast expanse of railroad tracks and mud, and a limitless murky lake beyond. I saw no stockyards, but the streets and avenues behind the hotel were shabby, remarkably like those in Dreiser's books. We went to lunch with the concert manager, a Mr. Neumann, who lived in a house on Lake Shore Drive. Lake Shore Drive was as grand and ostentatious as the streets around the hotel were mean and noisy. In the evening Mrs. Fels took Efrem and me to dine with her friends Mr. and Mrs. Alfred Sampson, a young couple who lived in one of the new apartment houses on the North Shore Drive. Mrs. Fels told us that Mr. Sampson had gone into the up-and-coming business of national advertising and had made quite a success. When we were shown into the apartment by a butler, I thought Mrs. Fels had understated the scope of Mr. Sampson's success in the new advertising business. The apartment was large and grand, and filled with fine, new, ornate furniture, and large paintings of flowers in the dining room. Mr. Sampson gave every evidence of being enthusiastically concerned with his business affairs. He related, with no outside encouragement, episodes of his early life. He told, with evident pride, how he had left school and run away from home at a youthful age, his subsequent struggles and his ultimate triumph in business. And looking directly at me, he said pointedly that we lived in a great country, where hard work and ingenuity were always rewarded. He said schooling was unimportant. He was very gracious to his guests, but his thoughts seemed to be on himself or elsewhere in the city. I asked him questions about Chicago in relation to the books of Theodore Dreiser. He said he had never heard of "the man." As for Chicago, Mr. Sampson said cryptically that "it was *the* place." I was too shy to ask him to explain what he meant.

After our recital in the Studebaker Theater, we put Mrs.

Fels on a train for New York and Efrem and I left for Colorado
Springs, our next stop. All the next day we rode through
Nebraska. I was amazed at the levelness of the land and the
signs (though it was winter) of its tremendous productiveness.
Efrem said he was reminded of Russia, and challenged me to
estimate the size of the annual wheat crop of the state. We
approached Colorado Springs at dusk. The Rockies suddenly
loomed up without warning, snow-capped, and I felt surprise
and awed disbelief as I had in the past at the final scene of
Das Rheingold at the Metropolitan, with its vapor-enshrouded
heights and crags surrounding Valhalla.

We went to the Antlers Hotel, the interior of which looked
as severe as a hospital, with the rooms white and immaculate.
I was not surprised. I had always heard that Colorado Springs
—indeed, the entire state—had curative properties for people
suffering from tuberculosis. I was worried, though, about contamination. At home on the East Side, where tuberculosis
struck in most households, people took the greatest precautions
against catching the disease. The dishes and cutlery a sufferer
used were kept separate. Each consumptive carried a little cup
with a lid, into which he spat. "Lungers" were not permitted
to spit on the floor, unlike well people. But in the Antlers Hotel
no precautions appeared to be taken. The patients—I assumed
that all the guests except Efrem and me were patients—
roamed around at will, and carried no little containers to spit
into. The next morning we walked in the town, gazed at Pikes
Peak, which seemed to be following us wherever we turned,
drove in an automobile to the Garden of the Gods and examined the fabulous caves with their pendent icicles (I thought
of Kublai Khan). After the concert that night, we were taken
by the local manager to a supper party at a splendid private
house a few miles out of town. There all the guests were in

evening clothes, the women looking very much like the ladies
at a fashionable New York "private." As at the Antlers, nobody
carried a little cuspidor, and people stood closely packed, quite
as if there was nothing the matter with any of them. I attempted to keep a safe distance, but the elegance and attractiveness of the ladies made their proximity pleasant.

The next morning we took the train for Los Angeles. It
took all day to ride through Arizona and New Mexico. The
skies were clear and pure, as if they had never known clouds.
The day took longer than any I could remember. I thought of
"a summer's day" in *Paradise Lost,* through which Lucifer fell
from heaven to earth. When the train stopped for water, we got
out to stretch our legs and breathe in deeply the warm, brittle,
strange-smelling air. At the station in Albuquerque, we had
dinner in a Harvey restaurant, to which we were summoned
by the clamor of an enormous bronze gong. I was delighted
to find Indians and cowboys idling about the station. The next
morning the train rode through orange groves, and at each stop
the ground, the trees and the flowers sparkled and glistened as
if they had been secretly rained on when no one was about.
We were approaching Los Angeles.

§ II

My brothers Solomon and Louis lived in Los Angeles. At
the Alexandria Hotel I found a letter from them. They had
seen the advertisements of Efrem's recital and had assumed
rightly that we would be stopping at the best hotel. I telephoned
Solomon and invited him and his wife, and asked him to invite
Louis and his wife, to have tea with me at the Alexandria that
afternoon. I waited for them in the imposing lobby. I hadn't
seen them in years, and I wondered if they had changed as
much as I had. When they arrived, I did not kiss them, as I
would have done in the old days. I had since learned that,

except on the East Side, men refrained from kissing each other
in public, even fathers and sons. But I kissed my sisters-in-law
ostentatiously. We moved over to a corner where there was a
table, and I called a waiter and ordered tea. My brothers were
diffident and self-conscious, as if from the weight of my importance in the world, the grandeur of the Alexandria lobby
and the ease with which I spoke to the waiter. The ladies, however, were voluble, even strident, I thought, as I glanced around
me to see whether they were being remarked by the people at
the other tables. I learned that my brothers were trying to gain
a foothold in the building trade, but had so far not gone beyond
small carpentry jobs. When I inquired whether they were
getting along, Solomon said he "knocked out" (presumably a
western phrase for "earned" or "made," implying a sort of
granitic resistance somewhere to earning a living) around
twenty dollars a week. He then asked he how much I might be
"knocking out," and I told him, but failed to add that I was
paying my own board and lodgings. After I disposed of their
inquiries about my father and mother and other relations, I
spoke about Efrem, the Felses, the Vanderbilts, the Burdens,
etc. My brothers were so impressed with these personages and
my intimacy with them that they involuntarily reverted to
Yiddish in their exclamations of surprise. *"Takke!"* (Really!)
they kept repeating. Louis's wife asked me to show them the
gold watch and chain that Mr. Zimbalist had given me. The
request puzzled me, but I was obliged to confess that I did not,
at the moment, possess a gold watch and chain. Louis's wife
blushed and began excusing herself. She said that a friend of
hers who was a friend of Mischa Elman told her that Elman
had presented *his* accompanist with a gold watch and chain.
Her friend had seen the watch, the inside of the lid of which
bore a warm engraved inscription from Mischa Elman. Louis's

wife had assumed that it was customary for every great violinist
to present a gold watch and chain to his pianist and traveling
companion. I laughed at her assumption. But my heart sank
at the thought that it might be based on fact, and that Efrem
was the exception. It was true that Efrem had given me many
things, but they were impersonal gifts. A gold watch would add
the touch of intimacy and provide me with a visible, costly
symbol of his regard for me. I could see myself being asked the
time and drawing out my gold watch, opening the lid and
remarking, "A present from my friend Efrem—Efrem Zimbalist." But how to induce Efrem to buy me a watch? There
was now no doubt in my mind that I could not be happy without one.

Solomon's wife invited me to dinner the following day. I
accepted, and casually asked if I might bring Mr. Zimbalist
along, hastening to add, provided he had no other engagement.
This created the sensation I expected it would. I was closely
questioned about Efrem's tastes in food. I said that there was
no need to fuss, that his tastes were the simplest. When they
were leaving, Solomon said, "Well, Sammy, you have gone a
long way since the Waterbury days. I am not surprised. I always
knew you would." Solomon had given me my very first piano
when I was a boy of eleven, in Waterbury, Connecticut. "It
was all your doing," I said with emotion. I was overcome by
a feeling of gratitude, affection and pity for my goodhearted,
uneducated, simple half brother. And without thinking about
the effect on the strangers around us, I put my arms around
Solomon and kissed him on the cheek.

Later I told Efrem about my tea party for my brothers and
their wives, and their dinner invitation to him and me. Efrem
said he would be delighted to meet my relatives, and he hoped
we would get a nice Jewish meal. I assured him we would. All
this time I was obsessed with the thought of a gold watch. The

next morning after breakfast, Efrem proposed a walk through the town. A few blocks from the hotel, he saw some colorful silk shirts in a window of a large department store. We went in. While Efrem sampled the shirts, I wandered over to the jewelry counter and looked at gold watches. Presently Efrem came over to me and asked me to pick out a silk shirt for myself. At this God-sent opening, I told him, with a boldness that astonished me, that if he wished to give me a present, there was something I desired more than all the silk shirts in the world, and I pointed to the tray of watches on the counter. Efrem looked at me sharply. Then his face broke into a broad smile. "I was going to give you a watch and chain after the season was over, but I'll be glad to give it to you now. Pick one out." I chose a large, handsome one of pinkish gold, and a chain to match, after I had made sure they were both fourteen karat (I thought fourteen karat represented the ultimate in quality and cost). Out of delicacy, Efrem took the clerk aside to discuss the price. He then wrote out a check for the amount, and I attached the chain to my vest and put the watch in my left pocket. Suddenly I remembered about the inscription. Efrem had not even mentioned it. "Wouldn't you like to have something written on the lid of the watch?" I asked him. Efrem said lightly, "Oh, have them write something." The clerk gave me pen and paper and I printed: "TO MY DEAR FRIEND AND ACCOMPANIST, SAMUEL CHOTZINOFF, WITH LOVE AND ADMIRATION FROM EFREM ZIMBALIST." Without showing it to Efrem, I gave the piece of paper to the clerk, who then took back the watch, promising to deliver it, duly inscribed, later that afternoon. We then went back to the haberdashery counter, where Efrem became absorbed in selecting a number of shirts, quite as if he had not, only a moment before, made me unutterably happy.

The watch was returned in time for me to wear it at dinner

at my brother's. I was overjoyed that Efrem did not ask to see
the inscription. Indeed, I was going to see to it that he never
would. But at Solomon's house I went into the kitchen to greet
my sister-in-law, and I showed her the watch and chain and
let her read the inscription. I told her that Efrem had that afternoon surprised me with the gift. Much to our disappointment,
Solomon's wife, perhaps hoping to make an impression of
elegance on Efrem, had prepared a non-Jewish dinner. Instead
of the gefüllte fish and sweet and sour meat we thought we
would get, she gave us lamb chops and French fried potatoes,
with Jell-O for dessert. Efrem was at his most charming, prais-
ing each dish lavishly and complimenting my sister-in-law on
the beauty of her bungalow, which was, in reality, a small, un-
edifying, mass-produced structure. Efrem talked all the time.
My relatives were so overcome by the honor of entertaining so
distinguished a man that they found hardly anything to say, and
kept smiling unnaturally. At the recital a few days later, they
sat stiffly in the fourth row (I had given them tickets) and at
the end they came to the artists' room to say good-bye, for we
were leaving for San Francisco the next day. I was touched by
the obvious pride they took in me. So we kissed, and I said
I hoped to see them again the following year.

§ III

We had hardly unpacked our things at the St. Francis Hotel
in San Francisco when Mr. Greenbaum, the local manager,
arrived to take us by ferry to Oakland for a recital that evening.
There we played in a large theater. To our astonishment we
saw, when we walked out on the stage, that the auditorium was
practically empty. Only the first four or five rows in the
orchestra were occupied. In the intermission Mr. Greenbaum,
a middle-aged, corpulent, benign, soft-spoken man, asked us
not to take the small attendance to heart. He said that he him-

self did not mind in the least, and that he was ready to book a second recital at the theater and at the same fee. He told us that the new tenor John McCormack had also played to an empty house, but had attracted a large audience at his second recital. "But these nice people who came tonight deserve your best," he added, and we agreed, though it was disconcerting to face a thousand empty seats. As we were about to resume the concert with Saint-Saëns' B Minor Concerto, Efrem suddenly decided to make some cuts in the last movement. He took the music and hastily indicated the pages and parts of pages he wanted to omit. The concerto went magnificently, and as Efrem played the slow, pastoral second movement with inimitable grace and ease, I thought how pleased Mr. Greenbaum must be that the tiny audience was getting what it deserved. I had no doubts about Efrem remembering the cuts in the last movement, for his memory was prodigious. And when he made the first cut naturally, as if the composer had written the music that way, I felt altogether secure. But when the second cut arrived, Efrem ignored it, and for a few bars I, who as agreed had turned the page, played harmonies that were at odds with the violin. Quickly realizing that Efrem had forgotten to skip a page, I hastily turned back to the passage Efrem was playing. At the same time Efrem remembered the cut, and he suddenly skipped to where I had been a moment before. The cacophony was dreadful, as we both jumped back and forth in our desperate efforts to arrive at the same place. Fortunately, this misunderstanding came near the close of the movement. I saw our cat-and-mouse game ending in disaster. I decided to simulate a finale by banging out a succession of tonic, dominant chords, fortissimo, the kind that ordinarily arrive at the close of a spirited movement. Efrem caught on at once and began playing brilliant arpeggios har-

monically consonant with my chords, and we finished triumphantly, with a great flourish. When we returned to the green
room, looking a little shamefaced, Mr. Greenbaum was beaming with pleasure. He had not heard anything amiss, nor had
the audience, nor the Oakland critic, judging by the next morning's paper. What had seemed like a catastrophe to Efrem and
me had miraculously gone quite unnoticed. And indeed, when
we talked the incident over in Efrem's room at the St. Francis,
we computed that we had been at musical loggerheads actually
for only thirty or forty seconds before we finished the movement with confidence, and even bravado.

The first person who called on us at the St. Francis was
Sir Henry Hyman. He sent up his card, on which was written
under his name "Friend of Paderewski." Efrem received him
with more than his usual cordiality, and I was duly impressed
at meeting a titled Englishman. "Welcome to our beautiful
city," were Sir Henry's first words. "Since it is your first visit,
we shall devote this morning to seeing the sights. I have a car
downstairs. We will lunch at a charming restaurant right at
the water's edge, where we can see the seals disporting themselves. Have you heard from Paderewski lately?" Sir Henry
went on. "You know him, of course. No? Well, then you don't
know the king of pianists. I hear from him frequently. The
other day I received this letter," and Sir Henry took out his
wallet and extracted carefully and lovingly an aging sheet of
paper. " 'My dear friend Sir Henry,' " our visitor read with an
effort, as if trying to decipher a difficult manuscript for the first
time. " 'I want to . . . to . . . thank you, dear friend, for
the . . .' and so forth and so on. It gets a little personal from
here on, so I'll spare you. Well, you can see what kind of a man
it is who will take the trouble to write an old friend," and he
folded the paper carefully and put it back in his wallet. Sir

Henry was middle-aged. He had a pleasant face, a mustache
and mutton-chop whiskers, and wore a light, checked vest and
a cutaway. There was a white carnation in his right lapel. He
took us on a tour of the city, and then drove us out to Palisades
Park, where we had a breathtaking view of the bay. In an
amusement place nearby, we went on the roller coaster and rode
a donkey. Sir Henry had himself photographed on the donkey,
first with Efrem, then with me. Afterward we lunched in sight
of many seals, who jumped on and off a large rock in the water
about a half-mile from the shore.

That night we visited Mr. Greenbaum and his sister in their
apartment in a residential hotel. The brother and sister, both
middle-aged, had never married. Miss Greenbaum was small
and frail. Both were quiet and soft-spoken. They gave us some
sherry, then took us downstairs to the dining room, which was
filled with middle-aged and old couples. In front of the Greenbaums were used napkins reposing in ivory napkin rings.
Efrem and I received fresh napkins. "Has Sir Henry Hyman
called on you?" Mr. Greenbaum asked us smilingly, "and did
he read you a letter from Paderewski, and take you on a tour
of the city, ending up with pictures of himself and both of you
sharing a donkey's back, and, for a finish, did he give you
lunch in front of the seals at Seal Rock?" I asked Mr. Greenbaum if Sir Henry's title was hereditary and, if not, for what
service to England he had been knighted. Mr. Greenbaum said
that "Sir Henry" was a "character," a "harmless" one, who
constituted himself the official greeter to all visiting musicians.
He was an American. He had lived for a time in Hawaii,
where, he claimed, he was knighted by his friend Queen Kali-
kahianna. He was a violinist of sorts, and gave lessons, but
what little money he earned he spent entertaining visiting
artists. "Poor fellow," Mr. Greenbaum said pityingly. "Many

years ago he got a formal note from Paderewski thanking him
for showing him the town, and since then he calls Paderewski
his intimate friend and pretends to get letters from him. I hope
you were nice to him. He is really a good fellow."

Mr. Greenbaum said he expected there would be a large
audience at Efrem's first San Francisco recital. But, he added,
the size of the attendance never worried him. He loved music,
and brought the very best artists to San Francisco. Quite often
he lost money on them, or broke even. He managed to make
a modest living for his sister and himself. As for the quality of
programs, he did not believe in playing down to the popular
taste. "Audiences have to be educated, even as I was," he said.
Mr. Greenbaum was indeed an unusual manager, the very opposite of the alert, business-minded agents I had thus far encountered. He and his sister took a liking to me, and I was invited to dine with them whenever I wished. They hardly ever
went out at night. Efrem had made several dinner engagements
with people who telephoned or came to see him. Those evenings I spent with the Greenbaums. My visits became so frequent that I no longer had a fresh napkin at dinner, but was
given an ivory ring like the Greenbaums'. After dinner I sat
around in the apartment, listening to records, of which the
Greenbaums had a fine collection, or talking about Japan.
Japan was the Greenbaums' hobby. They had made several
visits there, and fallen in love with the country and its people.
They presented me with books on Japan and introduced me
to the works of Lafcadio Hearn. Presently I, too, succumbed to
the fascination of Japan, especially its ancient customs. I could
understand not only the enthusiasm of the Greenbaums, but
the strange behavior of Lafcadio Hearn, an American journal-
ist who renounced Western civilization, married a Japanese
girl, wore Japanese clothes and became, in effect, a Japanese. I

began to dream of frail, enigmatic, kimono-clad Japanese girls with straight black hair and a loyalty to the death to me. Like Lafcadio Hearn, I would leave behind me forever crass, money-mad America and its glittering, ambitious women, marry a Japanese, beget many children whose little round heads with hair low on their foreheads resembled acorns, adopt the colorful Japanese religion, plant a little rock garden, and write books contrasting my life in my adopted country with the hectic, soul-searing civilization of America. Mr. Greenbaum thought that that would be going too far. But he advised me to go to Japan at the first opportunity and see and appraise things at first hand before I settled there.

There was a good-sized audience at Efrem's first San Francisco concert. In the green room afterward, I was delighted to renew acquaintance with a Miss Chapman, a Christian lady who had studied violin in New York with Mr. Sam Franko, and who had often played in our Educational Alliance orchestra. Miss Chapman was happy to see me too, and she invited me to visit her in the country near Berkeley, where she lived with her parents. I went to see her the very next day. I took the ferry to Oakland, and, by prearrangement, she met me at the pier and drove me in a horse and buggy to her parents' estate. It was an imposing rambling wooden house, with several outbuildings, and woods all around. Miss Chapman asked me if I would like a horseback ride before lunch. I said I would, and soon a man brought two saddled horses, and Miss Chapman and I mounted them and we cantered away through the woods. During the ride, Miss Chapman told me that in the summer she took her horse and went off for weeks by herself, sleeping on the ground with a blanket to cover her, and feeding on crackers and canned soups. It seemed to me the ideal way to live, and I thought of Thoreau and the austere life he had led. Miss Chapman said that if I was so disposed, I could join her next summer, and I could have the horse I was riding. I accepted her offer instantly, for at that moment, trotting alongside Miss Chapman through a wood the warm color of rust, a limpid sky overhead, I lost all feeling of responsibility for the welfare of my family, and thought mainly about myself. I would have to contrive somehow to get back to California and Miss Chapman in the summer. As for my family, if anything went wrong with them I could more easily be reached in Yellowstone Park than in Japan. I now abandoned the idea of emigrating to Japan—an impracticable idea at best—in favor of a life in the open, in the West, with its attendant release from family responsibility, yet with the knowledge that I could reach my family in case of need.

On the other hand, San Francisco itself now seemed a most desirable place to live in. It was a beautiful, exhilarating city. Now it took on an added interest because of Oscar Wile (I was delighted with the name). It was after Efrem's first recital that Mr. Greenbaum had introduced Mr. Wile to me as San Francisco's noted piano teacher and intimate friend of all the world's great pianists. Unlike Sir Henry Hyman, Oscar Wile was actually the intimate friend of Paderewski, Moriz Rosenthal and Harold Bauer. Mr. Wile was old and thin and ailing. He stooped, and his face looked ascetic. I was very flattered when he asked me to lunch with him. He took me to an unostentatious restaurant, where we stayed long after the other patrons left. He had some nice things to say about my piano playing and a few critical ones about what he called my "erratic" use of the pedals. He talked sensibly about technique. "Nowadays everybody has technique, and performers can no longer astound the public with it, as they used to in my young days. But astound the public they must, and if they can't do it

with technique, they do it with what they call interpretation—
that is, they do what they please with the music, to the injury
of the composer. I know an eminent pianist who says, 'Wait
till you hear *my* Beethoven'—or *my* Schumann, or *my* Chopin."
When we parted, Mr. Wile invited me to Sunday supper at his
house. He lived on the first floor of a wooden house, and he
was cared for by a middle-aged German woman servant. Our
supper consisted of cold meat and salad and beer. Mr. Wile
showed me some intermezzi of Brahms I didn't know. He himself could no longer play; his fingers were terribly gnarled and
the skin mottled like a snake's. He made me sit down at the
piano and read the intermezzi, and he offered penetrating comments and suggestions, and presently, what had seemed strange
in the music took form. He was rigid about observing the
nuances and directions printed in the music, and frowned at my
attempts to take liberties. At the same time he was never overbearing, nor did he talk down to me, but treated me as a colleague. It was only later that I realized he had given me a
lesson without my knowing it. The hours went fast, and I
would gladly have stayed on playing and talking all night.
But around eleven o'clock the German woman came in and
said it was the Professor's bedtime and I would have to excuse
him. Mr. Wile called her a jailer, and begged her to let him
stay up a while longer. But he looked haggard and the pallor
of his face accentuated blotches I had not noticed before. I
walked back to the St. Francis recalling all the things he had
said, and wondering if I could arrange to settle down in San
Francisco and absorb Mr. Wile's wisdom and knowledge in the
short time that remained to him on earth. And when he had
gone, I could perhaps, as his disciple, take his place, and
transmit his noble standards of interpretation to students who
would flock to me from all corners of America.

Our stay in San Francisco was coming to a close, and I was increasingly loath to leave. The precarious, hilly streets were adventures in themselves, the moist, scented air was heady, the women I saw were clear-eyed and pretty. Each morning I came down to breakfast in the great paneled restaurant of the hotel, feeling no timidity, and ordering strange dishes like scrambled eggs with mushrooms. An upright piano had been placed in my room, and I practiced on it for an hour or two, putting to the test Mr. Wile's theories and suggestions. I dined often with the Greenbaums, and I paid a second visit to Miss Chapman and rode "my" horse again before lunch, and discussed the possibility of my returning in the summer.

Efrem gave his third and last recital the night before we were to leave for New York. The audience was the largest he had had. I saw Mr. Wile sitting close to the stage. His small, wrinkled eyes were fixed on me, and I was conscious only of him in the big theater. We played the D Minor Sonata of Brahms, a favorite with Mr. Wile. I felt as if I were playing alone for him at his house. I played it well, and I knew I did, even as I played. At the end, the old man rose in his seat and clapped his hands significantly in my direction. He came to see me in the intermission, and told me how very pleased he was. I was unutterably happy. But when he began, "And now good-bye," and I saw tears in his weak eyes, I did not feel equal to parting from him then and there, perhaps forever, and I smiled and said I would run in to see him the next morning, before going to the station. But I knew I wouldn't have the courage to see him again. I would write him and explain.

When the concert was over, I invited Efrem to have supper with me somewhere, to celebrate our last night in San Francisco. But Efrem had already promised to go out with two ladies who were playing the feminine leads in a road company show at the Curran Theater. They were beautiful and vivacious, and I envied Efrem and felt sorry for myself. Sensing my loneliness, the Greenbaums asked me to go home with them and have a sandwich and a bottle of beer. Not wanting them to think that anything was amiss, I declined, saying I had packing to do. And indeed, I went to my room, and still in my evening dress, I began to pack my wardrobe trunk. But I was restless and agitated, and I left my packing in the middle and went downstairs and sat in the lobby, watching people arriving from the theater or dinner parties, or going away in taxicabs to find amusement. Couples openly showing their pleasure in each other passed by me. I caught sight of myself in a tall mirror. It seemed to me I looked interesting, even handsome, in my evening clothes and glossy pumps. I went outside and stood on the steps of the hotel. The stars were milky and very high, the trees in the little park in front of me very green, the air bracing yet soft. I looked down at myself, and a feeling of self-sufficiency and confidence stole over me. It was a pleasurable and a defiant feeling. I saw myself alone, late at night, in a city far from my home and my family and friends and all the once-treasurable associations of my childhood and youth, yet I was pleased with my isolation and my alien surroundings. I felt at the moment no longer dependent on anyone or any place. Standing on the steps of the hotel with no one looking at me, or giving me a thought, I felt I was perhaps the most conscious creature in all San Francisco, in all America, perhaps in the universe. My life had been, and was at the moment, unusual, because I was endowed with the faculty of tasting, of savoring nature and people and art, and the mysterious happenings in life, at the same time that I knew myself to be a helpless participant in life, like the most insensible, unaware person anywhere. More than anyone, I knew I *appreciated* every-

thing, good and bad. I did not like the bad. But when it came
along I found extenuation for it, as an aspect of poetry and
rightness. I saw the rightness of my father's rigid rabbinical
view of the universe, of my sister's frozen despair over the loss
of her child, of my mother's defiance of her God and the
religious injunctions of a lifetime, that she might satisfy her
desire to see me on the stage of Carnegie Hall. I now found
pleasure in being left alone by Efrem. I needed no one! My
ideas, my thoughts, my memories and my imagination were
enough for me.

I decided to celebrate this emancipation by myself. In a
sense I wouldn't be alone, for I was in myself many kinds of
persons. I hailed a taxicab and asked the driver where I could
go at that late hour. He drove me to a place in Chinatown
where there were music and dancing. It was a room in a basement, and it was filled with dancing couples. I was the only
man in evening dress, and the headwaiter, obviously impressed
with me, placed me at a small table at the edge of the dance
floor. I had twenty-five dollars in my pocket, and I felt secure.
No matter how large the bill might be, I would be able to pay
it. I ordered chicken à la king ($1.50) and a bottle of cham-
pagne ($3.00). The champagne arrived in a large silver cooler.
Before pouring it, the waiter turned the bottle around forward
and backward innumerable times. When the waiter poured out
a glass for me, I boldly stuck a fork in it and stirred the wine
ostentatiously. I appeared to be the only person drinking champagne, and I saw several people looking toward my table. I
was thirsty, and I finished the bottle by the time the chicken
à la king was set before me. Then I ordered a second bottle.
This one I drank sparingly, while I ate, so that I could justify
my lingering at the table and watching the dancers. The dances
were frequent. At the first notes of the cornet, drums, piano and

violin, everybody, so it appeared, instantly rose and made for the dance floor. Neither the men nor the women were exceptional. None of the men looked as romantic as I did. But the women dancers, as they brushed past me, smelled of different intriguing perfumes. One of them, a thin girl, had a strikingly beautiful face, and danced with an air of complete surrender to her partner. She was smaller than the man, and she rested her head on his chest and pressed her slim body close to his. She danced with her eyes closed. There was a faint smile about her lips expressive of some inward satisfaction. The man was better dressed than the other men, and his face was more refined. They were lovers, I was sure. I sipped my champagne, and tried to follow them with my eyes as they were momentarily obscured by the crowd of dancers and became visible again in some unexpected direction. The place was warm, and I felt warm inside me, and I had to use my handkerchief frequently to wipe the perspiration from my face and head. I began to look only at *her*. Each time she passed me I found something more to notice—the lovely color and soft texture of her dark-blond hair, the delicacy of her skin, the ease and grace with which she moved, the serious, solemn look on her face, accentuated by the half-smile. I could imagine the quiet joy of her partner as he held her close, his lips touching her hair. She had not noticed me. When she danced she seemed to see no one, and when she sat at her table her eyes never wandered around the room, but were fixed on her companion, who appeared to have a great deal to tell her. My second bottle was now empty, and I ordered a third. With my first glass from the new bottle, I determined to *make* her look at me. I stared boldly at her as she sat a few tables away, facing me. I never took my eyes off her. I looked at her steadfastly as she circled around the room. I was sure that she must feel my eyes on her,

even through her shut eyes. It was hours since I had entered
the place. The room began to thin out. Soon, only a handful of
couples was left. Presently there were so few dancers on the floor
that *she* was visible at all times. When she passed by me I had
to stifle an impulse to touch her, to call out to her. If she would
only look at me, just once, fleetingly, she would read in my
eyes my ardor, my longing. I wanted nothing more than a look
of recognition, one that would assure me of my right to appraise her loveliness. But she refused to look at me, or show the
slightest awareness of me. After each dance I told myself that
I must give her another chance, that at the next dance she
must give me a sign. But no sign came. I grew angry with her
for her insensitiveness, and with myself for my vanity and
conceit, and I called the waiter and asked for my bill. As the
waiter left, I saw her rise from her chair and excuse herself to
her companion, who remained seated. She made her way to
the ladies' room, and she skirted my table. She passed close to
me, her eyes looking into the distance, paused for a second before me and in a whisper said, "Darling!" I watched her as
she went on her way. She now looked less beautiful than I had
thought, but it didn't matter. The improbability of what had
just happened filled me with wonder and delight. It had not
been a mysterious, irrational accident of life. I had *willed* something to happen, and it happened! My confidence in the appeal
and influence of my proud, conscious, perceptive nature had
been tested and had triumphed. Now I was sure I needed *no
one*. People were not necessary to me, except, occasionally, to
attest my presence and magnetism. This had been proved to
me this eventful night. Art alone was the true necessity for
me; art and the ability to see life and myself in terms of art.

Happy in my triumph, and with my extravagant and grandiose deductions (I thought of proud and lonely personalities

of literature—Manfred . . . Onegin . . . Prince Andrei—and compared myself favorably with them), I left the basement dance hall without waiting to see *her* again. I asked the cab driver to stop for a moment at Mr. Wile's house. I had the faint hope that the old man might perhaps be still awake, and we could spend the rest of the night talking about music, especially about Brahms, who was his favorite and could easily become mine. The windows of Mr. Wile's house were all dark, and we drove on. As I rode through the hilly streets, there sang in my head the melody of "How Lovely Is Thy Dwelling Place" from Brahms's German Requiem. The dwelling place Brahms sang of was the Hereafter. But for me, at that moment, it expressed the serenity of my heart, and the loveliness of the world around me.